DICKIE BUCK
Robin Hood of Dennis

Scott E. McDowell

This book is available from Amazon.com, on-line book outlets,
bookstores and retail shops on Cape Cod.

View Scott's other literary works at:

www.scottemcdowell.com

Email Scott for purchase of copies signed by the Author:

scott_e_mcdowell@yahoo.com

Cover Design by E. K. King

The small town of Dennis on Cape Cod is famous for many things, as well as home of the Living Legend – Dickie Buck. From a young age, he was a scrapper and daredevil but always worked hard and respected others. In his middle years, he transformed into the Robin Hood of the North Side village, helping dozens in need. Some locals view him as Peter Pan, never wanting to grow up and always demonstrating the stamina of a young man. He has also raised a family within a marriage of fifty-five years. An extraordinary man who is never to be forgotten in Dennis.

Contents

Dickie's Genes

Elmer Newell – Dickie's Maternal Grandfather

Dark Night at the Bass Hole - 1928

Two 'salty', middle-aged Cape Codders quietly dragged the skiff into the rising waters of the Bass Hole. 'Ha'past midnight and pitch black – perfect!' Elmer had whispered to his partner-in-crime before rowing out to his wooden, double-ended boat on its mooring in the channel. They climbed aboard Elmer's 35-ft *Black Duck* with its cuddy cabin forward, two bunks and gas cookstove.

He started the small inboard engine which had an aligned shaft for propulsion. The two-cylinder engine was sufficient to move the old round-bottom boat at six knots but tonight they crept along, headed north in the channel toward Cape Cod Bay. Being quiet was more important than running fast. They purposely scheduled their covert activity on 'New-Spring' - the date of the New Moon when evening skies are darkest and on the 'spring' tide when tidal ranges are greatest, providing the deepest water for larger boats to approach the Bass Hole from the north, across the vast sand shoals.

The seasoned men knew the drill; no words spoken and with the extinguished oil lamp hidden beneath the oiled-canvas to avoid any salt spray. Upon reaching the outer entrance of the Bass Hole, Elmer slowed to an idle, needing only a bit of headway to oppose the incoming tidal current. There they sat, seemingly for hours. Neither had a pocket watch nor did it matter. If need be, they'd keep position until daybreak approached, being careful to head ashore under darkness and when the tide started to drop. They knew the Rum Runner delivery boat would enter the Hole only on the rising tide for fear of becoming grounded and thus a sitting duck for local police who were eager to nab the Bootleggers who would supply the Speakeasys of their town.[1] And, if the police didn't arrive, some pistol-packing local hoodlums might appear to nab the hooch from Elmer's easily recognizable double-ender headed ashore.

He and Cliffy sat in the cockpit with backs to each other; one faced eastward; t'other westward. Elmer shut the engine off near high tide when there was no drift current. Each man kept an eye trained offshore and t'other to the south. All ears were tuned for the slightest sound that could announce Fortune or Fate.

Cliffy gently tapped Elmer on the leg and pointed to the north. A dark shape loomed in the outer channel; no lights, just slow southward movement toward them. Elmer restarted the engine and idled northward. Cliffy lit the mantle, placed the oil lamp on top of the cabin and lowered the glass chimney to protect the flame from the gentle salt breeze. Next, he lifted the lamp three times at two-second intervals to present the signal given to them by the owner of the East Dennis Speakeasy who'd ordered this delivery of coveted moonshine. The large boat acknowledged, with a single flash of their lamp, and the visual handshake was done.

Within ten minutes, the *Black Duck* was headed ashore with six cases of hard liquor hidden beneath a canvas. Elmer slowly motored past their mooring and around three bends in the small channel that meandered through the expansive salt marsh.

A small light appeared ahead. It too blinked three times, signaling that Joseph P. (J. P.) Walker (a 9-year-old boy at the time) was there waiting in his small rowing dory. He had rowed from Chase Garden Creek to meet the incoming delivery for the Speakeasy on Sesuit Neck. Of course, J. P.'s father, Ben, had approved his son's mission. Ben was the Harbormaster of Nobscusset Harbor[2].

***

On another evening when Elmer and Cliffy Ellard were making one of their Rum Runs, they spotted the Coast Guard boat approaching and the East Dennis Harbormaster, Charley Ellis, surely was aboard. Quickly, Elmer turned the steering wheel 'hard over' and tied it to the starboard gunwale so the *Black Duck* would run continuously in a tight circle. The two men jumped overboard together and headed for shore before the Guardsmen could spot them retreating. There was one problem with this plan - Elmer couldn't swim (not unlike many Cape Codders of those days, even Sea Captains).

As described to Dickie Buck by Cliffy Ellard many years after the event during a drink at Dom's Bar in North Dennis, 'I told him… Come on Elmer, you can make it… Come on Elmer, we can get to shore together.' Fortunately, the water was shallow enough they could wade to shore most of the way. They ended up spending the night behind the large brick building of Orin Robbins' freezer plant, located on the shore between the Bass Hole and Barnstable Harbor inlet.

As Dickie and Cliffy drank that evening, many years after Elmer had been murdered, Cliffy expressed how he missed his old friend. 'If I could find out who killed Elmer, I'd choke him with my bare hands!'

***

It was also widely known in East Dennis that during Prohibition days, Joseph P. Kennedy, Sr. of Hyannis fame was actively involved with Rum Running. This was in the mid-20s when J. P. Kennedy was in his late thirties. In those days he owned a number of launches that would shuttle liquor from the larger, offshore boats into Sesuit Harbor. The cases were transported to the Pearce House on Harbor Road with an eventual destination of the Speakeasy at the hotel that later became the property of Bill Stone.

Elmer's Family

Elmer Nelson Newell of local Rum Running fame was Dickie Buck's maternal grandfather. He was born on October 26, 1884 in Yarmouth, Nova Scotia (NS) and lived in Yarmouth Port, MA nearly his whole life. He and his thirteen brothers had returned to NS during the smallpox epidemic of 1901[3] and most died, but Elmer survived and returned to the Cape.

Elmer was the 12th generation of his family that originally immigrated from England. John (Smythe) Smith (2nd generation) was born in Hingham, England in 1585 and died in Hingham, MA in 1640. Elmer's father, Archelaus Newell (11th generation) was born in 1838 at Cape Sable Island, NS and died around 1905 in Indonesia. Many Newells settled in Nova Scotia and probably continue there.

In 1914, Elmer married Eleanor (called Alma) Francis of Cohassett, MA, who was born circa 1891. They had their first daughter, Eleanor (called Ellie) Francis Newell, in April 1916 and their second, Zalma (called Thelma) Newell in July 1918.

Ellie (Dickie's mother) married Herbert Alwyn Buck (called Buckie) who was born in May 1913 in Wilmington, MA.

Ellie and Buckie had three sons:

Leo (Lee) was the eldest, born in 1934 and died in 2014.

Richard Daniel (Dickie) is the middle son, born on April 27, 1935.

Herbert (Bertie) is the youngest son, born in 1945 and living in Florida.

Elmer made 'good money' from Rum Running but it was a dangerous activity in the latter years of his life, especially for a man with wife and two daughters. His largest land-based, legal business development, the Rainbow Ballroom, is described below.

When Elmer and Alma's two daughters were born, they were living in a small bungalow in Yarmouth Port near the Bass Hole. By the time he was forty (1924), the daughters were approaching their teen years and his marriage was not going well. Alma had her fill of Elmer and insisted on marital Separation, for reasons that have not survived the years. She stayed in the small home and he moved onto his 35-ft boat moored at the Bass Hole. As a very 'independent' man, Elmer probably welcomed moving aboard his *Black Duck* whereas Alma was likely pleased with his exile.

There are no details on how Elmer 'wintered over' in his double-ender but suffice to say he was a hearty character. What's more significant is that upon the Separation, it was decided that daughter Ellie would live with her father while Thelma would stay in the house with mother Alma. There is little doubt that Ellie was adventurous in her youth and living aboard with her father at the Bass Hole surely expanded her life skills and independence. Furthermore, it's unlikely he could conduct his bootlegging activities with Ellie in the picture so that business venture probably ended for Elmer in the late '20s. His development of the large Rainbow Ballroom soon after, likely was built with rum money.

The Rainbow Ballroom

During his middle years, Elmer was a hard-working man who profited from a variety of activities and business developments. In 1930, Elmer built a large roller-skating arena called the Rainbow Ballroom on Route 28 in West Yarmouth. This was an excellent location for a new entertainment venue as it was across the street from a previously famous facility called the Mill Hill Pavilion[4] that was first opened in 1916. The Pavilion was very popular as the Cape's largest venue for Big Bands, Vaudeville and dancing during the Roaring Twenties. Later, it was known for exhibitions, boxing contests and basketball games. Unfortunately, the large Pavilion burned down in 1928 and was never rebuilt as an entertainment venue; a restaurant exists there today.

Adjacent to (and immediately to the west of) Elmer's Rainbow Ballroom was the successful Old Mill Tavern from 1924 to 1941. The Tavern later became the famed Mill Hill Club, an upscale Live Music and Dancing club in the '50s and 60s, which transitioned to a less-formal, music and happy-hour drinking scene in the '70s and '80s. The Club was closed in 2008 after a successful run of over fifty years. In 2014, it was demolished to make way for a housing complex.

Elmer Murdered

On November 19, 1938, Elmer was murdered in Yarmouth Port on the road to the Bass Hole. He was a mere fifty-four years old and supposedly killed for the cash he was known to carry in his boots. It occurred while he was returning home from card playing at Thatcher's Tea House located two doors east of the Yarmouth Fire Station on Route 6A. Mrs. Thatcher was adamant that card games never occurred at her 'proper' establishment but the local men knew otherwise. None of the 'North Side' characters were tea lovers, especially Elmer.

The citizens of Yarmouth viewed Elmer as a hoodlum compared to the person who was convicted of killing him. It's true that Elmer was a bootlegger and might have had other 'shady' ways to make a buck, whereas his assailant was a reputable businessman in town. For this reason, the conviction barely made the local newspaper; Elmer's death, unfortunately, was not important to many townsfolk.

* * *

Years later, an old man approached Ellie and confessed to killing her father. She hadn't known this man.

'I killed your Paw. Didn't mean to do it. I konked him on the head. I just wanted his money.'

Ellie decided not take this new confession to the police because many years had passed since the murder, trial and grieving. Consequently, the original verdict was never overturned.

Elmer's grave is located in the Ancient Cemetery on Center Street in Yarmouth Port, leading to the Bass Hole. Because his family was poor at the time of his death, they were unable to afford a proper gravestone. Some years later as a tribute to their beloved Bootlegger, some of the family members poured a concrete block and partially inserted a kedge anchor for easy recognition of his gravesite. It still exists today in plain sight.

Elmer's Old Boat

After Elmer's death, his wooden double-ended boat, *Black Duck*, washed ashore in a storm at the Bass Hole and came to rest east of the Center Street parking lot in Yarmouth Port. She laid there until 1947 when Dickie, his father, older brother Lee and friend Edgar Bearse, III, tried to patch her up and make the old girl seaworthy again. Their attempts were futile so there she lay in disarray for an estimated fifteen years. Over that period, thousands of photographs were taken of the *Black Duck* and tourist Post Cards were printed with various explanations of the old derelict. The Town of Yarmouth finally removed what remained of the famous Bootlegger's boat.

To this day, when Dickie thinks of his grandfather, Elmer, and his old boat at the Bass Hole, he immediately begins to recite one of his favorite poems of Robert W. Service: *The Cremation of Sam Magee*. In the story, the old miner Sam had requested that his best friend see to his cremation after death in the frigid Yukon Territory. The friend fulfilled his promise and cremated Sam within an old derelict barge found on the shore of Lake LeBarge.

The poem's narrator is Sam's friend in the story.

...Till I came to the marge of Lake Lebarge, and a derelict there lay;

It was jammed in the ice, but I saw in a trice it was called the 'Alice May'.

And I looked at it, and I thought a bit, and I looked at my frozen chum;

Then 'Here,' said I, with a sudden cry, 'is my cre-ma-tor-eum.'

Dickie felt it would have been appropriate for his grandfather Elmer to have been cremated in his own double-ender right there at the Bass Hole.

In the poem, the friend returns to the incinerated barge to verify that his deed was done.

Dickie continues with his melodic recitation:

...I was sick with dread, but I bravely said: 'I'll just take a peep inside.

I guess he's cooked, and it's time I looked'; ... then the door I opened wide.

And there sat Sam, looking cool and

calm, in the heart of the furnace roar;

And he wore a smile you could see a mile, and he said: 'Please close that door.

It's fine in here, but I greatly fear you'll let in the cold and storm—

Since I left Plumtree, down in Tennessee, it's the first time I've been warm.'

And like Sam Magee, Dickie loathes the cold. Recently, I asked Dickie of his plan for burial, if that day should ever come. Adamantly, he replied 'Cremation for me, like Sam Magee. I don't want to be in a box in the ground and forever cold!'

Dickie wishes he could still visit the ghost of his grandfather, the Bootlegger, in the burned-out hulk of his *Black Duck*.

Ellie Newell and Herbert Buck – Dickie's Parents

Ellie, the first daughter of Elmer and Alma Newell, was born in their small bungalow on Thacher Shore Road in Yarmouth Port. She attended public schools in Yarmouth but was likely more adventurous than other girls of her age as Elmer wasn't the typical father. As described above, she lived aboard her father's boat, *Black Duck*, in her teen years and may have been exposed to the Rum Running trade.

When only eighteen, Ellie married Herbert (Buckie) Buck, an off-Cape boy, and had her first son, Lee, the same year. Dickie followed a year later, in 1935. 'Definitely a fast start for their family, with two boys before Ellie was twenty-one. Her third son, 'Bertie', came along ten years later.

Times were tough for Cape families, with the Great Depression spanning from 1929 through 1939. Unemployment was 25% and the Buck family had to scratch to make a meager living. There was minimal money on the Cape for construction and the tourist trade had dwindled to almost nothing.

During the early years of their marriage, Buckie and Ellie worked many different jobs on the Cape to make ends meet. Their income was adequate during summer when the Cape's population rose and retail business peaked but each fall when business dropped, they had to move off-Cape to seek gainful employment. Packing up and driving away at Thanksgiving season became a yearly ritual for their family. Locals viewed the Bucks as 'drifters'.

First, they wintered in upstate New York then later in North Carolina. Eventually they chose Sarasota, FL as a good place for the family's winters.

Buckie's Cab Company and His Gambling Addiction

In 1940, Camp Edwards in Bourne, MA (which later became Otis Air Force Base) was established as a large Army training facility at the beginning of World War II. The facility was rapidly expanded to accommodate 30,000 soldiers and opportunistic businesses arose to handle retail needs of the many soldiers. Dickie's father wisely established Buckie's Cab Company to provide local travel for soldiers on Leave. Profits were excellent and most importantly, it was a stable, year-round business.

Buckie's cab fleet consisted of seven-passenger Plymouths, large Packards, Chryslers and a 1942 Cadillac. The Caddy was a special model because it was actually built in December 1941 as the last car of its type until the war was over. This same model was driven by President Eisenhauer when he moved around Europe during the war. Buckie's car was identical to the President's, with soft, leopard-skin rear seats and the intercom phone from the passenger seat to the driver. Ellie also kept a vehicle in Dennis to support local transportation needs.

The cab business was lucrative, with a one-way fare to New York City of $125; $75 for the return trip if Buckie was fortunate to find riders heading back to Cape Cod. In the '40s, $200 was a substantial sum of money, especially for a six-hour drive.

Gas was rationed during the war years, even for cab companies. Buckie had to collect gas tokens so he'd always have an adequate supply in the event that he had a fare to New York; if not, he'd have to refuse a big fare for lack of gas.

Gambling was one means of acquiring gas tokens so Buckie justified his hobby for the interests of his business. Often, he'd 'pitch pennies', other times he'd play cards for dollar bills which were big antes in those days.

Pitching Pennies was a game where players would throw a coin at a wall, from some distance away. The player whose coin landed closest to the wall was the temporary winner and permitted to collect all the other coins of that toss.

Buckie and his drivers had

considerable spare time each day as they waited for riders. When he wasn't gambling, he'd be playing guitar and he amassed a collection of guitars from gambling too.

Sadly for the Buck family, Buckie's cab business ended abruptly when the war ended and all the soldiers departed from the Cape. There wasn't much year-round demand for cabs on the Cape because people had their old cars for local transportation and a cab ride would have been a luxury for most townsfolk.

Although Buckie was making very good money from his cab company for four years, when it ended he had nothing saved. When Dickie was ten years old, his father admitted that he had no money – 'piss poor and barely enough to feed the family each day'. It was all spent by Buckie's gambling addiction. Very sad but also lasting in the memories of the children. Dickie recalls all the other young children wearing new clothes at Easter time but he and his brothers got nothing.

Apparently, Buckie was an excellent 'negative role model' for his sons. As a result, Dickie has never allowed himself to become a gambler. His limit is a few lottery tickets each year.

In 1940, Buckie and Ellie bought a small house on the east side of Paddocks Path near Route 6A and opposite Bohlin's Cape Cod Paper Company. They paid only $1,000 for the house and plot of land but it had no running water, no heating system and only an outhouse. Buckie gradually upgraded the home to standard conditions and functionality, also developing a fine vegetable garden for the family's subsistence.

Dickie remembers that his father loved gardening but didn't care to go to the beach like most families.

Their third son, 'Bertie', was born in the Paddock's Path house in 1945, with Christine Harriman assisting as the midwife.

Settling in Florida

Buckie never provided well for the family after his wartime cab business ended. In 1949 he and Ellie decided it best to re-establish the family in Sarasota, FL with the prospect of year-round income. They purchased a parcel of land on Almond Avenue with plans to build a house. Buckie built a concrete platform that would later become the foundation for their house but initially, it became the base for the family's tent – a 16-ft by 16-ft surplus Army tent. Because of their poor financial situation, the tent was their winter home for five years.

While working for the Sarasota Concrete company, Buckie used a portion of his weekly pay to purchase a small number of standard concrete blocks. When he had accumulated enough blocks, he constructed an 800-square-foot house that was completed in 1954. He was forty-one years old, Ellie thirty-eight and the three teen boys all lived in the small house. Nevertheless, it was nearly four-times larger than the tent that had been their home for five years. The youngest son Bertie is still living in the house today.

Dickie's Freshman, Sophomore and Junior years in Sarasota High School were spent in the family tent from Thanksgiving to April each year. For the other months of the school year, the family travelled back to Dennis and he was enrolled at Dennis-Yarmouth Regional High School. For his Senior year (1952-1953) Dickie was enrolled in North Carolina for the winter months.

When Buckie had vacation time, his preference was to travel to the mountains near Ashville, North Carolina where he enjoyed panning for gold and mining for rubies. He liked being alone and spending a bit of time with the local mountain people. On one mining vacation, he discovered a ruby that was nearly two carat-weight. Later as a gift to Ellie, he had it mounted in a setting for a necklace with gold pieces placed around the gem.

Buckie's Final Years

From 1958 to 1963, Buckie and Ellie lived in Pacoima, CA located about twenty miles northwest of Los Angeles, and within a few miles of the mountainous region called the Angeles National Forest. It is not known why they moved to Pacoima, especially hearing what the town was like back in the late '50s.

The Los Angeles Times wrote in 1955 that Pacoima was a 'smear of sagging, leaning shacks and backhouses framed by disintegrating fences and clutter of tin cans, old lumber, stripped automobiles, bottles, rusted water heaters and other bric-a-brac of the back alleys.' It lacked curbs and paved streets. Other than that, it makes total sense that Buckie and Ellie drove across country to settle there. It's likely they could have bought a piece of land for $500 and maybe pitched another tent. With the LA mountains only a few miles to the east, Buckie could have enjoyed mining for gold.

They retained ownership of the Florida home as a fallback if California living did not suit their long-term interests. One day in 1969, Buckie felt a bit under the weather. He called Ellie to his side and spoke: 'Well, I guess it's time to put me in the waste basket and take me across the country.'

Buckie died the next day at age fifty-six. He had given Ellie specific orders to have his body cremated and his ashes brought to the top of a mountain in Ashville, NC where he had spent many months mining. For the burial service, Dickie accompanied his mother and brothers to the mountain top where they met several of the native people who Buckie had befriended over the years. They were pleased he chose to spend his eternity on the mountaintop with them.

Throughout life, Buckie had always chosen what he wanted to do, whether it be gambling his (and the family's) money away or being buried far from his family's eventual gravesites. Family came second to Buckie and it was always apparent to Dickie.

***

One of the jobs Buckie had while living on the Cape in his forties was to work for an insulation company in Harwich. Daily, he was exposed to asbestos fibers and came home covered in asbestos dust. The cause of his death was believed to be stomach cancer but mesothelioma was not well understood back in the '60s. Today, stomach cancer is known to be a moderate risk from asbestos exposure.

Dickie remembers his mother having to dust off Buckie when he returned home from work each evening. Coincidentally, Ellie also died of stomach cancer. Their bodies were donated to the University of California - Los Angeles for use in cancer research.

Hold-Up at the Gas Station

After Buckie passed away, Ellie had to find things to keep herself occupied while living in Florida. For a while she worked at a self-service gas station. One evening, a hooded man entered the station with intentions of robbing the cash register. He passed a note across the counter to Ellie: 'Give me the money, or I'll shoot.'

Instinctively she replied, 'Show me the gun first, before I'll give you the money.' She certainly was brave (and maybe a bit daring?).

'Are you crazy?' the robber answered with surprise.

'I want to see the gun first!' Ellie said defiantly.

'You're crazy!' and the perpetrator ran out, empty handed.

No-way was Ellie going to give away the cash without a fight. She earned quite a reputation, especially when the local newspaper published an article, 'Brave Granny Stops Robber'.

More proof of where Dickie got his 'bravery genes'.

Ellie's Later Years

Ellie certainly was a free spirit; a Hippie of sorts who dressed with flair and was lively despite her age. Shortly after Buckie died in California, she decided to move back east to see her sons in Dennis before returning to her other home in Sarasota, FL. She was forty-seven years old at the time.

Dickie, his wife and two daughters were living on Black Ball Hill Road when Ellie pulled into their driveway at the end of her cross-country drive. She wasn't driving an ordinary car of the time – certainly not. She was behind the wheel of a long, black limo of the type that would follow a hearse for carrying many family members. Normal wheels for Ellie.

Spotting her alone, the family immediately inquired how she could have made the long, potentially dangerous trek by herself. Over the next few days, she told stories of how she picked up hitch-hikers and let them drive eastward as she slept comfortably and with no worries, in the back seat. Who would trust strangers to this extent, especially a middle-aged woman? Another example of Dickie having inherited his 'risk taker' genes from his mother.

For the next thirty-two years of her life, Ellie spent most of them in the Sarasota house. Occasionally she would travel north to spend summers in Dennis and every year was different, which she enjoyed. One summer she lived aboard Dickie's 40-ft Chris-Craft houseboat while she operated the seafood café at Sesuit Harbor Marina, under Dickie's management. Other summers she worked in various jobs and restaurants in the Dennis and Hyannis.

***

Ellie died in 1995 at the age of seventy-nine, twenty-six years after Buckie's death. As requested, she had her cremation ashes spread in Cape Cod Bay near the Bass Hole of Yarmouth Port where she grew up and her father was the Bootlegger. The ashes of her eldest son Lee also were spread at the same location years later. Both ceremonies were performed by Dickie aboard one of his boats, as discussed in a later Chapter.

Dickie views much of his personality being derived from his mother, Ellie. Enjoyment and helping people were her strongest virtues – Dickie's also.

Landmarks of Dennis Village:
1940s - 1960s

Cape Codders who lived in Dennis village during the mid-1900s have fond memories of their quiet, idyllic community. Just ask anyone from those cherished days. We all smile, amidst everlasting memories:

> "The village was a very safe place to live and raise your children."

> "After WW II, families were thankful to have a home and a car in the yard."

> "Police were visible but they were local men and friends of the village."

> "Things were easy and everyone enjoyed life, no matter how much money they had."

> "The Volunteer Fire Department on the North Side was amazing – all the men dropped their work and drove to the Station when the whistles sounded and CB radios beckoned."

> "Townsfolk represented many religions but the Dennis Union Church was open to everyone and a comfortable place for congregating, weddings, Christmas events and funerals."

> "The few village restaurants were all family owned, family oriented and affordable."

> "There weren't many regulations that hand-cuffed normal life and seashore enjoyment."

> "When individuals met 'hard times', police and townspeople were there to help."

> "Everyone loved when the Dennis Drive-In Theater opened for the summer season."

Most would say, 'It was the best of times…' This warm sentiment also was shared among families who summered in the village, many of whom later bought property and retired here.

This Chapter identifies prominent establishments and landmarks that were favorites of the village locals, from the '40s through the '60s. The list is not all-inclusive; exact dates of proprietorship are not provided; nor are names of all owners and staff. Many of the most prominent establishments in the village, such as the Cape Playhouse, are not included as they have been thoroughly addressed in other, historic compilations[5]. View this Chapter as a stroll down memory lane.

A final clarification: I herein use the designation 'Dennis village' as including (North) Dennis and East Dennis.[6] Therefore, consider my 'village' being situated between Cape Cod Bay and Setucket Road, which is oriented roughly east-west, as the waist of the town and a mere 2.6 miles wide. Nearly all of Dickie's life has been spent in the village, within a radius of only two miles, centered at Scargo Tower – definitely a small 'fish bowl' in which to work, play, harbormaster, politicize, fly, dive, misbehave, procreate and be a generous citizen. No wonder he's well known, albeit loved by some and scorned by others. You can draw your opinion later.

Indian Burial Ground and Chief Mashantampaine

The name Mashantum[7] is recognizably of Indian origin, even to those unaware of Native American history on Cape Cod. Mashantum Road is a small lane off Elm Street but its name is ideally suited for its location, in the area called Indian Fields when ownership of the land was transferred by the Nobscusset tribe.

The Nobscussets occupied what is now Dennis and spent their winters on the south side, along Bass River, to avoid the harsh weather on the Bay side. In spring, they'd migrate back to the area of Scargo Lake to plant crops. Indian Fields later became the common name for the tract of land bounded by Elm Street and Dr. Lords Road. Thus, Mashantum Road is appropriately nestled within the original Indian Fields.

The Nobscusset tribe inhabited this land before the arrival of the English settlers. Mashantampaine[5,9] was the Chief (also called Sachem or Sagamore) of the Nobscussets who were a part of the Wampanoag Federation of New England. In May of 1657, Mashantampaine transferred the deed of the large parcel of land to individuals who had recently settled in the area that we now call Dennis. It is believed that these Native Indians had occupied the Cape for thousands of years, and some still remained 150 years after the English arrived; until the late 1700s.

A small burial ground on the north shore of Scargo Lake is purported to be that of Mashantampaine's tribe. The town retained ownership of this strip of land, between 985 and 995 Route 6A. In 1829, the town constructed a metal-pipe and granite pillar fence around the Burial Ground to preserve this resting place.[5] The original fence and a commemorative metal plaque still stand at the cemetery today, with the following inscription: 'Burial Ground of the Nobscussett tribe of Indians of which tribe Mashantampaine was Chief'.

Readers are encouraged to seek out Mashantampaine's resting place and pay their respects to one of the town's earliest inhabitants. Visitors notice that no gravestones are present, as was the custom of the Wampanoags. Rather, visitors encounter symbolic offerings as tributes to the deceased Indians: sea clam shells, small stones, bracelets, feathers, dried corn cobs, etc.

You might see Dickie at the Burial Ground as he retains a strong commitment to the Indian history of the village. To this day, he takes personal responsibility for maintaining the physical grounds of the cemetery. He has always felt good karma from the Indians and states that he has done well by them. When Dickie visits the Burial Ground, he often calls the swans of Scargo Lake and they come to him from any direction.

***

Mashantum is also a familiar name for local tennis enthusiasts, since 1946 when Tom Dingman, Sr. began offering tennis lessons at his small club tucked in the pines west of Nobscussett Road, appropriately on Forehand Drive. The successful Mashantum Tennis Club, still in operation after seventy years, follows the goal of its founder: 'It wasn't only about teaching the game of tennis, but about building character so the kids grew up to be kind and contributing citizens.' Tom is remembered for 'his quiet strength, his nature, his commitment and willingness to work hard, his steadiness, the poetry he wrote and how he loved to dance.'[8]

As another piece of trivia, Bill Stone named one of his horses 'Mashantum'. Although it never was invited to the Derby, Bill loved his horses and cared for them dearly. Never did they see the glue factory.

Army Half-Tracks on Route 6A during WW II

In the early '40s during World War II, Army M3 Half-Track Personnel Carriers often traveled along Route 6A, distributing troops among Cape towns. When Dickie was seven years old, he and his older brother sold newspapers on foot to local residents. With a large, canvas sack on his shoulder, Dickie made daily deliveries to thirty houses within a two-mile radius of his home in East Dennis. To this day, he recalls standing on Route 6A watching in awe as the heavy Army vehicles rumbled down the road with young soldiers hollering to the boys. 'What's the news today, boy?' As the GIs lacked contact with up-to-date news, they gladly gave Dickie chewing gum in trade for the day's paper.

At the peak of the war in 1942, the federal government imposed a mandatory 'brownout' during evenings in all coastal towns along the east coast. This was a precaution against enemy aircraft and submarines that were known to search for lights to identify prospective targets. Lights were prohibited from Scargo Tower and auto headlights had to be partially obstructed. Further, it was mandatory that headlights be extinguished completely when autos headed north (downhill) on Old Bass River Road and on Route 134 approaching Route 6A, so that lights would not be seen from Cape Cod Bay.[5]

Coast Guard's Bleak House and Dog Training Facility

Bleak House Circle, located north of Seaside Avenue near Route 6A, is the site of a residential development with stately properties near the shore of Cape Cod Bay, east of Corporation Beach. The neighborhood was developed as Bleak House Downs in 1962, on property that had previously been acquired by the U.S. Coast Guard during World War II.

The original building at this location was a modest homestead, constructed in 1805 by Zachariah Howes, on a 25-acre parcel of land in the Indian Fields area. In 1888, grandson Ezra greatly expanded the house and named it Bleak House because it stood alone amidst clear land that extended from the Bay to Scargo Lake[10]

During the War, the Coast Guard established a headquarters in the Bleak House, with primary responsibility for patrolling beaches and keeping an offshore lookout for German U-boats (submarines). There also were cases of German spies coming ashore in rubber boats launched from their submarines.

Guardsmen were housed in a building called the Knoll House on Howes Street, immediately west of the Bleak House property. At the peak of the war, it has been estimated that two-hundred men were stationed at the Bleak House. Each night they'd conduct foot patrols along Dennis beaches looking for signs of the enemy; preferably not the real thing. On occasion, some of the Dennis girls would walk along the beach with the Guardsmen but their eyes were certainly not trained offshore.

In 1942, the Coast Guard recognized that dogs could enhance the beach patrols, via their keen sense of smell and ability to be trained for shore duties. On the Bleak House property, numerous small kennel buildings were built to house over fifty German Shephard dogs that were trained on-site. Thousands of patrol dogs were trained at coastal facilities in all Coast Guard Districts around the country during the early '40s.

My uncle and grandparents lived a short distance to the east of the Bleak House facilities and remembered when new dogs would arrive as they barked wildly each morning and evening, likely around feeding time.

The Bleak House and adjacent kennels were removed from the property or demolished in 1962 to make way for the privately owned Bleak House Downs development. Townspeople were permitted to take any of the construction debris for personal use[5,11].

During the war, the Guardsmen would communicate through wires buried in the beach sand rather than via radios that could be detected by the enemy. Today, when winter storms shift the sand along the dunes east of Corporation Beach, wires from the Coast Guard communications are sometimes uncovered.

While only eight years old, Dickie delivered newspapers to the Coast Guardsmen who were stationed at the Knoll House on Howes Street. The enlisted men enjoyed war-time news and young Dickie was more pleased, being able to view the 'girly magazines' that were plentiful in the soldiers' quarters.

The original, 600-foot-long stone wall of the Bleak House property still exists along Seaside Avenue, off Route 6A. It was constructed in 1901 by a local mason named John Murphy[12], from small, wave-tumbled stones that were collected from Sandy Neck in Barnstable. An identical wall can be found at 831 Route 6A.

Corporation Beach

Patricia A. Walker, a twelfth-generation Cape Codder, produced a fine book titled *Nobscusset Harbor at Corporation Beach.*[2] She grew up in the village and was blessed with a grandfather, Ben Walker, who was undoubtedly the 'saltiest' local since the Clipper Ship days. She begins with stories of the local Nobscusset Indian tribe, how the Nobscusset Harbor thrived during the days of coastal sailing vessels and the booming commercial business where today there's barely a trace. The history of breakwater construction is accompanied by many photos. Her 'Memory Lane' provides quotes from locals who recall enjoyable times at Corporation Beach from years past.

Below are a variety of interesting facts and fond memories from the '40s and '50s:

- Ben Walker was town Fish Warden from 1915 to 1932 and Harbormaster of Nobscusset Harbor from 1932 to 1952. The 1949 Annual Report of the Town of Dennis indicates that Ben was paid $5 as Harbormaster for the year. He had a fleet of a half-dozen flat-bottomed skiffs that he would rent for $1 per day to visiting fishermen. All were built by Warren Wigginton in a wood shop where the Encore Restaurant exists today.

- Ben initially sold lobsters for 15 cents each, regardless of size: 15 cents for a ten pounder! Later he realized that selling for 5 cents per pound was significantly more lucrative. Today's typical price of $8 per pound is 160 times more expensive than Ben's price! (Gasoline has increased by a factor of only 30 over the same time period.)

- He also was known to be a very competitive striped bass fisherman. When he hooked a large fish, he'd show no excitement and calmly motor his skiff away from the other boats with the fish still on the line.

When he was a fair distance off, he'd slide the big bass over the skiff's gunwale without the other fishermen noticing, then head back to where he had hooked it. He wanted no one to see his landings.

- Harry Hall and Francis Gibbs were additional skilled lobstermen back in the '40s and '50s. Francis was physically handicapped, with one arm ending just above his elbow. Regardless, he would pull the pot line with his complete arm then tuck the line under his shortened arm for each three-foot pull. Nowadays, some men complain that it's hard work pulling lobster pots using motorized winches!

- In the late '50s, Clarence 'Ginger' Eldridge was another Dennis lobsterman with a skiff in the harbor and the bearer of a big bushy mustache. As a ten-year-old, I sometimes accompanied him in his skiff and small outboard to watch him pull his pots. On other days, I joined him to visit his muskrat traps set in the backwaters of Brewster and Orleans. I still remember the look of panic on Clarence's face one day, when a large whale breached near our skiff off Nobscusset Harbor. He headed toward shore as fast as the little outboard would go.

- Smelly wooden skiffs always lay aground at low tide behind the breakwater, where water depths exceeded two fathoms, seventy-five years ago. Some of the 'salty' owners would purposely leave fish gurry and lobster bait (i.e., rotten herring) on the deck of the skiffs so they'd smell bad and keep children out. And they used old, metal automobile license plates to patch the largest holes in the skiffs.

- Dennis natives can date themselves by recalling how many vertical pilings existed when they first climbed on the eastern tip of the breakwater. Do you remember the large, circular-link chain that hung around the 'King's Chair'?

- Pristine, edible soft-shelled clams (steamers) could be dug in the harbor, inshore of the breakwater.

- Jack Ass Rock, north of the breakwater, was always prominent except at the highest tide. One story has the name originating from a man named Jack Sire who would sit on the large rock to fish during the upper half of the tide. Because he'd often fall asleep, he'd tie a fishing line around his toe to awaken himself when he had a bite. But the validity of this tale remains unproven.

- Most cannot remember the large hill that was originally located immediately to the west and southwest of the existing parking lot at Corporation Beach. It was excavated and the rocks used to build the first macadam surface on what is now Route 6A.

- The large, gray swimmer's raft was anchored east of the breakwater's tip, near the low-water line during summer months. For teens of the area, the raft represented a local 'Rite to adulthood' via proving your ability to swim to the distant raft at high tide.

- Many children of the '50s remember Mr. Tyler, the Town's summer swimming instructor at Corporation Beach. He'd be there at 8 a.m. sharp, rain or shine, north wind or not. We all hated going into the sea on those cold mornings when the wind and waves were approaching from the north. The young boys felt 'very small' from the cold as we stood in the frigid water with seaweed around our little legs. Of course, the weather didn't bother Mr. Tyler – he was on the Underwater Demolition Team (UDT) of the U.S. Navy during World War II. Today the UDT is referred to as the SEAL (Sea Air and Land) team.

Aircraft Bombing of the Target Ship in Cape Cod Bay

As Dennis teens sat in the dunes during covert, late-evening 'beach parties' of the late '40s through the '60s, all got excited watching the aerial bombing of the 'target ship' located well to the east of Dennis in Cape Cod Bay. They'd hear the characteristic rumbling from the propeller-driven aircraft that originated from Otis Air Force Base in Bourne and flew low and eastward, only a mile or so north of the beach. In later years, jets from South Weymouth Naval Air Station would approach from the northwest with guns and missile launchers trained on the target ship. The gunnery training operations began in 1945 and continued until 1970, despite World War II and the Korean Conflict having ended many years before.

Back in those days, we'd lose sight of the eastward-flying planes and the aircraft sounds would gradually fade but we knew to watch for the 'tracers' that would appear as white streaks across the low sky as the aircraft approached the motionless, partially submerged hull of its target. Within seconds, we'd see many bright flashes caused by live ammunition hitting the ship. From experience, we knew the lag-time between the flashes and the sound of bomb impacts would be around thirty seconds, due to the seven-mile distance for the sound waves to reach us (at the same speed as thunder traveling one mile in five seconds.)

Some nights the bombing was brief; other times it occurred as we lay in our beds on warm summer evenings with the windows open and large June Bugs buzzing, fortunately on the outside of our window screens. Room air conditioners were not yet in the minds nor budgets of most Dennis homeowners back in the '50s and '60s.

The doomed, sunken vessel was officially named the *SS James Longstreet* but Dennis locals affectionately called her the 'Taaagit Ship'. Stately at 440 feet in length, she was scuttled during a very high tide on New Found Shoal three miles west of Eastham in 27 feet of water. Her military career was short, having been built in 1942 but soon after, categorized a total loss after a collision with a British vessel and running aground off New Jersey in 1943.

The *Longstreet* had made transits across both the Pacific and the Atlantic, carrying cargo to support wartime operations, as did many of the 12,000 Liberty Ships built for the Navy in 1942-

1943. At least she became the most photographed vessel in Cape Cod Bay before literally being shot-to-pieces. She now rests on the seafloor as algae-covered scrap metal and home for assorted marine life. The old girl served her country well. Out of sight but not out of Cape Cod memories.

Sears, Roebuck and Company – Mail-Order Houses

As the village expanded during the early to mid-1900s, most of the new houses were constructed by local carpenters using standard building materials. In the later decades of the 1900s, prefabricated houses began to appear but they generally were small and intended as a low-cost alternative to normal construction techniques.

It will likely surprise most people born in the last forty years that large prefabricated houses were sold via mail-order by Sears, Roebuck and Company between 1908 and 1940. Three of their 'Sears Modern Homes' were constructed in the village and still stand today, at 563 and 889 Route 6A, and 29 Corporation Road. They were originally the homes of Mr. Earle Davidson, Mr. William Miller and Mr. Anson Howes, respectively.

Each single-family home was relatively substantial and based on wood construction. The components (25 tons for the average house) were shipped by Sears via railroad and off-loaded to trucks at the rail station on Willow Street in Yarmouth Port. The Sears houses were known to have excellent construction, as built from 'full-size' timbers versus the scaled-down lumber that is used today.

Sears offered 370 different architectural styles. It's estimated that more than 70,000 were sold in the United States and a small number in Canada. The 'kit' homes came with a 75-page construction manual and 10,000 to 30,000 pieces, some marked to aid assembly.

The houses were very popular in 1929, just before the Great Depression. The least-expensive model cost less than $1,000 (for components) while the highest was about $4,400, roughly $70,000 in present-day value. These costs did not include plumbing fixtures, heating elements nor wiring; nor the carpenters' expense. Nevertheless, Sears provided a strong house, proven to have survived many hurricanes.

Village Improvement Society

Around 1900, the population of Dennis was only 2,300 and there was no Public Works Department. Few businesses existed and consequently, town coffers were low and barely enough to build and maintain roads. Fortunately, a number of good citizens stepped up to aid the town, as volunteers, sweeping streets, decorating Veterans' graves and performing other civic activities.

In 1902, the Village Improvement Society of Dennis (VIS) was officially chartered by the Commonwealth of Massachusetts with the objective 'To improve and ornament the streets and public grounds of the Village of Dennis by gathering and cultivating trees and performing such other acts as shall tend to beautify the village.'[13] Improvement

Societies became prevalent in many Cape Cod villages around the turn of the century.

'The (Dennis) Society is committed to maintaining a quality of life in the village, and has supported issues that seek to improve its character.' as discussed on the VIS website.[13] The Society has been involved in designing several buildings in the village, installing park benches and fences, and adding a dock at the town landing on Scargo Lake.

Nobscussett Park was created from the 'un-development' of a parcel of land on the corner of Nobscussett Road at 680 Route 6A. Although the town owns the park land, the Society manages the maintenance and landscaping, with assistance of local citizens and business owners.

The VIS has demonstrated remarkable civic pride for over 116 years. Get involved, there are other projects underway that could use assistance from townsfolk.

Telephone Operators

Back in the '40s and '50s, some would say everyone knew each other's 'business' whether they liked it or not. Rumors spread quickly amongst the working men, most of whom toiled within a few miles of the Post Office. They also 'chewed the fat' during visits to the Post Office and Dennis Garage, where gossip was fertilized daily. Independently, the women had their own tight circles for discussion, especially when a new woman arrived from out of town.

As surprising as it may sound,

communications technology of those days surely helped the rumor mill. The terminus of each home or business 'land line' was the large, heavy phone with the rotary dial mechanism and characteristic bell ringer. Pertinent to this discussion is the simplistic means for making outgoing calls. This required a New England Telephone Company employee to mechanically link the caller with the intended party. This 'Operator' would sit in front of a vertical panel (TPX-1 switchboard) having one single-hole receptacle (phone jack) for each home or local business. When a call 'came in' to the Operator, she would connect a wire (phone cord with a phone plug on each end) from the caller's jack, to that of the intended party, which would cause their phone to ring.

In some cases, more than one house had to share a single line, thus the term 'party line' in such situations. For example, Dickie Buck's house was line 206M while his neighbor was 206W. If the incoming call had two quick rings, Dickie knew it was a call for his house; if only one ring, the call was for the neighbor. Few phone numbers were needed in the '50s. For example, Dennis Garage was 23.

Unlike today's fully-automated phone switching systems, the early Operators had the option of listening to conversations if they wished; not company policy but often done. Not only would the Operator learn who spoke with whom but she could follow the most intimate discussions without being suspected nor ever proven guilty.

Nationally, the very first telephone Operators, in 1878, were males but their lack of patience (and occasionally, inappropriate comments with customers) quickly rendered them unacceptable in this role. Soon, telephone companies hired women as they were generally more courteous and with higher-pitched voices which aided audible clarity, as proven for maritime radios. In those days, telephone companies also liked that women could be paid a fraction of the men's salary.

There is no doubt that the Operators who sat in the small telephone building on Route 6A in East Dennis enjoyed their job, probably beyond what it paid. Standard procedure was for Operators to work four-hour shifts then take a significant break. Dickie's Aunt, Thelma Jacobs, was an Operator as well as the Author's Aunt, Joy (McDowell) Boucher.

Operators were replaced with updated telephone technology in the mid-50s. The original telephone building is part of the house now located at 1687 Route 6A. If only those walls could talk.

Scargo Tower

The history of Scargo Tower has been well documented by others[5]. In brief, the initial, wooden tower was constructed in 1874 as a tourist attraction, with funding from a group of local residents. Tragically, a major storm blew the tower to the ground two years later. A second wooden tower was constructed in 1876 and later purchased by the owners of the Nobscusset Hotel for use as an Observatory by guests visiting the Hotel. A telescope installed in the tower supposedly could reveal the time on the large clock in Provincetown (22 miles to the north), as well as structures on Nantucket (38 miles to the south).

Fate again struck the tower, via a large fire that consumed the peak of the hill in the late 1890s. A new stone-and-concrete tower was constructed in 1901 by a local mason, John Murphy, who used stones transported from Sandy Neck in Barnstable. The tower was donated to the town in 1929 and a tablet was erected adjacent to the structure for recognition of the generous donors.

During World War II, drivers of autos visiting Scargo Tower at night were prohibited from illuminating their sealed beams (headlights) for concern they would be seen by enemy submarines. Additionally, citizens were prohibited from bringing hand lights, lanterns and radios up on the hill.

Army soldiers were stationed at the tower around the clock in 1943 and 1944. Dickie and his friends would sometimes go visit the soldiers to see their guns and ammunition. On occasion, they gave the boys a few unfired shells, knowing the rounds were 'blanks' containing gun powder but no lead shot. Dickie would take the shells to a garage, put them in a vice and hit them on the end with a nail and hammer to fire them. One time, a shell blew up and a piece of the metal cap flew through his thumb causing an injury that is still visible today. Crazy eight-year-old boys playing with live ammunition.

Most of the soldiers were only about seventeen or eighteen so they enjoyed joking around with young Dickie. 'Hey young fella, go see if you can find our big guns on the north side of the hill.' There were big guns like Howitzers hidden in small caves in the sand hillside below the tower, many of which Dickie found.

***

Dennis residents and visitors as well enjoyed Scargo Tower during the '40s through the '60s. Most memorable was the wooden, circular stairway that made three revolutions to reach the top viewing platform. Large, concrete openings were strategically placed in the circular walls to provide climbers a view from various compass directions while ascending. The soft wood of the stairs and handrails allowed easy carving of visitors' initials, often circumscribed by the shape of a heart, symbolizing their relationships. For many decades, Scargo Tower was the favorite spot for 'lovebirds' to share precious moments and drop a knee for marriage proposals too.

Unfortunately, the wooden stairs within the tower gradually failed and had to be removed for safety reasons. New stairs were constructed with galvanized-steel steps and strong wire fencing but the hundreds of carved initials were lost forever. Maybe some folks have pieces of those prized, wooden steps in their homes as souvenirs. Most disappointing is that tower visitors of today cannot return to see the carved initials of their grandparents who kissed in the tower at a young age.

D. H. Sears' General Store – Later, Hodsdon's Ice Cream

East Dennis had been known as the site of fine confectioneries since David Henry (D. H.) Sears opened his general store at 23 School Street in 1887.[5] By the time he was twenty-two years old, his reputation for creating the best ice cream spread among the prestigious Cape Cod resorts of the day, as well as to distant shores by travelers who retained a craving for their favorite summer dessert.

In addition to his special recipe, it was essential to have a substantial source of ice throughout summer months. This was accomplished by cutting thick blocks of ice from frozen ponds in late winter. Both Scargo Lake and Cedar Pond were excellent northside sources as they had clear water and were mostly protected from winter winds that would prevent ice formation. 'Ice houses' were built lakeside for storage of the ice. These small barns had walls one-foot thick filled with sawdust or seaweed that was effective insulation for the large blocks of ice that were stacked tightly to fill the entire house.

D.H.'s ice cream was sold from his store until his death in 1952; a run of 65 summers making ice cream! For a few years after, his grandsons Dave and Bill Hodsdon (sons of Gertrude Sears Hodsdon) continued the summer ice cream business from a new building at 33 South Street. With the advent of refrigeration, pond ice was no longer necessary in the late '50s, making the ice cream process much easier.

When the business closed, Dickie purchased all the ice cream making equipment. It may still reside in the basement of the Lost Dog Pub.

Ezra H. Baker School and Dennis-Yarmouth Regional High School

The term 'Consolidated School' is foreign to most Dennis townsfolk in the twenty-first century but prior to 1931, children from Kindergarten through Grade 8 were educated in a variety of small buildings. Fortunately for the town, Mr. Ezra H. Baker deeded a large parcel of land at 810 Main Street (Route 28) to the town for construction of a large school that would allow consolidation of all grades prior to High School participation. The new Dennis Consolidated School, completed in 1931, had nine grades and only nine teachers were needed in the first few years.

When eighth-graders graduated from the Consolidated School between 1932 and 1956, they were transferred to the Yarmouth High School for their last four years of public education. This 'regional bussing' was necessary because the small Dennis North and Dennis South High Schools could no longer accommodate the growing school enrollment of the town. Interestingly, the High School graduation exercises for Dennis students were conducted at the Cape Playhouse for these years.

In 1949, a special ceremony was conducted at the Consolidated School for the purpose of renaming the facility as the 'Ezra H. Baker School', in honor of the original land donor. Also that year,

Mr. Baker's wife deeded an adjacent parcel that could be used for the ballfield and later building additions to the school, which were constructed in 1961.

Dickie was a sixth grader at the 1949 renaming celebration but as a 'skilled' trumpeter, he was selected to play at the commemorative flag-raising event. Another boy, Lincoln Thacher, also played trumpet while positioned across the large field. He and Dickie perfected an echo-effect that added to the significance of the celebration.

In 1957, the Dennis-Yarmouth Regional High School (D-Y) was opened to thereafter accommodate all students from Dennis and Yarmouth, who had been attending the overcrowded Yarmouth High School. Additional students from Brewster also began enrolling at D-Y.

Starting in 1969, children from Grades 6, 7 and 8 could no longer be accommodated at the overcrowded Ezra H. Baker School and consequently were transferred to the new Nathaniel H. Wixon School at 901 Route 134 for their schooling. Thereafter, the Ezra H. Baker School accommodated students up to grade 5 (and only to grade 4 a few years later).[14]

Willows Inn and Howes Street Beach Pavilion

Another fine summer resort developed in the village was the Willows. Located at 77 Seaside Avenue, patrons have expansive views of Cape Cod Bay from guestrooms, as well as from the front porch that was surrounded by a stone wall that still exists today.[15] In the '40s, Heddie Howes was the owner of the property and ran the Inn which consisted of the large Guest House and eight small cabins. When ten and eleven years old, Dickie worked for Heddie two summers in the mid '40s. His duties were to wash the sheets from the guest rooms and mow the large lawn with a push-style reel mower, for fifty cents per hour; pretty good pay for a young boy in those days.

The Howes family also owned a large hay field across the street from the Inn. As a boy, Dickie rode the cows that grazed there, as well as the Howes' horse, Nelly. Also part of the Willows facility was a significant stretch of private beach on Cape Cod Bay at the north end of Howes Street. Old timers had initially called this beach Seaside Beach or Bathhouse Beach.

Back in 1903, the Howes family constructed a wooden boardwalk over the sand dunes and a beach pavilion for use by the summer guests. In 1939, the town purchased the beach property from the Howes family and converted the pavilion into a public bathhouse with individual changing rooms that beachgoers could rent for the day. The facility and snack bar were managed by Harold Dixon until the structure was damaged by a major storm in the '50s. Soon after, the facility was demolished and removed. Today, only the town parking lot remains at the north end of Howes Beach.

In the late '40s, Dickie and other teen boys hung around the bathhouse in summer when girls would be in the changing rooms. The boys would temporarily remove a few of the circular, wood knots from the pine wallboards which allowed them to peek-in through the small holes. Also, there were no ceilings above the rooms; only wide sections of chicken wire to prevent entry from overhead. This also gave the boys a fine vantage-point when they shinnied across the roof rafters. Boys will be boys!

As late as the '60s, there were no homes situated north of Seaside Avenue, opposite the Willows. Dickie used to ride a mare on that field and young Nate Howes would cut and bale hay there. Today, the field has been replaced by a neighborhood of densely spaced homes overlooking the Bay. Progress?

Hokum Rock – The Necking Spot

In the '40s and '50s, only a dirt road led to the cluster of large rocks fondly called Hokum Rock. They lay tucked in the scrub pine forest at 170 Hokum Rock Road, midway between Old Bass River Road and Route 134. It is believed the name Hokum originated from the native Indian word 'hoccanum', meaning 'back bend' because the largest of the rocks was bent, similar to that of a man bending over.

Reid[5] presented two additional theories for the origin of the rock pile's name. The first is associated with a local Indian named Hoken who was an incorrigible thief and dangerous individual. Local (English) authorities punished him repeatedly and later sent him to prison but he managed to escape. He was finally sentenced in 1674, under terms that if captured, he would be sold or banished to Barbados, 'to free the colonie from so ill a member'. But

Hoken's fate is still unknown.

A second legend, from the 1880s, is that an aged descendent of the Nobscusset tribe lived in a cave under the rock pile. When someone approached, he would call out 'Who Come?' – possibly the origin of what we now pronounce as 'Hokum'. Could the elderly tribesman have been a descendant of the scoundrel Hoken, of two-hundred years prior?

Regardless of its naming convention, Hokum Rock had never been a tourist destination. The rough road leading to it was riddled with vast pot holes, making it off-limits for the average vehicle and driver. But its secluded, unlit setting made it a perfect spot for 'necking' in the large back seat of cars from the '40s and '50s. The spot was so dark that if another car approached in the night, a busy couple could rustle up their clothing in time, in the event it was the police investigating whether 'everyone was OK?'.

Hokum Rock Road gained significant summer traffic with the opening of the Dennis Drive-In Theater, located west of Route 134. The road remained a dirt/gravel surface for many years until the town created a paved road that spanned the distance from Route 134 to Old Bass River Road. With all privacy now gone at the 'Rock', necking ceased at this location but the fond memories of those nights linger forever in the minds of those who received their first kiss (and more) in the darkness behind Hokum Rock.

Lido – Today's Royal II Pizza; Earlier, Deacon's Perch

The Royal II Restaurant and Grill at 715 Route 6A in Yarmouth Port, near the Dennis town line, is a fine restaurant with Mediterranean, Italian and American cuisine. Since opening in 2013, it has earned an excellent reputation for pizza and Greek specialties but the history of eating and drinking establishments at this location certainly predates the present business.

Prior to the Royal II, the Deacon's Perch operated in the same facility, as a summer bar known for its excellent live entertainment during the evening. The 'Perch' was built in the early '70s and continued operation until approximately 2002.

Ken Manzer was the main entertainer at the Perch; a renowned pianist who captured the attention of everyone sitting at the bar and surrounding tables. Ken was a faculty pianist at Westfield State College and had played for Arthur Fiedler with the Boston Pops. Anyone who visited the Perch to enjoy the music quickly learned that Ken 'ruled the roost' in the establishment. If any patron spoke while Ken was playing, he'd immediately stop his keyboard mastery and loudly scold the patron; warning that he/she would be escorted from the premises if another word was spoken during his performance. The rules were simple: enjoy the music, be silent or leave. People generally obeyed because Ken's piano performances were excellent.

Hardly worth mentioning was the small chicken and egg farm located across the street from the Perch. Tucked away in the pines, the farm was operated by a kind, strongly accented Swedish family who sold eggs to local patrons. They also were pleased when customers would fill their trucks or car trunks with fresh chicken manure for composting of their home gardens. I did not enjoy accompanying my grandparents on these odorific trips, back in the late '50s.

Prior to establishment of the Deacon's Perch, old timers from Dennis and Yarmouth remember the Lido. Dickie recalls the Lido having a bar/restaurant in the main building, plus eight small cottages situated back from the road, which were rented to overnight guests. He retains vivid memories of the Lido because he worked there in 1949 while fourteen. His duties included cleaning the cottages and making beds, as well as helping make spaghetti and salads in the restaurant.

By the early '50s, the Lido had gained the reputation of being a popular watering hole where the town's more 'seedy' characters would quench their thirst. Later, the establishment gained immense notoriety for another cause: The owner/proprietor, Mrs. Grant, chose to conduct another type of business from the small cottages behind the Lido. Her intentions may have been good, to help women with unwanted pregnancies, but abortion was illegal in those days. That didn't stop Mrs. Grant nor her partner in crime, a reputable medical doctor who was highly acclaimed in Hyannis. He and Mrs. Grant were arrested in 1950 and put in jail for many years. That proved to be the end of the Lido establishment as well.

Carleton Hall – Minstrel Shows and Children's Square Dancing

Carleton Hall, located at 1006 Old Bass River Road, has a history that dates back to 1830.[5] Originally constructed by the Reformed Methodists, it was purchased by a group of Dennis residents, led by Captain Carleton Howes, and modified for use by the community. In 1954 it was given to the town by citizens who owned original shares in the property, with stipulation that it be used by 'Benevolent, charitable and recreational organizations' of the town. Two widely different uses are indicated below:

Minstrel Shows

The village has been void of bigotry since anyone can remember. It is thus, with great irony, that men conducted Annual Jubilee Minstrel Shows, at Carleton Hall, starting around 1950. Slavery, religion and other controversial topics of the first minstrel shows of the early 1800s, in southern states, were purposely absent from the Dennis productions. But the local men adopted the minstrel format to air their strong opinions on local topics of the day.

Most of the townsfolk attended to see their middle-aged, male relatives and friends performing on stage, dressed in the colorful garb of professional minstrels and singing in chorus. Wives had obviously toiled on costumes to make their men stand-out on stage.

The typical Interlocutor and End Man played their parts well, with rehearsed banter that everyone could relate to, on issues in the village or surrounding towns. One of the most memorable Minstrel characters was tall Howard L. Hall, dressed in tails and top hat, and masterful playing the bones. And his young grandson, Billy Thatcher, also carried the skill for later generations, as demonstrated during a short Minstrel production that was conducted by the sons, in the late '50s. Joel Crowell played the Interlocutor finely. I too participated.

As an example (from the 1956 Jubilee Minstrel) of how the local men expressed their strong opinions on topics of the day, somewhat in jest and via the Minstrel format, the following lines made it clear that most individuals didn't want the Cape to become over populated:[5]

'We don't want no Mid-Cape highway, we don't want no tourist boom.
We just want to do things our way, all we want is elbow room!'

Square Dancing Lessons for Early Teens

'Al-a-hand left with a monkey on your right.' This verbal command was 'as clear as mud' to many of the ten-year-old boys who'd been delivered to Carleton Hall on Wednesday afternoons in winter. The boys had no idea what was said nor what it meant, so their interpretations were askew, wicked awful.

Dapper Mr. Anderson, who was the 'Caller' for the Children's Square Dancing Lessons was a Master in his realm. Dressed in jacket and bow tie, with a short crewcut and corded microphone in hand, the slight man was determined to keep the attention of the children, who might someday become dancing stars on Community Auditions in far-away Boston.

How Mr. Anderson was able to control his focus and keep his wits, with all the mischievous boys joking around and snickering at the young girls, was truly remarkable - not unlike herding cats. For the boys, it was their first opportunity to touch the hand or arm of a GIRL who wasn't their pesky sister. Most preferred to be male Wall Flowers. They muffled their objections when the Caller ordered the boys to pick a partner. And the girls weren't keen either, as some of the boys smelled like fish or grease from their father's garage (both in my case). Later, the girls got to choose their partner, from the Flowers who couldn't possibly back any farther into the wall.

Remarkably, all the children managed to survive each one-hour dance lesson, with smiles, only to return the following Wednesday with similar trepidation. Years later, the participants may have learned the meaning of Mr. Andersen's exact words: 'Allemande Left with the Lady on the Right.' One of the simplest square-dancing calls, whereby a dancer changes position in the circle via turning and ending with their back facing the past partner so each can move on, greeting the next person in line. The children actually liked this maneuver because they weren't 'stuck' with a single partner for long.

Kudos to the Town Fathers for investing in Mr. Andersen's lessons. A gallant attempt to introduce dance and culture to the village children.

Sign of the Motor Car – Where Dennis Village Theatrics Originated

The history of theatrical productions in the village is an interesting tale that began in a small cottage immediately east of the prominent Scargo Manor B&B at 909 Route 6A. The cottage no longer resides at its original location, having been moved decades ago to Route 28 in West Dennis, but the tale deserves being told, especially as it involves many Dennis residents, including Dickie and his relatives too.

Mrs. Margaret (Howes) Richardson (1876-1948) was a descendent of the Dennis Howes family. She and her husband Hayden Richardson (1869-1922) lived a creative life in New York with various business ventures, including a jigsaw puzzle-making business.[5] Margaret's strong desire to return to her ancestral village led the couple to purchase a cottage at 919 Route 6A. In 1910 they opened an Inn and Tea Room, promoting their facility as the 'Sign of the Motor Car' and hoping to attract tourists who were driving through the village. Business was initially slow but they used clever means to attract patrons and eventually establish a viable business.[5]

Most pertinent to the local history of theatrical developments, Margaret became a 'close' friend of Raymond Moore after her husband passed away in 1922. To this day, locals are very familiar with Mr. Moore as he developed the Cape Playhouse in 1927.

Raymond arrived in Dennis in 1925 after developing theatrical productions in Provincetown. Margaret ('Mags' as she was called later in life) was 49 at the time, financially comfortable and very willing to assist her friend Raymond. The story has it that Mags (twenty-two years older than Raymond) loved the arts and was very influential in the Playhouse development. Unfortunately, Raymond died in 1940 at the age of 42 when Mags was 64.

One may expect this to be the end of the tale of early theatrics in the village, especially at the small Sign of the Motor Car – not the case.

Mags deeded the property and business to her niece Susie Lutz. Coincidently, she and her husband Herbert ('Whitey' to his friends) also loved the arts.

After Susie died, Whitey married a wealthy woman whose family had extensive holdings from a female cosmetics business. She was the ideal supporter for Whitey, providing sufficient financial backing for him to pursue his theatrical interests, as had Raymond Moore with funding from Margaret Richardson, the wealthy Aunt of Whitey's first wife Susie.

Dickie recalls that when he was a young boy, his father 'Buckie' participated in a play that was produced and directed by Whitey Lutz. The play was performed outdoors and adjacent to Scargo Lake on the grounds of the Sign of the Motor Car Inn. Dickie has a photo of his father dressed in an angel's costume while playing the guitar in the play.

The production, called *The Ballad of Bill*, was cast with wildly costumed players, many with big-headed masks.

Most of the participants were residents of the village, including the Author's father. One of the central ballads in the production was *Streets of Laredo*, the story of a young cowboy who had done much wrong, was shot in the chest, then was gone. The ending was, 'We all loved our comrade although he'd done wrong.' Dickie still recites every line from this ballad, possibly because he can relate to it?

Was it actually Whitey Lutz who was lamenting, having done something wrong? Truth be told, he later died under mysterious circumstances. His body was exhumed for concern that his late wife's children had facilitated his ending. The outcome is unknown.

Raymond Moore and Herbert Lutz certainly created a colorful beginning to the performing arts in the village.

Dennis Garage

Another long-term business was the gas station and auto repair business called the Dennis Garage, located on the south side of Route 6A, nearly opposite from the original Post Office at Goodspeed's Store. Initially, Dan Walker was the business partner of Chippy Whittemore. In 1947 when Chippy retired, Dan and Paul McDowell formed a partnership to continue operating the SOCONY-Mobil[16] gas station. After 18 years, they moved the business to a newer facility owned by Getty Oil, located at 680 Route 6A, opposite from the Dennis Public Market. A Tydol gas station had existed previously at that facility, originally operated by Bob Servidori, then later by Peter Tufts and Bill Kelly.

In 1978, the Cape Cod Standard Times published an article on the partnership which was being terminated after 31 years. 'Dennis Garage is where people go to make politics and repair American cars. Paul was widely known for disliking foreign cars, stating that 'We believe in the American Economy.'' Understandably, as he had begun working with Dan immediately after returning from Active Duty with the U.S. Merchant Marines in the Pacific.

Dan continued to run the Garage for another five years, with his son-in-law, Billy Bell. Through its long history, the Dennis Garage certainly was a landmark, run by hard-working local men. The business finally closed in January 1983. Soon after, Cumberland Farms purchased the property from the owner, Getty Oil, and planned to build a convenience store but local opposition convinced the town to buy the land.

***

In the early days, Dan and Paul sold gas and repaired cars six days per week, with extended hours in summer. They remained open late on summer evenings to catch business from cars leaving the Cape Playhouse after the show. Dan, Paul and many other Dennis natives enjoyed poking fun at drivers who needed directions. Their favorite skit was play-acted often, in connection with the Cape Playhouse which was across the street, only a short distance to the east of the Garage. A car would pull up to the gas pumps and ask Dan for directions to the Playhouse. With pipe in mouth, Dan would shake his head no, then holler, 'Hey Paul, ever heard of the Cape Playhouse?'

Paul would reply, 'Nope, what's the name again?'

'The Playhouse, Cape Playhouse I think.' Dan clarified.

'Damn f'I know.' Paul would say, then walk back inside the Garage.

By then, the wife in the car would normally have spotted the very large Playhouse sign across the street. Typical antics of Dan and Paul.

For the convenience of their trusted, long-term customers in the early years, the Garage offered credit to those who filled up often but sometimes arrived at the pump with no cash in their pocket. Dan or Paul would write down the gallons and price of each sale on a ledger. At the end of each month, they'd have the wives 'do the books' and mail monthly bills to the customers. This was common practice in the trusting village, before the arrival of credit cards and automatic metering on the gas pumps. The honor system worked back then.

Furthermore, in those early years there wasn't much concern about groundwater contamination. For example, the proprietors of the Garage would pour waste oil from automobiles on a large patch of bare ground behind the garage building. When asked many years later why this was their method of waste disposal, Dan smugly answered 'Dust Control'. He certainly was a funny Dennis native!

Another important role of the Dennis Garage was coming to the rescue when vehicles were stuck in the sand on North Side beaches, most often during summer when tourists would get their fancy, two-wheel-drive cars stuck in the soft sand. The worst-case scenario involved cars getting stuck or breaking down on the vast Chapin sand bars at low tide. Quickly, the rising seawater would overtake the vehicle before a wrecker could be summoned. In such cases, the car would be watched by many amused onlookers (except the owner) as it disappeared underwater, reappearing six hours later as the tide receded. The Dennis Garage would eventually be called to tow the waterlogged car ashore. With a restrained chuckle and comment 'stupid tourists', Dan or Paul would explain to the naïve owner that although the car looked fine, except for some sea weed and sand inside, it would be a total loss as the saltwater would ruin the wiring and internal combustion engine.

The final and most overlooked duty of the Dennis Garage was to remove cars from the scene of accidents in town. Most occasions did not involve injury to drivers and/or passengers but each year there would be a few horrific accidents, with loss of life. The worst normally occurred at 'Dead Man's Curve' on Route 6A near the early Durham's Gas Station (1098 Route 6A), where the road bends sharply at the intersection of Route 6A, Dr. Lord's Road and Sesuit Neck Road.

Dan had a strong stomach but Paul was squeamish and had gastric difficulty at the scene of gruesome accidents.

Dan's fine sense of humor arose even at the most inopportune times. One day, he received a call from the police that a terrible accident had occurred and the driver had perished. Dan immediately called Paul to tell him to delay, as the crash site would be too gory for him to cope with. On his way to the site, Dan stopped by Louie's meat counter and purchased a very large piece of raw, bloody and gristly beef, which he proceeded to place on the driver's seat before Paul arrived. Paul did encounter the offal mass and immediately 'tossed his cookies' thinking it was the real thing. He wasn't pleased when he later determined it was just another prank by his deadpan partner Dan.

Beach Buggies

The long stretches of white sand extending from Chapin Beach to the Bass Hole and at Crowe's Pasture in East Dennis were perfect playgrounds for beach lovers with vehicles they trusted in the sand. Like its neighbor Sandy Neck, North Dennis beaches received many vehicles during summer months. This activity certainly has gained popularity since the proliferation of four-wheel-drive vehicles that most anyone can drive without getting stuck; even people from off-Cape (a native joke).

Before the '60s, trucks and Jeeps were the primary vehicles for off-road travel but the early Jeep models were uncomfortable for family travel.

Consequently, only a small number of hardy characters 'road the beaches' from the '30s through the '50s. They were practical fellas who owned 'second cars' that were used primarily for beach play. Most were in poor condition, outdated and of no value (the cars; not the men). Consequently, if the cars 'died' in the dunes, there would be no major loss. Some wives may not have cared if the men didn't return either.

These jalopies were called 'beach buggies' by the locals. Although common in other coastal regions around the country, North Dennis in the '40s and '50s certainly had its buggies and characters behind the big steering wheels and sitting atop whining, manual transmissions. The Dennis Garage was pivotal to the activity, having a large wrecker that would be summoned whenever a buggy would get severely stuck (unable to be towed out of the sand by another buggy) or partially underwater with the tide coming in.

The beach buggies were large, heavy, old, manual shift, rear-wheel-drive vehicles. Typically, back seats were removed to lighten the load. Intuition would say these heavy vehicles were the worst type of machine to take on the beach, which was true, but the drivers didn't give a damn, even if the buggy was making its last ride. They put on the oldest, widest and baldest tires they could fit on wide rims and lowered the air pressure down to nine pounds-per-square-inch versus thirty or more in today's tires. This made the old tires squishy and they had no tread at all; like riding on heavy-duty air balloons. The men knew that coarse treads were bad on the beach, as they dug into the sand

versus bald tires cruising along. 'Start off slow, maintain your speed and down-shift quickly if the sand slows you down. Just keep her moving.'[17]

These buggy guys weren't interested in riding on the horizontal beach; they wanted to drive up the side of the tallest dunes they could find. Even going airborne with these multi-ton hunks of rusted metal if they could find a dune with a sharp edge at the top. The thrill was not knowing what was on the other side of the dune crest. Hopefully it was flat and broad; wide enough for the buggy to stop on the crest; and for the driver to show off to his buddies that he was 'King of the Dune'.

Realize that it was very difficult to get the heavy buggy going fast enough to ride up a 45-degree dune face; maybe 25 or 30 miles-per-hour speed for a tall dune. This meant a long running start was necessary. Sometimes when the tide was low at Chapin, the buggies would drive out a quarter mile and line up side-by-side with their big front bumpers headed toward the dunes. When someone honked the starting horn, they'd all put the gas pedal to the floorboard and race to the tallest dune each guy could see. (Of course, during winter when not a soul was lying on the beach.)

Alas, sometimes a driver would race up a dune, then immediately encounter a sharp drop on the other side. (Dune profiles changed often, as sculpted by winter-storm winds.) Unable to stop in time, the buggy would head straight down on the steep, back side of the dune, stopping instantly with its front bumper buried in the horizontal sand and with rear-wheels pointing up-slope. Of course, no seat belts in those days.

No matter what happened, everyone laughed; at themselves, at each other and at their poor buggies. How better for a tired, old 1942 Dodge to spend its final hours screaming through the dunes at the Bass Hole? Like taking your 15-year old mutt for a swim in the Bay on his final day.

No one got hurt, as these were rugged men - buggy men; they could almost always fix what broke. The dunes took some wear and tear, and some beach grass was ripped up in the tire tracks but all this was minor compared to the environmental havoc of a single Nor' Easter. There were likely only six to ten buggies playing in the dunes each year.

Louie Terpos' IGA Grocery Store – Today, Dennis Public Market

The Dennis Public Super Market (DPM), at 653 Route 6A, initially opened as a franchise of IGA (the Independent Grocers Alliance) which was founded in 1926 and quickly grew to eight-thousand independent markets nationwide. Mrs. Estelle Savage and her husband were the original proprietors, then in 1941, Elias 'Louie' Terpos and his wife purchased the market. After the sale, Mrs. Savage had life tenancy above the market and worked behind the register nearly until she passed away.

Today's prohibition of vehicles riding in dunes is wise, as the number of off-road vehicles has increased, likely by a factor of one-hundred. Without this prohibition today, the dunes would surely be decimated and many people would likely be run over as they lay on the leeward side of steep coastal dunes. The days of the big, heavy beach buggies are gone but not forgotten.

Village folk quickly became fond of hard-working 'Papa Louie' even though he wasn't a native (having migrated from the 'city' of Hyannis). The children of the village grew up with Louie's son, Jimmy.

For the next 49 years, the family business earned respect for consistent quality, affordability and employment for many locals. The Dennis Public Super Market was affectionately called 'Louie's' by all the townsfolk. Beside his hardworking business acumen, Louie also was an effective Selectman for six years in the '60s.

In 1981, a major event was held to celebrate the 40th anniversary of the market. Louie's son Jimmy and assistant Tony Zombas continued operating the DPM until it was sold in 1990. Subsequent owners have maintained the neighborhood market charm into their 28th season.

For locals who frequented Louie's from the '40s through the '60s, Mrs. Estelle Savage will always be remembered as well as 'Baby Jane' Dixon who worked behind the counter in the Luncheonette, located at the east end of the building. Jane certainly was a jovial and 'robust' woman, also famous for having two adjoining seats designated for her use at the Hyannis movie theater, where the Author's mother worked during her High School years.

***

Dickie Buck's wife, Judy, was the store manager at DPM for twenty-four years, having been trained by Mrs. Savage. Vi (Viola) Sencabaugh (Dickie's mother-in-law) and Carol Sears also were long-term employees at Louie's Luncheonette and Soda Fountain. And friendly Billy King worked in the meat market for five decades. Ruthy Lynch also was a long-term employee at Louie's and lived in one of the apartments upstairs.

Some townsfolk remember that notorious Lester Hallett would visit the market each fall season to pick a fight with Louie. No one can recall what the long-term disagreement was based on (or even if there was one) but it happened like clockwork. Lester would arrive, inebriated, and make quite a scene, 'calling out' Louie and threatening to 'Knock him to the moon!'. Quickly, the police would be called to prevent the ensuing scuffle. The friendly local police knew the routine and would handcuff Lester and take him to the Barnstable County House of Correction. There, Lester would stay for the fall and winter; eventually being released in spring when he could be gainfully employed again, as a skilled gardener. More details about Lester are given later (see Notorious Characters Chapter).

Next door to the DPM, at 633 Route 6A, was the long-term home of the Dixon family. In the '50s, Maud conducted her Real Estate business from that location. Her husband Harold was the operator of the Willows' Bathhouse on the beach at the north end of Howes Street. The Dixons sold Sunday newspapers from their front porch on Route 6A. It was their daughter Jane who worked behind the Luncheonette counter at Louie's.

My grandfather, Walter McDowell, one of Maud Dixon's siblings, was born in the family home next to the DPM, in 1896. Walter also sold Real Estate, during his retirement years, and developed the area known as Newcomb's Hill, extending from Route 6A to Cape Cod Bay, west of Dr. Lord's Road. Three roads were constructed in the new neighborhood, all named after Walter's children: Paul Street, Peter Road and Joy Lane.[18]

Dennis Drive-in-Fly-In Theater

Cape Cod's first outdoor movie theater was officially named the Dennis Drive-In-Fly-In Theater.[19] Opened in summer of 1949, it was located at 300-326 Hokum Rock Road, a parcel that is now owned by the Dennis Water District. The Annual Town Report of Dennis for that year indicates that a $10 license was granted for the private theater business. The Drive-In was the dream of Louis Segrini, a true visionary of his time, and off-Cape developer from Mansfield, MA. He even posted a notice of the Drive-In's Opening in the May 1949 issue of 'The Billboard' magazine, which was 'The World's Foremost Amusement Weekly' of its time.

Louis planned to 'Show Cape Codders how to live'. His facility was built with a ground-level restaurant but Louis didn't stop there. On the roof was a dance floor, a bar for selling alcohol, a live orchestra that played before and after the movies, and seating to watch the movies. A bit grandiose for Dennis standards, especially in 1949! The roof activities quickly went bust but the ground-level concession stand continued for years, offering 'theater quality' fare.

Widely advertised with capacity for one-thousand cars, the theater welcomed patrons to 'drive in or fly in' via automobile or airplane, to view evening movies during summer months. Double features (back-to-back on the single, large screen) were shown after sunset – certainly a bargain for families with a flock of children. Typically, a children's movie played first then a more adult-oriented feature was shown later when the children were (possibly) asleep. Freedom to bring your own refreshments was much appreciated, as well as room to set up chairs in front of your car. Some children sat on the roof of their parent's car too. The only down-side was the mosquitos that often-necessitated car windows to be closed or bug repellent to be applied liberally to the entire family.

Below are fond memories that many Dennis locals recall from their Drive-In days:

- Packing many teen kids in the large, rear trunk of autos from the '50s to evade the movie admission charges. Quite often, the ticket attendant and accompanying policeman (Don Parker or Dick Sylver) would suspect a prank was underway and insist on opening the truck.

- Taking your first girl- or boyfriend to the Drive-In and appreciating the full-width bench seats of cars from that era. The newly designed bucket seats of the '60s were not enjoyed by many Drive-In patrons.

- Upon completion of the double feature movies (typically around 1 am), auto drivers would be tired and eager to leave the theater. In haste, they'd forget to rehang the heavy, wired speaker back onto the adjacent, well-reinforced pole. Upon driving away, the speaker would either pull the driver's side window out of the door, or the car would pull the speaker and wire from the pole; sometimes both. Either way, the result was not well appreciated by someone. Local boys had a collection of Drive-In speakers at home – strong, water-proof and ideal for other usages.

- The long Intermissions between movie features were fun for the kids, flocking to the concession stand for popcorn and to see their friends. But we also remember the Jimmy Fund collections for cancer research at the Dana-Farber Cancer Institute. Ted Williams of the Boston Red Sox was a prestigious representative, making his heart-felt 'pitch' on the big screen and encouraging everyone to make donations into the cardboard cups when theater employees visited each auto before the second movie started.

The Drive-In Theater operated successfully for thirty summers, until 1979. Dickie worked at the theater in 1952, during his junior year in high-school. He and friends wore zip-up, one-piece, white suits[20] while parking cars and directing traffic upon departure. The large concrete screen was finally demolished in 1987.

***

On the opening night of the theater in 1949, Mr. George Parmenter and his wife Doris (a descendent of the original Howes family) arrived in their private plane, landing on the small runway behind the theater. A photograph of their plane, situated among the parked cars at the Dennis Drive-In, is shown in the book on Dennis history.[5]

George and his wife were co-founders of Cape and Island Flight Service. Later, he became a senior pilot and co-founder of Air New England. She too was a pilot and highly educated.

Tragically, on a foggy night in June of 1979, George crashed in the Yarmouth Port woods (near Camp Greenough) while piloting a flight from New York to Hyannis. He was the sole fatality, while nine other persons survived the crash. George will forever be remembered as one of the most influential men in the development of air travel in New England.

Miraculously, a nineteen-year-old passenger on that ill-fated Flight 248 survived the crash and was able to make her way through the dense forest in darkness to reach Route 6 and obtain help for the other survivors. Susanne Mourad was the hero, then residing with her parents on Whig Street during her summer vacation.

Gina's and Rose's Restaurants in Little Taunton

Gina's By The Sea (originally Gina's House) is both quaint and the longest-running restaurant in the village. Operating since 1935, it's a true landmark, providing culinary specialties and fond memories for many residents and summer visitors. Within walking distance of the beach, at 134 Taunton Avenue, white beach sand accompanies you through the doorway of this restaurant and tiny bar that's still paneled with the original knotty pine boards.

As told by one of Gina's granddaughters, Gina was born in 1900 and immigrated from Italy to Dennis in 1925 with her husband, Gerino Uguccioni, who was an avid hunter. He built some of the shacks at the Bass River Gun Club, along with the cottages adjacent to their home on Taunton Ave. Gerino kept bringing hunters to the house to eat and Gina thought she might as well open a restaurant. During summers, Gina's House was operated truly as a family business for three generations.

The restaurant was a favorite of many actors who performed at the Cape Playhouse, including some who became movie stars. Young Jane Fonda and other big names were patrons multiple summers.

We all remember Gina in the early '50s, when she visited each table to greet her patrons with a friendly Italian accent. Always wearing an apron over her big flowered dress, she'd personally deliver each meal to the table and announce 'Here's a cumma you pizza. Here's a cumma you pizza.' It didn't matter whether you ordered pizza or spumoni, 'Here's a cumma you pizza.' Everyone felt at home. Wonderful Gina passed away in 1986.

We children were fascinated with the empty, straw-covered bottles of Chianti wine that sat atop each table. Red candle wax had dripped down the bottle sides for dozens of summer evenings. The captivating smell of Gina's 'gravy' (spaghetti sauce) wafted through the entire restaurant, saturating our minds and clothing as we sat for hours in her 'home'.

Gerino also was very friendly to patrons, visiting each table during meals. The unfortunate man had a medical condition that required surgical removal of his larynx (voice box). He had to use a hand-held, vibrating wand (electrolarynx) placed at his throat when he spoke. Although his speech was understandable, it did frighten young children (and me) who did not understand why he spoke like a robot. Such memories we have from our childhood days.

Larry Riley was the bartender at Gina's for a number of summers then in 1979, he, his brother Ross and Bill Farnsworth leased the restaurant. In 1984 the threesome bought the restaurant outright and Larry became the sole owner a few years later. The fine, seasonal restaurant has been operating ever since and patrons from near and far always look forward to opening day each year.

***

Rose's Italian Restaurant also was a summer favorite, beginning in 1946 and continuing until closure in 2000; an impressive 55 summer seasons for the family owned business. Rose's, located at 27 Black Flats Road, was the first local restaurant to serve rectangular, thin-crust pizza - her specialty. Rose provided excellent meals while she and her husband brought up three children in the home-style restaurant. A full menu of Italian specialties was enjoyed by all patrons for six decades. It was sad to see this terrific restaurant close.

Driving north along Beach Street, you encounter a point where three optional routes are posed: Black Flats Road at the left, Taunton Avenue in the center and Horsefoot Path on the right. All are wonderful options as they provided access, respectively, to Rose's, Gina's and at the far right, access to what later became Mayflower Beach. Locals were well aware that the left and center routes led you to 'Little Taunton', a primarily summer neighborhood fondly named for the Italian heritage of families, most of whom originated from Taunton and Mansfield, MA.

Early records of Dennis reveal that Italian immigrants had moved to this neighborhood in the late 1800s while participating in the construction of the new Cape Cod railroad.

During summer months, nearly all of the road-side homes along Taunton Ave. were filled with happy Italian families; three or four generations in most. Evenings were special as many backyards were lit with strings of red and green lanterns hanging from pine trees, as signs of their Italian heritage. Old men hunched over picnic tables sipping their red wine or playing bocce in rectangular, beach-sand filled pits, while apron-wrapped mothers and grandmothers were toiling indoors, simmering their special 'gravies', rolling pasta and freezing their home-made spumoni. We townsfolk drove slowly through Little Taunton with car windows down, purposely inhaling the tomato-scented air of the wonderful Italian neighborhood.

Dennis Inn – Originally, Windswept; Later, La Coquille

The Dennis Inn, located at 25 Scarsdale Road, has a long history as a comfortable Cape Cod Inn and picturesque venue for family celebrations. The property was originally the spacious home of Willie Nickerson, built in the early '20s. Howard L. Hall (of Dennis Minstrel fame) purchased the property in the '40s and his two children (Budge and Anne) later ran the facility as an Inn and restaurant called Windswept. In the basement, Captain Luther's Liquor Locker became the favorite local bar for the enjoyment of many thirsty patrons who were heading home from the beach. Live music on weekends drew large crowds including famous actors who were performing at the Cape Playhouse. Dennis locals certainly enjoyed partying with the stars.

In the '70s, the facility was recreated with an upscale French flair, as the La Coquille restaurant with its Metro Café. Howard Hall's granddaughter, Jane, was the proprietor in those days and Bob Hayes was a popular attraction at the piano. The '80s led to another change, with the facility reopening as the Dennis Inn which has successfully focused on weddings and other private galas for over thirty years. Many locals have enjoyed their special days at the Inn. In later Chapters, stories are told about Dickie's experiences at the Inn, as well as some of his 'run-ins with the law'.

The Dennis Christmas Tree

A warm description of the Dennis Christmas Tree (shortened to 'Tree' in discussions among locals) has been provided by Carole W. Bell:

"The 'Tree' began in the early 1900s by Hayden Richardson, a wealthy resident who sought to provide every child in the village with a gift from Santa on Christmas Eve. He recruited the 'Chatterboxes', a local women's group. They divided up the streets and solicited donations along with the names and ages of the children in the household. They made note of shut-ins and anyone over the age of eighty. No child was turned away and the shut-ins and elders received gifts as well.

Membership in the newly formed Tree was strictly controlled. No member was accepted unless she had a direct line through a family member. The night before Christmas Eve was a huge undertaking in Carleton Hall (at 1006 Old Bass River Road), with a large cedar tree placed on the stage, decorations hung and chairs assembled. Local men took turns playing Santa, arriving via the wood fireplace and faux brick chimney handcrafted by carpenter Willie T. Nickerson.

Vintage sleigh bells announced Santa's arrival and a hush would fall over the packed hall. Kids in their finest clothes sat glued in their seats breathlessly waiting to hear their name called. The gifts were tagged with each child's name and age, so of course, Santa would call each child to the stage, sit them on his knee and have a short 'chat'. One little girl asked Santa for a 'daddy' and Santa had a tough time composing himself.

Walter McDowell, who worked for the Sunshine Biscuit company, provided for each child a box of real graham crackers in the shape of circus animals. Each small, oblong box had a string handle. Years later, the company changed to a type of sugar cookie in a similar box with animal shapes but the kids didn't like these as much. Now, for the sake of being Politically Correct, the manufacturer does not show circus animals depicted in cages on the outside of the boxes.

Ice cream was distributed as individual slices, chocolate and vanilla, separated by stiff cardboard in a long oblong box. Much later they switched to Hoodsies (ice cream in a small cup) and Louie›s (later the Dennis Public Market) continued to donate. Caroling around the piano, played by Mrs. Estelle Savage and later Mig Maher, rounded out the evening.

Back in the '50s, the population of the north side was small but by 1990 the town had grown substantially, a new school was added and the number of children had grown to 300! Consequently, the Tree could no longer provide for ages infant through grade 8; thereafter it was limited to grade 4. The Tree was moved to the larger Dennis Union Church hall at 1713A Route 6A.

In an effort to continue on, and recruit volunteers, the party was even moved from Christmas Eve to the week before Christmas. The last Tree was held in December 2001 and so died a village tradition."

County Fair Restaurant – Later, the Red Pheasant; Today, The Pheasant

In this instance, the interesting story isn't about the fine restaurant nestled in the trees by Scargo Lake. What's most significant is the woman, Ms. Marguerite Ickis, who founded the restaurant, among many other accomplishments for which she excelled. The dear Ms. Ickis has passed away but will never be forgotten, as she was a generous philanthropist for the Town of Dennis.

Upon her death, she bequeathed considerable wealth to the town for construction of physical assets that will be enjoyed for years. One example was funding for a recreation room at the Dennis Senior Center. This was appropriate as much of her life was devoted to teaching the importance of traditional arts and crafts.[21] Additionally, Ms. Ickis' memorial fund established a well-equipped playground for children at the Johnny Kelley Park in South Dennis.

Ms. Ickis was born in 1896, originally lived in Ohio, spent many years in North Carolina and the latter part of her life in Dennis with a home near the intersection of Hope Lane and Whig Street. Her life was full of diverse achievements, as a researcher, botanist, editor, dean, quilt designer, author of twenty books, restauranteur and painter. Internationally, she is remembered as an early authority on quilting, having published *The Standard Book of Quilt Making and Collecting* in 1949.[22]

In the summer, she would often have friends from North Carolina visit.

Mrs. Ruth Faison Shaw was her closest friend and they spoke of each other as sisters. Mrs. Shaw was a famed artist and inventor of the Art of Finger Painting, as an art education medium. She developed her techniques while working in Rome, Italy and in 1931 patented a safe, non-toxic paint for child play.

Another 'cousin' of Ms. Ickis was Mr. Claude Hunter Moore, a fine gentleman from North Carolina who spoke with a significant southern accent. He visited Dennis for over ten summers and would stay with Dickie Buck's family. Mr. Moore is discussed later as he helped Dickie get enrolled in a High School in North Carolina at which he was the Principal. Not surprisingly, Ms. Ickis' restaurant fare included many southern specialties, including true southern fried chicken, grits, collard greens and other items that were foreign to most Cape Codders.

When she opened the County Fair restaurant at 905 Route 6A, the original structure had been a barn and storage building for components of Clipper Ships. The odor of horses lingered for the first year but was eventually displaced with scents of her fine cuisine. Marguerite ran the restaurant for fourteen years. She passed away in 1980.

When Dickie was in his early teens, he worked one summer as a dishwasher and potato peeler at the restaurant for Ms. Ickis. He lived in a converted chicken-coop on the property of the Sign of the Motor Car Inn, two properties to the east of the restaurant. He recalls Ms. Ickis being a wonderful lady and kind employer.

***

Dickie also remembers having fun in Scargo Lake during the warm summer nights. He, his older brother and a couple of his young guy friends would paddle canoes to the north end of the Lake, near the public swimming area. They knew that girls from the Cape Playhouse would go there late, after the shows had ended.

The boys would paddle up close to the noise of the girls' swimming then quietly roll their canoes over. The canoes would then have a low profile in the water but the boys could breathe inside the air pocket beneath the hull. It was a perfect spot for the young boys to view the naked girls who were skinny dipping, especially when they entered and exited the water.

***

The restaurant was next sold to Mrs. Leah O'Leary who ran the business as Mrs. O'Leary's County Fair. She and her two daughters successfully operated the restaurant for an extended period before selling the facility, which was later reopened as the Red Pheasant restaurant. In 2018, ownership of the restaurant changed again and it now operates as 'The Pheasant'.

When Mrs. O'Leary sold the facility at 905 Route 6A, she moved her County Fair restaurant to the renovated home of the late Gerard Chapman at 799 Route 6A. Years later, that property was sold again and the Scargo Café was established in 1987.

Dickie washed dishes and was later a bartender at the County Fair restaurant, as well as bartender at the Stagedoor restaurant (at 36 Hope Lane), both operated by Mrs. O'Leary. And Dickie's mother-in-law, Vi Sencabaugh, worked as a cook at both restaurants.

Players Plaza

In 1947, Phil Dubin and his brother Lenny established the first 'shopping plaza' in East Dennis, at 1582 Route 6A, the intersection of Bridge Street and Route 134. It was considered a busy corner in those days. The complex was constructed with a substantial pharmacy on the left, a small barbershop in the center and a gas station on the right, at the east end of the building.

The pharmacy had large letters on its high façade, designated as 'Players Pharmacy' and unofficially capitalizing on the well-known Cape Playhouse. Two thespian masks (representing comedy and tragedy) were positioned on either side of the business name. Note they are still displayed at the newer Plaza, mentioned below.

The pharmacy was typical of an old-style general store, with a linear 'soda fountain' running along the left side with a dozen stools aligned from front to back. Phil was the owner but robust Fred Jakes was the on-site pharmacist who attended to daily operations. As years progressed, Phil's son Michael took over the business and Judy Scarafile became the pharmacist. Judy remained for decades, partly for the wages but more likely for the on-site entertainment.

Although the business was normally slow, the pharmacy was a popular meeting place for East Dennis folks and especially, Dickie Buck. Most days, you could find Dickie visiting with Mike and Judy in the pharmacy, with spirited conversations on all topics, especially local gossip. The boys pulled many local pranks and constructed a crude bedroom upstairs for various activities. Rumors have been told that they installed panes of one-way glass in strategic locations of the building. Likely only rumors.

Occasionally, Mike's wife Judy would stop at the pharmacy; sometimes, Dickie's wife Judy Buck also would visit, making it a triumvirate of three Judys. They still laugh about those good old days when work didn't get in the way of simple enjoyment at Players Pharmacy. An example was the day when Dickie walked in wearing a full-body gorilla suit.

***

Roger Lindstrom was proprietor of the barber shop. Roger was 'hard of hearing' but that didn't prevent gossip to flow amongst 'Roger the Dodger' and the elder local men who would occupy the barber shop for hours.

The small gas station on the east end of the complex also was owned by Phil Dubin. He always hired local men to run the gas business; the first being Ralph Richardson of East Dennis. Minimal auto servicing was conducted on-site; the primary income was from retail sales of gasoline. Cape Oil supplied the gasoline and Phil received a few cents for each gallon sold, in payment for the proprietor's use of the facility. The wholesale representative from Cape Oil, Adam Fletcher, was certainly a character that Dickie enjoyed, as described in the Chapter on Notorious Characters.

Sinclair gas was sold at the station and the company's mascot was 'Dino', a green brontosaurus dinosaur, remembered by all. The founder of Sinclair Oil Corporation had made a big marketing campaign at the 1933 Chicago World's Fair, promoting his oil products via a correlation between underground oil formation and the era of dinosaurs. This was highly effective because dinosaurs were loved by everyone and Sinclair's green Dino toys appeared in households throughout the U.S. On occasion, Dickie gave free plastic Dinos to all the customers when he ran the business.

Sinclair Oil Company was eventually sold to ARCO then later acquired by BP but today, Sinclair gas stations have reemerged in twenty U.S. states throughout the West and Midwest.

After Ralph Richardson 'retired' from the Players gas station, Ejner C. (Big Chris) Myland, Jr. took over proprietorship. Although Chris was known to have exceptional mental abilities, he chose to expend minimal effort running the gas station. During his 'spare time' he became a skilled, self-taught guitarist, with Chet Atkins as his idol. Gas patrons learned that music was more prevalent than gas at this station, which became obvious to owner Phil as well. If a car pulled up to the pumps, Chris wouldn't tend to their needs until he was finished playing whatever song he had begun. Often, Chris would have reason to leave the station for periods of hours; his young son Christopher was left to run the station.

Dickie worked part-time at the station for Chris. This was while Dickie was on a Pass from his Active Duty at Otis Air Force Base in Bourne. Additionally, he lived in the attic of the station, from which lascivious stories abound.

Big Chris eventually 'moved on', becoming a commercial cod fisherman on George's Bank, using an old Novi-design boat that he berthed in Chatham Harbor. Anyone who had the opportunity to fish with Chris will not forget his 'mate' Edgar (pronounced 'Egga') who was an old, gravelly voiced fisherman with a strong Swedish accent. More could be said about Egga's persona, odor and collection of 'girly pictures' in the forward cabin of *Tuffy Two*. Billy Brister (senior), of local fame, fished for a number of years with Chris and eventually purchased his own boat for commercial fishing off Chatham and later in Cape Cod Bay.

***

In the late '60s, the pharmacy business had to close on account of strong competition from national pharmacy chains such as CVS and others. Contractors were hired to move the pharmacy building about two-hundred yards northward on Bridge Street. Later, the building underwent significant modifications to become the original Marshside Restaurant at 28 Bridge Street. In recent years, the original structure was razed and a new building constructed for the Marshside that prospers today.

A new Shell gasoline station was constructed in 1967, at the site of the original Players complex. Additionally, a new shopping complex (named the Players Plaza) was constructed a small distance to the east, at 1616 Route 6A and back from the road. Stapat Market (from proprietors Stan and Pat) was the primary store in the complex but others settled in over the next few years., including a Liquor Store and Fishing Tackle/Bait Shop. Tedeschi's Market followed Stapat Market then 7-Eleven which exists today.

Bucky Beaver's Magic Garage

Continuing on the topic of the gas station at the original Players complex at 1582 Route 6A, in 1961 at age twenty-six, Dickie became the next proprietor of the Sinclair station after Chris Myland's departure. Whereas Chris was generally unsociable, Dickie was the complete opposite; an extrovert. He loved having people visit his station, even if they didn't need gas or repairs. Having collected many friends (and some enemies) by his mid-twenties, he was always 'chewing the fat' in the parking lot with people of all ages, gender, race, intellect and finances. Everyone knew Dickie; most smiled when they heard his name; some just shook their head and grumbled a profanity, refraining from explanation of their personal encounter. He ran the station for ten years.

The popular folk group of the '60s, Peter, Paul and Mary, once stopped at the gas station and of course, Dickie chatted them up thoroughly.

Over the years, his diverse friends also proliferated numerous nicknames for Dickie:

- *Buckie*
- *Buckster*
- *Buckie Beaver*
- *The Beave, and*
- *Derogatory names that do not warrant printing.*

Buckie Beaver worked hard but he partied hard as well. He welcomed the notoriety and reputation that his station had become a 'happening' place. He even posted a large sign on the front of the garage, for viewing from Route 6A: *Bucky Beaver's Magic Garage.*

When asked about the origin of the name 'Magic Garage', Buckie said, "Shit if I know! But people would come in with their cars, wanting to know what was wrong with it. When the car left, it was running fine. They'd ask what I did but I enjoyed keeping it a secret. I'd just raise my finger, twirl it around and whistle an eerie sound. Then I'd say 'Magic!'

Back in those days, I'd repair a tire and remount it for only $2. A lubrication job was only $1.75. It's unbelievable what they charge today for the same services. I'd fix anybody's lawn mower; it didn't make a difference what was wrong with it, just $3! And only 25 cents for a gallon of 'regular' gas; 27 cents for 'high-test'."

The Magic Garage also gained the reputation as the first self-service gas station in the region (maybe country?). Locals knew this meant pumping your own gas and paying via the honor system. Buckie posted a sign inside the station's office: 'Help yourself and leave the money in the drawer.' Everyone was honest in those days so the procedure worked, or so it seemed.

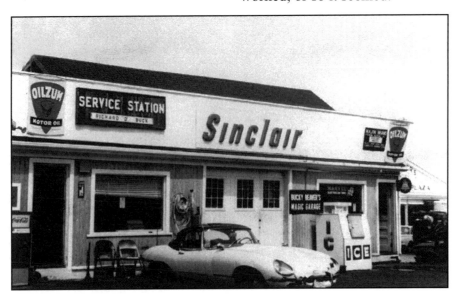

Mrs. Lisa Goodell, an eighty year old woman from East Dennis, would frequently drive up to the station and pump her own gas. She knew Buckie well, as he often mowed her large lawn by using her push-powered reel mower. She also knew that if Buckie was not at the station, he'd be away attending to his 'other interests'.

Buckie loved this ingenious system because it allowed him to leave the premises and go boating, play the trumpet at the marina or whatever mischief he chose to pursue at the moment. Sometimes he'd ask Billy Thatcher or one of the Lowther boys to watch the station but they'd often choose to avoid the responsibility.

Friends of Buckie Beaver remember his ritual for celebrating the end of summer and the departure of all the 'pesky' tourists, never mind that their revenues paid the bills of all shop owners. Ceremoniously, Buckie would lie down in the middle of the intersection of Routes 6A and 134 to prove the streets were clear or tourist vehicles.

***

Activity continued to increase at the Magic Garage but Phil Dubin gradually learned that more people hanging around the station didn't necessarily translate into more revenues from gas sales. The reason was that Buckie had become very interested in Scuba diving while Chris was proprietor of the station.

In those days, people called the underwater breathing device an 'aqua lung' following Jacques Cousteau's invention in 1943. Buckie remembers,

'How better to learn Scuba than from the expert, Phil Amero?' Amero had both the reputation and the credentials of the big-time Scuba diver, as president of New England Divers, but his chutzpah was even more grandiose.

When Phil Amero came to town in the mid-1950s, Chris and Buckie 'dove in' to this sport, head over heels. They loved diving and soon fabricated their own wetsuits, Scuba equipment, air compressor, etc.

Unfortunately and within a year, it became clear that Phil Amero was a total 'con artist', even tapping money from Buckie and Chris whenever possible. For example, there was a big spearfishing tournament planned in Cape Cod Bay and Phil was determined that he would win, for the visibility and fame. Prior to the tournament he offered a free trip to Aruba for Buckie and his best friend, Jimmy Drake, it they would catch a very large fish and place it underwater at Tautog Rock for he, Phil, to find and use for the winning prize. The two accomplices did their part and Phil won the tournament but Buckie and Jimmy never got a dime.

Soon after, Phil Amero was 'run out of town'. Chris moved on to a fishing career but Buckie continued his love of Scuba diving. The floor of Bucky Beaver's Magic Garage was often too cluttered with dive gear to accept any cars for repair. This became evident to Phil Dubin, as revenues from the gas station seemed to decline simultaneously. Buckie eventually shifted to other forms of employment, as described in a later Chapter, but diving remained one of his favorite hobbies. Later, he had a small business at the marina for Scuba instruction.

***

In the summer of 2018 at age 83, Dickie was still diving in Sesuit Harbor, replacing zinc anodes on the bottom of boats and performing other physical tasks. And if anything valuable was lost over the side of a boat, Dickie got the call, as had occurred since the '50s.

Bass Hole at Chapin Beach

The town line between Dennis and Yarmouth at the Cape Cod Bay boundary is delineated by the entrance to Chase Garden Creek, west of Chapin Beach. Yarmouth Port's Gray's Beach is situated to the west of the entrance. Locals fondly refer to this tidal inlet as the 'Bass Hole' although there is no hole nor striped bass resident through the colder half of the year. Nevertheless, the name has stuck. Fortunately for Dennis, the western tip of Chapin Beach has slowly migrated westward, from accretion of sand during winter storms that resuspend beach sand and transport it westward alongshore during strong northeast winds and waves. One hundred years ago, the northward flowing channel of the Creek, coincident with the Bass Hole, was actually located greater than one-hundred yards east of the present tip of Chapin Beach. Dennis natives enjoy having their beach continually lengthen.

Starting in the early '50s, the Bass Hole became a popular place for locals to party on summer weekends. They'd fill their beach buggies with family, clam rakes, fishing gear, beach chairs, ice, booze and food, to spend the day and early evening in the dunes. Families would gather closely while children would purposely try getting lost as most of the parents drank, smoked and spent simple times. On windy days, they'd all settle in behind the tallest dunes to enjoy the lee. When the tide was out, there was no seawater to be found except in the shallow channel of the Bass Hole.

The men would dig steamers for the afternoon meal, as well as sea worms for use as bait on the next incoming tide. Mary Jo Walker would often arrive on her Quarter Horse, Palm Beach, for the thrill of the children. When the tide was high, swimming was great and sometimes stripers were caught near shore. On more than one occasion, Dickie Buck arrived via sea in his Amphicar (amphibious vehicle) having 'cruised' all the way from Corporation Beach. The weekend beach parties were pure enjoyment in a variety of flavors.

Consider this: If you stand at the tip of Chapin Beach today, and conduct an unlawful activity (although not recommended), a Dennis National Resource Officer should not have jurisdiction to arrest you because you are actually standing on land originally designated as the Town of Yarmouth. But be sure to have an accurate map of the two towns from at least fifty years ago, with your GPS position charted on it, proving that you are in Yarmouth. The younger Officers might be surprised.

Dennis Pines Golf Course

After years of deliberation in Town Meetings and among the Town Selectmen and Finance Committee, the decision was made for Dennis to construct a public golf course. Yarmouth had been successful with the Bass River course and Blue Rock too, so Dennis was keen on establishing a new revenue stream, especially with the expansion of tourism on Cape Cod.

The significant tract of treed land east at Route 134 and opposite Hokum Rock Road was ideal for a full 18-hole course. A town road was constructed and appropriately named Golf Course Road for access to the new course.

The initial task of clearing the trees for the planned fairways, tees and greens was a major undertaking, especially with hills and numerous ponds (Funn being one of them) scattered through the tract. Construction was finalized in 1965, with all holes complete, clubhouse built and parking lot paved. Official opening of the course occurred in late May 1965.

Mr. Lou Thibeault was selected as the first Golf Professional for the club. He was definitely an off-Cape personality, a 'city guy' as viewed by Dennis townsfolk. Lou had class, wore woven dress pants with cuffs and even alligator shoes. He was tall and stood out in a crowd. Charisma shone brightly from his big smile; he certainly was enjoyed by numerous ladies from the town. His golf bag was huge and his name was painted on the side – such elan had never been seen in this neck of the woods, especially on the links! [23]

Dennis Pines was a success for the town and remains one of the most challenging public courses on Cape Cod. Lou will be remembered too.

Joe Mac's Bar and Grill – Originally, Dom's; Today's Chapin's

In the mid-60s, Joe McAleney, originally of Hyannis, purchased a building at 85 Taunton Avenue to open a family style restaurant at the location of a prior drinking establishment called Dom's. For many years, Joe and his hard-working wife Rosemarie ('Roe') ran an excellent business that included the restaurant, an extensive bar for liquor patrons, game room for children, a billiard room in the rear and a small seasonal grocery store. 'Joe Mac's' became a Dennis landmark and a favorite of patrons from all around the country. The Thursday night special of Roast Prime Rib of Beef for $2.95 (initially) was the real hit and the 35-cent frosty mugs of draft beer attracted many thirsty patrons, as well.[24]

Well before Joe Mac's, the original establishment on that parcel of land was a grocery and liquor store managed by Secondo Servidori. Secondo was a hard-working, likely first-generation Italian with a very strong accent. He and Dickie had disagreements on occasion, especially when Secondo saw Dickie Scuba diving near his lobster pots off Corporation Beach. All divers knew that lobsters seek rocky habitats, which coincide with the location where lobstermen would set their pots.

One day, Dickie happened to be diving in the general vicinity of Secondo's pots and he immediately thought Dickie was robbing from his traps. With his small boat and outboard motor, Secondo tried to run Dickie over, while yelling: 'You stealy my lowbsta. You stealy my lowbsta. I cutta you fucking throat. You stealy my lowbsta.' Both men survived the skirmish.

Years later there was a fire at Secondo's Little Taunton premises and the facility was later rebuilt as a drinking bar (e.g., gin mill, watering hole, beer joint). Dom Seccocia was the proprietor of the new establishment named 'Dom's', collaborating with his wife Lillian as the front-manager. 'Diamond Lil' was the nickname she earned with great flair, colorful clothing and large wild hats. Gregarious she was, bashful she was not. Everyone enjoyed Diamond Lil.

Dickie used to frequent Dom's and remembers the owner being cantankerous. Dom didn't like it when patrons would mostly socialize and not purchase drinks. He'd holler at these culprits: 'Hey, you buyin' a round or hanging around?' Sometimes Dom would announce that he would buy a round of drinks for everyone in the bar, 'Except you!', pointing a finger at Dickie. And Dickie would do the same in return, partially joking with the owner.

As Little Taunton evolved into a family neighborhood, the decline of Dom's bar was inevitable. And Joe Mac, a wise businessman, recognized the opportunity for a friendly restaurant near the beach; one that parents could visit with their children who were mesmerized by the pin-ball machines and early video games. Standing on their tip-toes to put quarters in the juke box was also great fun for the small children. The whole family enjoyed going to Joe's. Even the spirited employees are remembered – Kenny the manager, Jim the day bartender, John, Stacey, Jack and others characters behind the bar year-round.

Norman Lyman would often arrive on Friday nights, creating a big scene as he slammed the door open while entering. He'd plunk his ass down at the bar and like a big spender ready to buy drinks for all the patrons, he'd holler: 'Set up the bar…from here…to here' while his outstretched arms would move continually closer together so he'd essentially instruct the bartender to buy drinks for himself only. Furthermore, he had to be loud and create a big scene in order to be noticed because 'Stormin Norman' was barely five feet tall and had a blonde, flat-top crew-cut. Another colorful character in the village. It made sense that he dated Dickie's cousin Trudy Jacobs.

Like many good restaurants, Joe Mac's closed its doors in 1996 after more than thirty years of success, enjoyment for many and solid employment for numerous locals. The entire building complex was demolished in May 2002.

New life was given to the parcel, with the construction of the present-day Chapin's Restaurant in 2003. The new restaurant quickly became a year-round success, with seafood focus and beachy atmosphere, including a mini-sand dune and beach grass in front of the facility. As a tribute to Joe Mac's, the prior restaurant's sign is hanging in full view inside Chapin's.

Hamburger Galley

The big craze for cheap, low-cost burgers swept across the U.S. in the '50s, with both McDonalds and Burger King establishing thousands of franchises beginning in 1954. Sleepy Cape Cod is often a bit behind the times (intentionally) but in the mid-60s, partners Bob Hayes and Jim Miller opened the Hamburger Galley to the excitement of many burger-craving locals who wanted a cheap meal and soft-serve ice cream on the north side of Dennis. Prior to the Galley, a restaurant had been operated at that facility by Kay Harper.

The Galley was located at 1381 Route 134, the present location of Northside Liquors on Route 134 and across from the Lost Dog Pub. The Galley and adjacent mini-golf facility were very successful for nine years. Lines were long outside the Galley, with patrons eager to purchase the famed 14-cent burgers and 8-cent orders of French fries. In 1975 the Galley was sold to the Mitchell family who ran it until the mid-80s.

Bob Hayes and his wife were well known from the Windswept Inn on Scarsdale Road. Captain Luther's Liquor Locker, the tavern located in the Inn's cellar, was a favorite summer watering hole for people returning from a warm day on the beach. Bob played the piano to many appreciative patrons.

Most people knew Bob from his small, local businesses, but his notoriety was large in the music world, warranting mention here. In the Army he played piano for the Special Service Band, then went on to receive a B.A. in Music, M.S.

in School Administration and at the age of eighty-one, earned his Ph.D. in Music. While running the Hamburger Galley, he was the Instrumental Director in the Chatham Public Schools for eleven years. From 1950 to 2016, Bob played piano professionally on Cape Cod and in Florida. In the '50s he performed several times at the Cape Playhouse with people such as Sid Caesar and Jane Fonda. 'Bob Hayes & Society by the Sea' was the house band at the Wychmere Harbor Club and the Hyannis Yacht Club for many years. He was fortunate to play with well-known musicians and singers including: Bob Hope, Connie Francis, Robert Goulet, Jerry Jerome and the Ink Spots. Bob was certainly more than a just a hamburger flipper! He died in 2017 at the age of ninety.

Stageway Restaurant

From 1954 to 1972, Nicholas Fournaris and his family operated the Stageway restaurant at 700 Route 6A, where ERA Cape Real Estate is located today. Stageway was another establishment drawing name association with the Cape Playhouse. The fare was primarily seafood[25] and Greek specialties, based upon the family's heritage. Dickie was a bartender at the Stageway and his wife, Judy, was a waitress there for many summers.

The Fournaris family also operated a miniature golf course situated on the east end of their property at 716 Route 6A, where the Ice Cream Smuggler is located today. As a thirteen-year-old, I worked at this modest golf facility during the summer of 1964.

In 1973, the Miragliotta family took over operation of the Stageway until it burned to a total loss on January 19, 1975. Mr. Fournaris foreclosed on the property in 1977.

As a bit of Cape Cod trivia, Nick Fournaris also ran the food concession at the Kennedy Memorial Skating Rink in Hyannis during winter months. Opened in 1957, this was the first skating rink on Cape Cod having artificially produced ice. The Author and many Dennis boys started playing PeeWee and Bantam hockey in the early '60s at the Kennedy rink, with mothers sharing the 'long' (ten-mile) rides to Hyannis. The rink had no roof initially and rain would often make conditions difficult; miserable actually, for players and spectators. When it snowed hard, winds would form large drifts in the rounded corners quicker than the Zamboni could clear them out. Often, pucks would be lost, mid-game.

The same fate would occur during night games of the Cape Cod Men's Hockey League, with many village men playing on the Yarmouth-Dennis ('YD') team. This was great entertainment for families to attend games on Sunday and Wednesday nights. Kids were in awe watching these big 'pros' play, with frequent fights.

One of the most notorious players in the League was Attorney F. Lee Bailey; definitely an off-Cape character who played on the Hyannis Elks. When he arrived in the locker room before a game, dressed in a tailored, three-piece suit and with hair combed back smartly, everyone knew he was from over the bridge.

In the professional world, Bailey was a high-profile criminal defense attorney,

licensed in Florida and Massachusetts. His most notable case was the re-trial of Osteopathic Neurosurgeon Samuel Sheppard who had been convicted for murdering his wife in 1954. Seven years after the conviction and life sentence, Baily as Chief Counsel for the Defense, was successful in Sheppard's exoneration. The murder story became the basis for the movie *The Fugitive*.

Bailey participated in many other cases, most recently as part of the Defense team in the O. J. Simpson murder trial. As a fiery character, Bailey had a number of defeats, legal controversies and personal troubles with the law. He was eventually disbarred in Massachusetts and Florida for misconduct while defending a client. Hockey seems to have been a good outlet for his aggressive personality.

Bailey was born in Waltham, MA in 1950, studied at Harvard College but dropped out in 1952 to join the U.S. Marine Corps. He served as a jet fighter pilot then a squadron legal officer. He was later admitted to Boston University School of Law in 1957 and achieved the highest grade-point average in the school's history. He graduated with an undergraduate law degree (LL.B.) in 1960 and ranked first in his class.

***

Many of us have a vivid memory of the cold Sunday night at the Kennedy rink when the British group *The Beatles* played for the first time on United States soil, broadcast live from the *Ed Sullivan Show*. We huddled together to watch the small television positioned high above

Nick Fournaris' hamburger grill in the heated rink building. That was Sunday, February 9th, 1964.

Lower Deck Lounge; Now, the Lost Dog Pub

The Lost Dog Pub, located at 1374 Route 134, has been a popular restaurant and social bar for decades. Before the business opened under that name, the facility was run as the Lower Deck, which opened in the early '70s. Being the first liquor bar in East Dennis, it immediately became a favorite of locals.

Starting back in the early '50s, Hudson Eldridge had a local excavation and contracting business, situated where the East Dennis Branch of the Cape Cod Cooperative Bank is located today. His wife Shirley had recently developed a successful Real Estate business in collaboration with Dickie Buck. The three decided that establishing an office on Route 134 would be a wise decision for business visibility and expansion.

Originally planned as a sole Real Estate office for Hudson Eldridge and Associates, the parcel of land was purchased, the building was constructed and named the Ship's Chandlery. Soon after, Dickie was able to negotiate with the town to obtain the first-ever liquor license in East Dennis and the Lower Deck was born. Initially, the bar was on the left (north) side of the building and a small eating area was to the right, much like the Lost Dog is configured today. The Lower Deck became so successful that it displaced the Real Estate office.

As a bit of local trivia, Hudson was contracted to build the numerous pools at the Sea Land Aquarium facility on Route 6A in East Dennis near the Brewster line. Dickie purchased the concrete forms for use on the project, in collaboration with Hudson. The forms were subsequently used to build the concrete foundation for the Lower Deck. For whatever reason, the forms were not removed from the ground after the concrete walls hardened and they still reside there today.

Dickie was a bartender and manager at the Lower Deck for nine years. At the south end of the building they opened a small ice cream shop called the Dennis Scoop. It became a very successful summer business with long lines of patrons outside. Two college girls ran the business for Hudson. He and Dickie made the ice cream from equipment that Dickie salvaged from the original D. H. Sears store in East Dennis.

Eventually, after Hudson passed away, Shirley leased the facility to someone who ran the bar as an Irish Pub. Later, she sold the property, which subsequently became the Lost Dog. Many remember Shirley as an accomplished and very pleasant woman whereas most people recall 'Huddy' as a cantankerous man in his later years.

Town Dump

Last but not least among memorable locations is the Town Dump off Route 134. Dump deserves capitalization, along with the prestigious name for its entrance: Theophilus F. Smith Road. Mr. Smith was an extraordinary Dump Keeper (Superintendent) and the road was dedicated to him just before he passed away in the late '60s. Ben Thacher has told a wonderful, boyhood story about his interactions with 'Thoph' in his *Recollections of Cape Cod Yesterdays.*[26]

Prior to the '70s, all refuse was piled on the ground at the dump site and the Keeper would continually till it over with a pitch fork and toss all combustibles into an open fire that he would keep active all day. What remained was mostly metal and other solid trash that was eventually covered with dirt. There was no separation of materials for recycling. The pile kept growing and the unseen, contaminated ground-water spread continuously. But community spirit was thriving, as 'good' items were set aside for use by the next needy person who came along. Exactly as the expression goes: 'One man's trash is another man's treasure.' Free pickin'.

Today, Dennis refuse is recycled in myriad categories and the rat population of bygone days is absent (at least not visible to the naked eye). Groundwater quality in South Dennis has probably improved also.

So why has the Dump earned notoriety herein? Ask the Dennis girls who were in their dating years back in the '50s. The Dump is where some of their boyfriends brought them, for an evening's entertainment. Yes, it's true and many of the Dennis guys, including Dickie, were on the front line with rifle in hand. He's made it clear that he didn't bring Judy to the Dump (for that reason), but only because she was troubled at the thought of animals being shot, no matter what species.

Imagine a number of cars parked in the dark, immediately in front of the pile of ripe swill delivered that day. Headlights were extinguished but aimed at the invisible rising stench. Men stood beside their cars with pistols, shotguns and rifles aimed toward the mound. The most experienced men could hear lots of tweeting noises from little critters that lived in the dark piles.

The unsuspecting girlfriends were sitting inside the cars, on the front seats and with trembling hand ready to pull the big headlight knob to trigger full illumination from the sealed beams. Everyone was silent and still, then the assigned man yells 'Shoot' and the girls knew to pull their (the cars') knobs. Within a fraction of a second, guns blared and lead was flying toward hundreds of feasting rats that scurried around the pile seeking darkness and protection.

The firing continued for about 30 seconds until no further motion could be seen on the pile. All the guys were proud of their accomplishments. No counting of dead rats; the guys just reached for their bottles of beer sitting on the hood of their car, and toasted to each other.

When all was silent, the girls would open their eyes and begin to scream at their guys, nearly in unison. 'I hate this killing! You bring me here on a first date? How dare you?'

All the guys laughed and congratulated themselves for aiding the town via vigilante pest control. Of course, the town police knew there would be shooting at the Dump on weekend nights. They could have blocked the entrance road but they didn't. Times were different back in those days. And fortunately, dating in Dennis has become more sophisticated, I suspect.

It must be acknowledged that a few shotgun-toting Dennis girls also joined the front line, proudly. Being politically correct today, they'll likely not admit that their trigger finger participated at the Dump events.

As a final example of the chivalry of certain young Dennis men back in the '40s and '50s, another Dump story lingers in Dickie's aged but crisp mind. He had a roommate named Peter Alby and Dickie admits that Peter was not your 'average guy', seriously lacking all hints of etiquette.

Peter would often hang out at the Players Pharmacy with Dickie close by. In summer, girls from off-Cape would come down to search for summer jobs; many stopping at the Pharmacy. One afternoon, a group of three or four nurses entered and sat at the soda fountain. Peter quickly began to make conversation with them, 'So what are you girls doing while you're down here?', trying to sound sophisticated. He continued, 'Perhaps you'd like to go over to the dump and shoot some rats, with my musket.' And he actually owned an antique musket.

With tongue-in-cheek, that was his line to catch the girls and he used it frequently; not surprisingly, with little success. To Peter and Dickie, the boyhood humor outweighed his fruitless attempts at landing a date.

Dickie's Early Years

Starting from an early age, Dickie was very active and ambitious. His parents' finances were meager so he quickly recognized he'd have to buy his own toys and other items whereas most children had parents who could afford such niceties.

By the time he was fourteen, he had worked numerous jobs as described in other Chapters; some examples are given below:

- Reciprocal babysitting with his brother, one year older, for $2 per week while his mother worked
- Delivering newspapers in the village and to WW II soldiers, for $3 per week, starting at seven years old
- Washing dishes and peeling potatoes in numerous restaurants
- Cleaning rooms and changing linens in local Inns
- Catching herring for Bill Stone

The various jobs necessitated his freedom to roam the village starting at the age of seven. His mother knew he was capable of navigating around, on foot or his peddle bike, and nearly everyone knew Dickie. He seemed to pop up everywhere, even at night when he became a teenager. He was an independent, high-energy boy.

Dressing Up

The village has always been a place where many houses are vacant during winter months, only to be occupied when families return to their 'second homes' for the summer season. Later in life, Dickie became a winter caretaker for numerous homes, but as a young boy, he and his friends would sometimes sneak into these vacant properties to explore.

There was a substantial property on Route 6A near his home on Paddocks Path which he would walk past on his way to the school bus stop. It was a favorite of the local boys because its attic was full of dresses and colorful accessories of the

Competing on Community Auditions

In the '50s there were few programs on television and knowing they were produced in the big, far-away city of Boston added to the aura for children who watched the weekly talent show *Community Auditions*. It's unlikely that Dennis children would imagine themselves competing on this program that is watched by thousands of families throughout New England. Would they ever be chosen as the 'Star of the Day'? Dickie was eager to give it his best try.

fashionable woman who lived there in summer. He and his friends would enter the house a few days each winter. Dickie had no sisters, nor did his guy friends, so when they encountered the colorful dresses, hats and frilly undergarments, it was definitely a new experience for them. Sometimes they'd dress up in the gowns, put on the strings of beads, perfume and even lipstick when they ran around all pretty. It was just fun dressing up as girls. Nothing more shall be said about that.

Never were they arrested or interrogated by the owner so it stayed off the police records.

Acrobatic Adagio Dancers

Dickie and two of his girl-cousins, Charlene and Trudy from Hyannis, competed on *Community Auditions* in 1950. One girl was a ballet dancer and the other a gymnast. Dickie was the strongman at fifteen years old. As a group, they 'headlined' as the 'Adagio Acrobatic Dancers'.

Adagio is a type of performance acrobatic dancing where a pair or trio performs feats of stationary balance, lifting and acrobatic movements. The two girls were the dance 'fliers' and Dickie was the 'base' who remains in contact with the floor while the fliers balance in the air. In professional adagio, the fliers balance on the base's feet, hands, shoulders, knees or combinations of these in a variety of orientations including horizontal, vertical or upside down.

Dickie and his cousins skillfully performed a variety of acrobatic poses, flips and somersaults but unfortunately, were not chosen as the 'Stars of the Day'. Regardless, they competed on television with hundreds of friends and family watching the Cape Cod team.

***

Community Auditions first aired in 1950 and was a family tradition on Sundays until the program ended in 1987 after a successful run of thirty-seven years. Gene Burns was the original host, followed for twenty-five years by Dave Maynard, a popular Boston radio host. Each half-hour episode featured a combination of singers, musicians, dancers, magicians, comedians, impersonators and jugglers. Six contestants performed during each show. At the end of the program, viewers were encouraged to mail in postcards, voting for their favorite contestant. No internet nor email voting back in those days. Do you suppose any families ever mailed more than one postcard?

On the following week, a winner was announced and would appear again on that week's show. Winners walked away with bragging rights, a trophy and a prize such as a new television set. At the end of each episode, the host and contestants would sing the show's beloved theme song *Star of the Day*:

> *Star of the Day*
> *Who will it be?*
> *Your vote may hold the key.*
> *It's up to you*
> *Tell us who…*
> *Will be Star of the Day.*

Many of us who were children back in the '50s still remember this tune fondly. The show returned to television in 2007, paying homage to the original but with focus solely on musical performances.

Dickie's High Schools

After years of unsuccessfully trying to make a year-round living on the Cape in the mid- to late '40s, Ellie and Buckie made the decision to move to Florida for the winter season. Warm weather and better job prospects were worth the attempt. Each year starting in 1949, they packed their bags and three sons at Thanksgiving and drove south.

In December of that year, both Lee and Dickie were enrolled in Sarasota High School and Bertie went to the public grammar school. But when spring arrived, the family packed their belongings again and drove back to Dennis. On the following Thanksgiving Day, they shut off the water in their Dennis home and departed again. No one ever locked their doors in those days as there was no vandalism.

This relocation upheaval was difficult for the boys, as their enrollment in Dennis schools occurred from September to mid-November then again from April through June. Integration within the Sarasota school system was for the brief period from December through March each year.

Dickie had done this school-hopping for his Freshman and Sophomore years but during his Junior year, he was fed up with Florida and missed his friends in Dennis. He informed his parents that on his sixteenth birthday, April 27, 1951, he was going to quit school in Sarasota, move north to Dennis and live alone as an adult. Details of the parent-son conversation have been 'lost' but it was likely an interesting discussion with the strong-minded young man. It's important to mention that another reason for his obstinance is that he refused to be at home by 9 p.m. each evening. He would not live 'that way' with minimal freedom.

On that memorable day of departure, Dickie's parents gave him new suitcases, a check for $20 and a 'good luck' farewell. It was solely his responsibility to hitch-hike to Cape Cod with the money in his pocket. Cleverly, Dickie arranged a ride with the father of a friend who drove him from Florida to Boston. From there he hitched down to Dennis.

At the time, the family owned three small houses in Dennis. Lacking maturity, Dickie moved into one house; when it was filthy he moved into the next house that was clean; then on to the third. Not a nice surprise when the family arrived a few months later.

In May of 1951, Dickie had no friends to play with as they all were still attending school. He decided to again visit Dennis-Yarmouth Regional High School and request to be re-enrolled. Surprisingly, he was allowed to start the next day.

Living on his own and needing money, he obtained a night job at the Dennis Drive-In Theater and also worked cleaning the aisles of the Cape Playhouse and Cinema; later he was an usher at the Playhouse.

***

In the spring of 1952, Dickie's father had a job opportunity to drive bulldozers in upstate New York. Dickie's uncle, John, contacted his brother to work on the construction of the Downsville Dam project in the Catskill Mountains region. The Downsville Dam led to creation of the Downsville Reservoir which later was renamed the Pepacton Reservoir. This source supplies New York City with nearly one-quarter of its drinking water. The Dam was completed in 1954 and the flooding was completed in 1955.

From April through November, Dickie's parents lived in the small town of Roscoe, NY which had a population of only a few hundred people in the '50s. In those days, it was famous only for the Roscoe Diner that had a waitress who would pull pranks on unsuspecting patrons by pretending to squirt ketchup all over them. Today the town is known as Trout Town USA due to excellent fishing in the rivers and reservoirs of the area.

In September of 1952, young Dickie decided it would be difficult to survive the winter in Dennis on his own so his Aunt drove him to his parents in Roscoe and he enrolled in the local High School to begin his Senior year. Little time passed before he disliked being in New York, as well as its cold weather. Roscoe was surrounded by the Catskill Mountains and Dickie hated the feeling of being 'hemmed in' by the significant topography. He quickly became homesick for Dennis and it's flat, spacious ocean.

When Thanksgiving arrived and his last football game was over, Dickie quit school again. At the same time and independent of Dickie's decision, his parents decided to head back to Sarasota. They still had only a tent on the Florida property due to insufficient funds to build a house but that made no difference. The parents loaded Dickie and Bertie into their 1941 Chevrolet ¾-ton panel truck and headed south.

***

Mr. Claude Hunter Moore was the Principal of the public High School in Clinton, NC. He had previously boarded with Dickie's family for a number of years during summer. Ellie called him with news that Dickie had quit school again and asked for his advice. Knowing Dickie's personality and intellectual potential, Mr. Moore replied slowly and wisely, with his strong southern accent. 'You have Dick come down here and try my school. If he likes it, he can stay. If he doesn't, he can quit.' Clear as a bell.

On their drive south, Dickie's parents dropped him in Clinton to resume his Senior year there. Fortunately for Dickie, the school building had two bedrooms and Mr. Moore made arrangements for Dickie to stay there. He had to work at the school part-time as compensation for meals he received.

As a surprising turn of events, Dickie liked the school, performed well and went from being a D-minus student to achieving all A's on his report card. He was ahead of his class because the New York curriculum was advanced from that in North Carolina. For example, he knew Shakespeare plays and he quickly developed typing skills (78 words per minute) that exceeded those of his instructor. Interestingly, typing skills greatly benefited him in the Air Force and helped him become a Corporal much faster than normally possible. Typing became his pass for waivers of other requirements and technical deficiencies.

His fellow students in Clinton High School graduating class of 1953 really liked Dickie and identified him as the 'Funniest' student in the class – not surprising. Of course, Dickie boasts that his girlfriend was the prettiest in the school – also not surprising. Dickie didn't travel to Clinton for the graduation ceremony but he was remembered with writings in the Senior yearbook.

Years later when he contributed as an alumni donor, the organizers remembered him fondly. And to this day, he likes the kind people of North Carolina.

Sarasota – Circus Town

In the 1920s, John Ringling, of Ringling Brothers and Barnum & Baily Circus fame, moved to Sarasota with much visibility and grandiose. He and his wife had a magnificent home and art museum constructed, and circus elephants were used to build the first bridge to their private island. In 1927, the circus' winter home and training grounds were moved to Sarasota, creating a new identity as the 'Circus Town'. Today, Sarasota is known as the 'Circus Capital of the World', being home of many circuses and the Ringling Clown College. (Can we think of any nominees from Dennis?)

Imagine Dickie and his family of five living in their small tent in Sarasota. Their neighborhood also was extraordinary, with the winter practice grounds of the Ringling Circus across the street. Circus performers were frequently doing handstands on the back of horses as they ran fast in circles. Trapeze artists could be seen practicing their high-wire acts dressed in tights and flowing capes. And a man was occasionally shot out of a body-size cannon, but for some reason there was no boom. Extraordinary visuals right next door.

A few houses away from Dickie's tent-home lived the Wallendas. This German family certainly weren't average neighbors. They were the 'Flying Wallendas', known worldwide for their death-defying aerial feats.

In 1922, father Karl Wallenda formed a group of family acrobats that toured Europe, performing daredevil acts on a tightrope high above the ground. The Wallendas debuted for the Ringling Brothers Circus in 1928, performing in New York without a safety net because it had been lost during their travels. The act was definitely a crowd-pleaser and the Flying Wallendas continued performing for decades although many family members have since perished from high-wire accidents. On March 22, 1978 in Puerto Rico, father Karl fell to his death from the high-wire at the age of 73. His great-grandson Nik still performs today and has set numerous records for aerial feats worldwide.

In another house near Dickie's family tent lived the Zacchini family. Not a familiar name to most but everyone has certainly heard of the 'Human Cannonball'. That was Mario Zacchini, father of the family. He was proud of this job description: 'To be explosively propelled ninety miles an hour out of a cannon across the circus tent into a net.' He and four of his brothers spent years being launched from a silver-painted cannon, three times a day with the Ringling Brothers Circus. The Zacchinis have acknowledged that their ear-shattering cannon blasts were purely sound effects, created by igniting a cup of black gunpowder; thus, no booms during practice. They never revealed the secret of the cannon's launching mechanism but Mario joked that 'Flying isn't the hard part; landing in the net is.'

Sarasota Sailor Circus

In 1949, the gymnastics program at the Sarasota High School was expanded to include various tumbling and acrobatic skills. Originating as an acrobatic demonstration during half-time performances at football games, the program evolved into the Sarasota High School Sailor Circus (Sailor being the school's mascot). It has become a full-fledged circus of student performers that receive training from faculty and parents, some of whom are or were professional circus performers.

2019 will mark the 70th anniversary of the Sailor Circus. It is no longer affiliated with the Sarasota High School but is now operated by the Circus Arts Conservatory. This circus is officially known as 'The Greatest Little Show on Earth'.

The circus program is still very active within the public schools of Sarasota and is one of the top in the U.S. for students from fourth through twelfth grade. Sailor Circus Academy, as it's now called, is a highly-disciplined, after-school training program and its students are recognized as future leaders and contributors to the circus legacy in Sarasota.

Dickie was enrolled in Sarasota High School for parts of his Freshman, Sophomore and Junior years. He too was involved with the Sailor Circus practice activities which were the equivalent of normal gym classes but the skills were at a substantially higher level in Sarasota. Dickie had learned trampoline flips, spins, pike jumps and other moves while in school at Dennis-Yarmouth Regional High School so that became his specialty in the Sailor Circus. His skills advanced each year with the excellent coaching in Sarasota but during the winter seasons when he participated with the Sailor Circus, there were no scheduled performances with audiences. Such a shame the world did not get to marvel at Dickie's trampoline skills.

He fondly remembers some of his classmates were who professional circus performers. For example, one classmate was Carla Wallenda, born in 1936. She is the daughter of Karl Wallenda, founder of the Flying Wallendas. She is famous for having performed most of her life on the high-wire. She's still active and performed on television as recently as 2017, climbing an 85-ft pole and performing balancing acts at 81 years old. She sounds like 'Dickie's kind of girl'.

***

Why is all this circus business relevant to Dickie? He wasn't employed as a circus performer but many of us think it would have been an ideal career path for Dickie. The circus impact was, however, subtle and indirect, via immersion with circus-minded students at school each day. And circus acts were continually being practiced across the street from where he lived.

With this constant exposure to physical-performance arts, it's logical that he would develop confidence in balancing acts and taking physical risks beyond those of the average citizen on Cape Cod. Such an individual would certainly earn much visibility in the small village of Dennis.

As mentioned in a later Chapter, Dickie's antics of performing handstands, riding backwards or lying prone on the seat of his motorcycles are consistent with his early exposure to circus life in Sarasota. Also, what employee of a home heating oil company would do a backflip from the top of the delivery truck?

Might this be why Dickie has always been comfortable with physical stunts and risk taking?

Wisdom from the School Bus Driver

Dickie still appreciates the common-sense guidance he received while enrolled in Dennis schools. Not from a specific teacher; rather, from a school bus driver named Mr. Theodore Sears. He would often give one-line, practical advice to the young children – his thoughts of the day. For example, Ted would start off by saying,

'I'll tell ya sonthan.' ('sonthan' was Dennis-talk for 'something') then follow with his advice:

'Hey boy. You got to get up in the mornin, or don't bother gettin up a t'all.'

or

'Hey boy. You got to make more money than ya spend, or don't spend nothan a t'all.'

Definitely good, timeless advice for work ethic and spending within your means. Simple words that may not be shared by today's teachers abiding by strict curriculums and language. Leave it to the bus driver. It's also noteworthy that Dickie doesn't recall any such useful advice from his parents.

He still repeats some of these valuable gems today and proudly lives by them too. He always has a wad of cash in his pocket but you can be sure he wouldn't spend more than he carries. Wisely, he doesn't gamble, with exception of a few lottery tickets each year, whether he wins or not.

It's apparent that Dickie's aversion to gambling was a lesson learned from his father's spending demise.

Notorious or Gracious Characters of the Village

The village was quaint in the mid-1900s, absent glamorous estates and expensive restaurants. But it certainly possessed 'spirit', mainly through the personalities of its townsfolk. Books on Dennis History have rightly focused on the Town Fathers who advanced the town's government and infrastructure; they certainly were fine men and women. Our fondest memories and immediate laughs are however, spawned by recollection of the 'characters' in town. These individuals didn't raise attention from their wealth nor their stature. Most were known simply for their good will or odd behavior. We mustn't forget these characters, be they notorious or gracious. Given below are the favorites of Dickie, with whom he interacted and created fine memories.

Bill Stone

When Dickie was a young boy, he made 'spending money' any way possible, including selling freshly caught herring to the man who lived in the large house overlooking Cape Cod Bay at 200 Bridge Street. His name was William Prescott Stone (1897-1988). Here's the story:

***

Ten-year-old Dickie coasted on his bike a short distance downhill on Bridge Street from its intersection with Route 6A. The year was 1945, two years before Players Plaza was built and seven decades before a streetlight was ever imagined in East Dennis. He stopped beside the small bridge and with bucket in hand, climbed down the abutment to Sesuit Creek. Next, he entered the 30-inch-diameter culvert pipe that allowed saltwater to flow beneath the dyke and westward into the upper saltmarsh. He slowly crept into the pipe, shuffling eastward in the knee-deep water. It was dark but he spotted dozens of herring, swimming side-by-side, with tails moving rapidly to maintain their position against the outgoing flow. The boy's biggest fear was that a snapping turtle may be lurking in the darkness, ready to take a taste of his little leg. He carried a stick for defense, albeit mostly to boost his courage. He certainly was a brave young boy.

The 'run' of herring normally coincided with Easter week but the boy's mother had explained that the Catholic holiday could occur in late March or as late as mid-April, Easter being assigned to the first Sunday after the first full moon of spring. Because herring have no concern for human holidays, they arrive according to their biological clock. The wise boy had already learned that a good harvest of herring was likely in late April. As the 27th was his birthday, he always chose that to be his first day for herring gathering.

From many visits to his secret 'honey hole', the boy was skilled at quickly snatching one fish at a time with his small, bare hands. 'No need to squeeze each fish to see if it discharged red roe or white sperm, as the boy's client wanted all he could catch. Having filled his bucket in less than ten minutes, he hung it from the bike's handlebars and peddled to the north end of Bridge Street to make the sale to the man who lived in the white mansion that overlooked Cape Cod Bay.

It was Bill Stone who smiled when ten-year-old Dickie knocked on his door with thirty fresh herring still flapping in the five-gallon bucket. Bill was always happy to receive his first delivery of the year. He also had growing respect for the young boy's work ethic that undoubtedly would help him throughout life.

Dickie and Bill developed an interesting and enjoyable friendship that persisted until Bill passed away forty-three years later, in 1988, when Bill was 89.

***

The dark culvert under Bridge Street became Dickie's hiding place when escape from family or childhood enemies was necessary. It also provided a perfect spot for him to cool off in the dead of summer when time was too short for a trip to the beach or aboard a skiff in Sesuit Harbor.

One afternoon in mid-August of that year, Dickie began to hear loud noises while enjoying the cool saltwater of the culvert. Upon crawling out of the pipe, he heard church bells ringing, cars honking and the Fire Department whistle blaring from atop the telephone pole on Route 6A. The day was August 14, 1945 and the entire country began celebrating the end

of World War II – it later was designated as VJ Day. Dickie vividly remembers where he was on that historic day.

For many years thereafter, Dickie returned to the saltwater of 'his culvert' on his birthday, April 27th, for an annual swim. The waters were often cold and sometimes cluttered with herring but this represented his near-to-home pilgrimage and time for reminiscing about his childhood and VJ Day memory.

A fine life example, where the view can sometimes be less important than the experience.

***

Bill Stone and his brothers John and Todd (Leroy) all grew up in the village and graduated from North Dennis High School, located about fifty yards north of the existing Dennis Northside Fire Department off Old Bass River Road. John was the eldest, Todd the middle and Bill the youngest, with Todd four years apart from both of his siblings. Their personalities were very different. Bill was a 'go getter', willing to pursue a variety of local jobs and having dreams of prosperity. Most people said that when he was young, he 'didn't have a pot to piss in', not unlike other boys in the village.

One story to exemplify Bill's modest boyhood finances (some say, his 'cheap' nature) recounts that when he invited girls on dates for a movie in Hyannis, he insisted they meet him inside the theater so he wouldn't have to pay for their admission. Wise girls probably avoided a second date.

Bill was active and spent as much

time as possible with affluent people; intentionally bumping elbows with people having 'deeper pockets' than he. This would occur when he caddied at Cummaquid Golf Club, located at 35 Marstons Lane, off Route 6A in Barnstable. This Club opened in 1895; the first in Barnstable County. The only years it was closed was in 1918 and from 1942-1945 on account of the local men participating in the World Wars.

The original name of the Barnstable village was spelled Chummaquid, derived from the Indian name for Sandy Neck.

While caddying, Bill met Mr. George Barton of Long Island, New York. The Bartons had significant wealth and chose to construct a large home on Scarsdale Road. As a hobby, Mr. Barton owned many horses, some of which were accomplished race horses. A few were kept at 'Mel-Pet Stables' originally located at 812 Route 134 in South Dennis. Bill took a liking to horses and later owned a few of his own.

Bill's life certainly changed after he met the Bartons. George's daughter Julia was a lovely girl and Bill set his sights on her; presumably, the reverse is also true. Many townsfolk described her as very classy but always sweet; a fine lady in all respects. To this day, those who remember her respectfully call her 'Miss Julia'.

Bill made many wise business decisions in his day, the most significant was his choice of Julia for his wife. In appearance and poise, she was as opposite as one could be from Bill, who was very 'rough around the edges'. They proved to be a good couple and

Bill did very well with investments of her financial holdings. To illustrate the positive effect Miss Julia had on Bill, he gradually earned the nickname 'Dapper' Billy Stone.

Whereas most townsfolk of those days were content to own a modest house on a cheap, half-acre of land, Bill and Julia set their sights high. This was the mid-40s, long after prohibition had ended and high profits of 'Speakeasy' establishments were a thing of the past. The large hotel on the bluff at the north end of Bridge Street was no exception. That Speakeasy closed and the owners could not cover taxes nor expenses. Word spread quickly that the entire property was to be auctioned for sale to the highest bidder, in 1943. This was a vast and unique property as it included the large hotel, a substantial barn and out buildings, as well as a large parcel of land that extended to Sesuit Creek – encompassing nearly the entire north side of Sesuit Neck. All that was needed for the acquisition was Julia's financial backing and Bill's gumption.

Note that the original building on the Stone property was built (circa 1772) by a Captain Crowell as a home for his wife. In 1925, all property boundaries and ownership in Barnstable County had to be redefined by the Land Court because records had been lost in a fire at the Barnstable County Court House. When Bill Stone purchased the property and large house, it included nearly the entire strip of land extending eastward to Sesuit Harbor. In 1946, he subdivided and sold the land (to Austin Kirkbride) that is today occupied by the Northside Marina. That contributed significantly to the expansion of boating and commerce at Sesuit Harbor.

Of course, Bill wouldn't just attend the auction like any other bidder. Being street-savvy, Bill knew that appearing prosperous and having 'deep pockets' would drive the price upward. Accordingly, his strategy was to appear as a man with minimal financial resources. He first visited his friend William Ernest Crowell[27] to borrow his oft-seen, full-length, shabby raccoon coat to wear to the auction. Beneath the coat Bill wore tattered clothes and he went unshaven for two-to-three days.

He arrived at the auction in his Ford pickup truck which had seen better days. He definitely personified the 'Jed Clampett' image from *Beverly Hillbillies* of mid-60s television. Needless to say, Bill won the auction and 200 Bridge Street became known as Stone's Point, a prominent landmark on Cape Cod Bay.

In 1996, the Stone estate was sold, including the forty acres of land, main house, summer portico addition, hip-roof barn and outbuildings. The new owner was Dr. J. Richard Fennell who made his fortune from medical research, owning and expanding Bioran Medical Laboratory before it was sold to Corning, Inc. He also owned Thompson's Clam Bar, Snow Inn and the Wychmere Harbor Club in Harwich Port.

Dr. Fennell intended to demolish the original buildings on the property but this was denied by the Dennis Historical Commission. The main house and barn were spared and relocated elsewhere on the property; they are still visible today. Most of us have heard of post-and-beam construction but the original house was

more impressive, with massive tree trunks situated in the four corners to support the entire building - nearly 250 years old today.

A new mansion was built at the location of the original house and later Speakeasy. This new structure became the epitome of architectural transformation along Dennis' Bay shoreline. Many long-term Dennis residents adamantly resent the proliferation of 'Mega-Mansions' along their coast, even though they meet the town's building codes and coastal set-back guidelines. It's clear that the 'long-timers' want their village to remain quaint, rather than transform to the ideals of wealthy, off-Cape persons.

***

During Bill Stone's mid- and later years, he did well trading in the stock market and their financial estate continued to grow. Anyone who lived or worked near the north end of Route 134 in those days can remember Bill Stone honking the horn of his Caddy as he drove down the hill approaching Route 6A.

One day, Dickie asked Bill what that frequent commotion was all about. He replied that his honking signified he had an excellent day trading stocks with assistance of his broker from Hyannis, Richard J. Buck (no relation to Dickie). Who the hell cared? No one from East Dennis, but it seemed that Bill felt he was the nucleus of the community from which all importance shone brightly. In other words, to himself, he was a Very Important Man.

Of course, important men drove

large, expensive cars. Bill would be seen driving in his Cadillac or one of his impressive Buick Roadmasters. That model was built from the late '30s to 1958 and was famous for having the longest wheelbase of any non-limousine vehicle. An impressive automobile and a reminder of Eliot Ness who battled the Chicago Capone Gang during the final years of prohibition in the mid-30s.

It's not known how long Bill kept his 1942 Ford pickup truck on the road, but for years he drove it whenever wanting to appear poor.

***

For decades, people have repeated the story of a man who drove up to the gas pumps of the Dennis Garage in his big Cadillac and honked the horn repeatedly. This was the driver's technique for demanding immediate service. Dan Walker, the proprietor, came out of the garage and slowly shuffled to the car. As always, Dan was dressed in his blue coveralls with 'Dan' imprinted on the chest, his briarwood pipe in his mouth and his blue work hat on his noggin. He lifted the massive hood of the car, yanked the horn's power wire out with his bare, oily hand then walked back into the garage to continue with his repair business. With teeth clenching the stem of his pipe, he mumbled out of the corner of his mouth, 'I guess Bill Stone's horn won't stick any more'.

Pete Petersen (who Dickie Buck nicknamed 'Ali Barber') also vividly remembers the second time Bill Stone drove into the parking lot of his barber shop at 585 Route 6A. Bill started honking the horn before his car had even come to a stop, as if it were emergency. Then he stormed through the doorway stating that he wanted to be sure he could get into the barber's chair without delay. Unpleased, Pete immediately told him he'd never again receive a haircut in his establishment. Vamoose! Ten years later Bill returned and pleaded to get a haircut.

***

Bill became very fond of horses, originating from care of Julia's father's steeds. Gradually, Bill purchased horses to keep on his East Dennis estate but he also developed an interest in horse racing and gambling. This led to the idea of purchasing a race horse of his own. He must have been very persuasive because he convinced two of the village's most conservative chaps (Charlie Johnson and William Ernest Crowell) to invest in the purchase of the race horse, with joint ownership and shared winnings. Rumors from those days say the horse never won a dime.

***

Bill and Julia had two daughters, Alison and Sheila, and a son who lived for only a short period of childhood. Alison was the eldest, having been born in 1938, a few years after Dickie. They were good friends until her unfortunate death in 2003 at age sixty-five.

During her High School years, Alison hosted parties in her parents' extremely large house that was the prior hotel of the Speakeasy. Lots of noise could be made at one end of the house without the parents knowing. The perfect party venue.

Following graduation in June of 1956, Alison threw a pajama party with fifteen of her girlfriends; no boys allowed – parents' orders. From first-hand accounts (i.e., my Uncle, Peter McDowell), about twenty-five boys gathered around the house, climbing the trellises and downspouts, even reaching the roof over the girls' party room. Two boys apparently fell of the roof and fortunately landed on their heads so no damage was encountered.

Eventually, father Bill 'got wind' that the boys were swarming around and ordered them off the premises. Peter fled through the large barn but tripped over a piece of rigid hardware in the darkness. This happened to be the water meter and shut-off valve for the main house. As any teen boy would do, he immediately shut off the water and headed home. A funny prank at the time.

By ten o'clock the next morning, the police knocked at the McDowell home on Whig Street. The Officer quickly interrogated Peter, who couldn't tell a lie. Punishment was for Peter to visit Mr. Stone who was 'very angry' that all toilets had been inoperable on the night that sixteen girls were sleeping over. Consequently, Alison was unable to host another party for the remainder of the year, but Peter and his buddies cherish the memory to this day.

***

Dickie remained a good friend of Bill and helped with many projects on his estate. Occasionally, Bill would ask Dickie to do something a bit out of the ordinary. He knew that if anyone would attempt it, Dickie was the guy.

For example, Bill loved fresh trout that Dickie would sometimes deliver after a successful morning's fishing on Scargo Lake. As explained in a later Chapter, Dickie wouldn't go fishing in a conventional boat; he'd troll around the lake in his small Amphicar with a rod streaming behind.

Bill's subsequent request was for Dickie to set up a fishing trawl-line across the short, northeast end of the lake. He suggested rigging a number of baited hooks along the line so many trout could be caught from a single deployment. Dickie says it was never attempted but not for fear of getting caught. Fish wardens were hard to find in those days, except on Opening Day of trout season after the lake had been stocked with hatchery-raised trout.

Another obvious example of how 'times have changed' since the '50s, is regarding the use of firearms. Close friends of Bill Stone knew that he possessed many shotguns, with one positioned near each of the exterior doors in his large house. It was not uncommon for Bill to see a deer, fox or rabbit on his property, soon to be shot by Bill standing in his doorway. Hunting license, time of year – none of those mattered to Bill in those days. He did what he wanted on his property.

***

From these examples of Bill Stone's flamboyant lifestyle, it's not surprising that he was well known in the village.

Yes, he was financially successful, as well as helpful on certain town committees such as the development of Sesuit Neck and the first marina, but he certainly was notorious for his high-profile behavior. Many people in town were 'sick and tired' of his occasional rudeness, inopportune horn blowing and middle-of-the-night phone calls to many townsfolk. Fortunately, the Minstrel Shows provided an excellent forum for the village men to poke fun at Bill. Retaliation in a partially respectful manner.

Exact details of Bill's antics were held back for sake of privacy but everyone in the audience enjoyed having the jokes pointed at him. To the 1896 ragtime tune of *A Hot Time in the Old Town Tonight*, the Minstrel players sang in unison:

> *Late last night I heard the telephone,*
> *I answered it and heard a muffled tone,*
> *My wife said 'Oh My God, I'll bet it's Billy Stone'*

***

The take-away message is that Bill Stone prospered well from a modest beginning, being an aggressive 'wheeler dealer' on properties and making an excellent choice for a life partner. He lived a colorful life but not at the expense of others. Another unforgettable, high-profile character from the village.

Lester Hallett

Everyone in the village knew Lester Hallett back in the '40s and '50s. And they shared a common view of Lester: an excellent gardener but he had a drinking problem – a big drinking problem! Stepping back in time, this was commonplace for many seafaring Dennis men in the early 1900s (before Lester's birth), likely due to the decline of the fishing industry and maritime commerce. Enactment of Prohibition in 1920 was expected to solve the alcoholism problem, but this backfired with proliferation of local Speakeasys and problems with coastal Rum Runners and Bootleggers. Consequently, Massachusetts repealed Prohibition laws in 1930 and alcoholism did begin to decline. For whatever reason, this didn't seem to curb Lester's drinking. He was unquestionably the most prominent drinker in the village.

Lester had many relatives of the Hallett and Walker families, with numerous descendants still living today. Those who knew him understood that Lester had two modes: either sober and friendly or totally inebriated. Regardless, the village treated Lester with respect and they took care of him when he was 'under the weather' even though he could be very unpleasant. Most knew he had been married, early on, but after he and his wife split up, he hit the bottle and it hit back.

The purpose of describing our friend Lester is to illustrate the close camaraderie that existed in the village during that period of time. Townsfolk had the attitude that 'Lester is one of us.' and they did what was necessary, as described below.

***

Dickie remembers Lester fondly, having helped him when he was down and gave him rides around the village, as Lester was 'on foot' for most of his mid- and later years. Through this friendship, Dickie became very skilled at impersonating Lester's unique way of speaking and pronunciation. Additionally, Lester's speech was challenged by a significant 'dental deficiency' at least in the front, which allowed his tongue to escape through a major gap. This resulted in a 'Fa' sound that preceded many of his words. For this reason, his friends affectionately called him 'Fa'Lesta'.

Sober Lester was a proud man and bragged about his landscaping skills and his fine income. In addition to doing yardwork for many residences, he was the designated gravedigger for the town cemetery adjacent to the Dennis Union Church.

During his bragging he'd explain that 'I do the business! And I have fa'thousand dollars right here in my ass pocket. I work for Judge John J. Crehan, as a matter of fact!' He was proud of his prestigious clients such as the Judge. Next, he'd reach behind and start to take his wallet out of his rear pocket but it didn't escape, probably because he knew he didn't have a thousand dollars inside.

Frequently, Lester would ask Dickie if he could borrow a few 'dolluz' for a bottle of booze. Dickie would never say no, often driving Lester to Blanch's Liquor Store on Route 6A just east of the Brewster town line.

'How about trying something new, Lester? I hear that Wild Irish Rose is good hooch?' (The Rose is still identified as one of the best-selling, cheap 'Bum Wines', created from grape wine and artificial flavoring, then 'fortified' with sugar to reach 18% alcohol.)

'No!' was the quick answer. Lester insisted on his favorite – Muscatel. He'd holler, 'It gives me the fa'feeeeeeelin!' Dickie knew not to argue with a drunk about his booze. The big M actually has cheap brandy mixed in, making it one of the favorite 'wino wines' following Prohibition, carrying into the '50s.

When you have a habit (big addiction, in Lester's case) you get proficient at supporting it, no matter what time of day nor where you are. Case in point – Lester would stash bottles of Muscatel in many locations so he could always find a swig close-by. The Sears boys would find half-full bottles in the rafters of the shed next to Obed Shiverick's house, at the intersection of Nobscussett Road and Route 6A, as they waited for the school bus, opposite Louie's IGA.

When a teen, Joshua Crowell (retired Pastor and long-term heritage in Dennis) had to clean out the barn of his Grandfather, Charles Lovell Goodspeed, who owned the grocery store and Post Office on Route 6A. It was a difficult task as his Grandfather had recently passed away and the scale of the job was daunting. For years, Lester had faithfully performed odd jobs for Mr. Goodspeed and had entered the barn hundreds of times. Not surprisingly, Joshua found about fifty bottles of Muscatel stashed in strange places throughout the barn, some full, others half-empty. Certainly, a gold mine for a wino; like a squirrel stashing nuts for the winter.

As another comment on Lester's careful work ethic, Joshua vividly recalls one spring when he had to install the window screens in the front sunroom of his grandparents' (Goodspeeds') house, where the present Post Office is located, at 766 Route 6A. Being careless, Joshua stepped through two panes of glass with a loud crash. The Post Master of those days, Fred Maher, happened to be looking out the window from the nearby Post Office, where the Pack Rat antique shop later was established. Fred witnessed the damage and hollered to Joshua, 'Lester's been doing that chore for thirty years while dead drunk and he never broke a single pane. You smashed two, sober.'

Lester also was known to stash bottles of Muscatel in the branches of trees at the cemetery where he dug graves. He knew the cemetery better than anyone in town and could always find his way to a nearby swig.

When Annie Walker took ownership of the original Henry Hall cranberry bogs on the east side of Scarsdale Road, she had to remove many cedar trees that had grown up in the unkept bog. There too, she found old bottles of booze that had been stashed in the branches, some of which were totally entombed by bark. Best guess is that they were owned by Lester, from decades earlier. Or possibly predating Lester's days.

***

As explained in a later Chapter, Dickie has been known for purchasing the newest and most irregular vehicles on the market, one being an Amphicar that was fully registered for driving on public roads but it also could float and had a small propeller at the rear end of the car for propulsion. This was back in 1970 and his Amphicar was a bright red convertible so everyone in town knew it was Dickie driving by in one of his newfangled vehicles.

One day when Dickie had chauffeured Lester to Blanch's for another bottle of Muscatel, he was driving his new Amphicar which Lester had not seen previously. Without Lester understanding the procedure, Dickie took time to close the doors and lock the 'dogs' (firm levers) that would prevent water from entering the side doors and cause immediate sinking. After the stop at Blanch's, Dickie drove westward and turned left into the Fisherman's Landing entrance to Scargo Lake at 961 Route 6A. Without stopping, Dickie drove into the water with a big splash and proceeded to motor out to the middle of the lake. Lester held on tightly with both hands and let out a scream, 'Highty Tight! It's not the day boys!' This was his way of saying 'Today's not the day for me to die!'

Dickie calmed Lester's nerves after they crossed the lake, explaining that everything was going to be OK. Lester replied, 'Well, I'll tell you 'sonthan', I never fa'thought in my long days I'd ever drive in a fa'automobile across Scargo Lake!' Dickie recalls it was a wonderful experience for Lester, after he realized he wasn't going to die. Over the next year, Dickie took other unsuspecting friends out on the lake in his Amphicar without them knowing their destiny. He was the ultimate prankster, often fueling the fears of his cohorts. No one died.

***

Louie Terpos' IGA was one of the busiest places in the village as it had a substantial grocery store and a luncheonette (soda fountain) on the east end of the building. Natives would often sit at the counter for a basic breakfast or lunch. Some of the single men in town enjoyed chatting with the girls behind the counter, including Carol Sears, Vi Sencabaugh (Dickie's mother-in-law) and 'Baby Jane' Dixon. Lester was another frequent patron of the luncheonette but the ladies were always leery of his condition upon entering. When sober, he was polite and respectful but with Muscatel in his belly, he could be boisterous and disrespectful to the ladies. Sometimes he'd say 'I'll take you over the top of the fa'moooon!' which we believe was his way of flirting, saying he'd give the ladies a wonderful time, which they did not appreciate. Lester may have thought he had 'a way' with the ladies in town; not so.

Dickie the prankster, would often go into Louie's luncheonette and impersonate Lester in voice and actions. The ladies working behind the counter loved it, as Dickie was always a performer.

If Lester entered the store inebriated, he'd get very belligerent and become

physical – a bad drinker he was. Louie would call the Cops and Chief Earl H. Whittemore, Jr. would arrive to deal with Lester. 'Come on Lester, it's time to come with me.' Handcuffs were the next step.

More often than not, Lester would stand and take a big, round-house swing at Earl who knew how to avoid the drunk's inaccurate punch. Off balance and tipsy, Lester would miss his target then fall in a heap on the floor and bark, 'Help me up so I can knock ya' agin.' After a short scuffle, Earl would stuff Lester in the police car and transport him to the town police station and lock him up for the night.

Every one recalls that when very drunk, Lester had additional speech characteristics that were memorable. Lacking most of his teeth, he'd slobber like an overheated Boxer dog. Before he would say something ('sonthan'), he'd use the back of his hand to wipe the slobber off his mouth, sling it on the floor with a sharp wrist action, then begin to talk. When addressing Earl prior to application of the handcuffs, he'd come out with his favorite line, only slightly modified from when he was flirting with the counter ladies: 'I'll knock you over fa'moon!'

Fortunately, there were men at Louie's store on most days when Lester entered drunk. They knew the drill and quickly wrestled him outside before he could hurt the ladies, patrons or himself. On more than one occasion, the men put Lester's back up against a sturdy tree and lashed him there so he wouldn't fall into the traffic on Route 6A before Chief Earl arrived to take him away.

***

Like the stately elm trees on Route 6A, Lester had a seasonal behavior pattern. Because his living conditions were marginal, at best, and his income from gardening and gravedigging would be nil in winter months, he wisely developed a plan for 'wintering over'. And he acted this out each year to the full awareness of the village.

When cold weather would set in, Lester would arrive drunk at Louie's. Sometimes he'd enter the store or luncheonette and 'Call Out' Louie, taunting for a fist fight with the owner. Louie was a gentleman with no intention of fighting but Lester's attitude would quickly become aggressive and frightening to all, so a call to Chief Earl was made quickly. A scuffle would ensue but the cuffs would be on Lester in short order.

Some years, Lester would make his autumnal, drunken arrival at Louie's when the store was closed. If neither Louie nor patrons were there, he'd throw a brick through the window, knowing he'd be arrested soon as no one else in town would vandalize the grocery store. To be sure, he'd always use the same type of brick so the Cops would know 'who done it'.

Those who lived outside of the village might ask what these early winter shenanigans were all about. But anyone who knew Lester would quickly explain that in winter he needed 'Three hots and a cot', meaning three hot meals and a bed to sleep on.

Backing up a bit, remember that Chief Earl would take Lester to the Dennis police station and lock him up for the night or a few days, depending upon the intensity of his 'bender' (drunken state). Earl had learned from experience that Lester's most inebriated condition would occur after the coldest night in Fall. Eager to move him out of the cell and police station, Earl would make a call the next morning to the Barnstable County House of Correction, asking if he could bring Lester to their facility for an extended period to 'dry-out'. Fortunately, two of the constables (Dick Sylver and Don Parker) at the House of Correction were from the village and they knew Lester, terribly well. They were good men and very kind during inmate 'processing' of Lester upon his arrival. He'd still be drunk, belligerent and physical, to the extent that any other constables would likely have had to manhandle Lester (i.e., rough him up) but Dick and Don didn't want this to happen to the man from their village. Fortunately, Dick had long arms and could keep Lester's fists out of punching range which was essential. Despite Lester's shortcomings, the two men treated him like family, got him stripped, washed down, clothed and in his cell for the winter.

Within a few days, Lester transformed into the kind, polite and gentle man that our village knew well. He also proved to be ambitious, which was very helpful because the Barnstable County House of Correction facility had a large plot of land for raising crops and animals. Note that most locals referred to the facility as the 'County Farm'; definitely a more pleasant moniker than the County Jail or the House of Correction.

The original House of Correction was built in the '30s but replaced in 2004 with a new facility, thereafter named the Barnstable County Correctional Facility. For over one-hundred years, the facility has been collocated with a 99-acre parcel of land on Route 6A which is still the largest piece of land under cultivation on Cape Cod. Beginning in January 2009, the County Sherriff's department has no longer operated the farm; it is available via lease to interested parties.

Lester was a great worker and soon proved his skills to the Warden at the House of Correction, to the extent that they liked having Lester on the premises, as a reliable laborer. He was likely a better worker than many of the employees at the facility. Additionally, the County Sheriff would enlist Lester to do the gardening at his home behind the County Courthouse in Barnstable Village. Joshua Crowell knew of this arrangement and would occasionally drive by the Sheriff's home to wave hello to Lester, who would smile back as he pruned the shrubs, like being on vacation. When spring arrived, Lester knew he would soon be released to Dennis.

This arrangement worked so well for all involved that the House of Correction came to expect Lester's arrival each fall when the cold weather would blanket Cape Cod. Handcuffed Lester would be 'escorted' through the big iron door in his nasty drunken state, slobbering at the mouth and cussing in all directions. Within a few days, he'd sober up and be a pussy cat, willing to work hard like no other inmate.

Lester was content being locked up for the cold season because he'd be guaranteed his 'three hots and a cot' daily. The Sheriff was pleased to have a free, skilled gardener. Chief Earl was happy that Lester was off the streets and Louie was relieved to have his nemesis out of town. Sober Lester was a good man.

Epilogue: During fall of one year, Lester's annual arrest was made in early October. After spending the night in the Dennis jail, he was driven the next morning to the District Court House in Harwich for arraignment. Judge Gersham Hall listened to the police's arrest statement but having seen Lester more times that he wanted, the Judge immediately made a sentence of three-months incarceration at the House of Correction. This would sound harsh to the average drunk, but Lester was special. Quickly visualizing the calendar, Lester realized he'd be released in January which would be a terrible fate as his living conditions were insufficient for cold months and he'd have no gardening work for income.

To the surprise of everyone in the courthouse, Lester pleaded for a longer sentence. Without hesitation, the Judge banged his gavel on the block and barked, 'Five months it shall be!' Lester was relieved and proceeded to thank the Judge, while those in attendance roared with laughter.

***

There is no doubt that much of Lester's later years revolved around alcohol, which was not a positive trait. Ironically, many teens appreciated Lester for his generosity linked to alcohol.

Lester was known to be very cooperative, which meant he was willing to purchase alcohol for teens who were underage, according to Massachusetts law. Of course, he didn't have spare cash, but the teens always gave him money for the goods and Blanch's Liquor Store at the Brewster line was the normal (and easiest) scene of the crime. Many of the local Juniors and Seniors attending Dennis-Yarmouth High School would have their friend Fa'Lesta purchase mass quantities of beer and alcohol for their parties at Chapin Beach. This meant he became a local hero of a special kind: 10-proof.

Cleverly, Lester was 'memorialized' in the D-Y Yearbook for the Class of 1969. On one two-page collage of student photographs, the word 'Lester' was over-printed in large letters, some presented upside-down, possibly typifying Lester's varying condition. The teachers and Yearbook editors would not allow the yearbook to be formally Dedicated to Lester, the notorious town drunk, but the appreciative Seniors found a way to extend thanks to their best Buyer.

***

When nine-year-old Annie Walker stepped off the school bus as it stopped across the street from Louie's, she was sometimes greeted by 'Mr. Lester'. The little 'peanut' of a girl enjoyed meeting her elderly friend because she still hadn't recovered emotionally from the sadness of losing her mother to cancer that year. 'Mr. Lester' was always kind and frequently took her for walks in the large cemetery where he worked digging graves. She liked holding his big hand while they roamed around many lichen-covered headstones, with he showing where her many relatives lie; his relatives too. It didn't matter that he took swigs from bottles he grasped from branches in the trees. He was always kind to little 'Girly'.

Annie remembers that on a few occasions, the local police stopped them and asked if she was Okay. 'You shouldn't be with him alone in the cemetery.' they said. She got very upset and replied, 'But it's Mr. Lester.' The little girl needed her special time with her friend, who also was a distant relative of hers.

Although Annie could trust Lester, the police were just doing their job, ensuring the safety of the village children. Never were the two obstructed from taking their heartwarming walks. Tears come to Annie's eyes today, as she describes her special time with Mr. Lester.

***

The village certainly was a safe place for children back in the '50s. When they got off the school bus in the afternoon, the boys would typically rush home for a snack (yes, mom's cookies and a glass of milk) then head off to 'play' with their friends. For some, this meant playing ball while others would bike down to the 'haahba' to motor around in the skiffs. All that mother need say was 'Be home for supper.' and the boys knew exactly what that meant. She needn't give instructions on where not to go as it was dangerous, nor whom to stay away from as he might hurt you. It was all safe in the village.

Also significant was that mothers in the village were friends who shared a common belief in how to raise their children, with a significant dose of discipline. It began when the moms would take their young'uns to Corporation Beach most days in summer. The toddlers would play, eat sand and learn how to interact with each other while mothers sat close-by in their beach chairs, ready to scold their kid when she (or he, most often) was 'bad' – maybe not a politically correct term today, but kids learned what 'bad' meant, even if from watching other kids get scolded.

As the kids grew into their mid-teens and roamed the village with their friends after school, from fall through spring, they shared the common understanding of what was right and wrong. When they'd misbehave, it was normally within earshot of someone's mother and she'd do the scolding of all boys involved. For example, if anyone misbehaved near Miss Anna (pronounced 'Anner'; my grandmother), they knew she'd quickly inflict the wrath of God on the boys, then later inform the mothers. It was accepted that all mothers had the right to discipline the village boys. This worked well.

The boys learned they had to behave at all times and everywhere, not just when their own parents were watching. Being a good citizen, consistently, was paramount. It was how kids grew up.

It's a damn shame that some kids don't live by that tenet today. I blame it on the parents and the lack of community collaboration.

***

Lester lived into his early eighties and is buried in the Dennis Village Cemetery. Dickie recalls one day when Lester told him that he was seventy-seven years old. It certainly was a linguistic challenge for Lester, given that he was toothless, drunk, drooling and his tongue slithered out as he began each word, and with an 'f' preceding the first consonant. 'F'theventy-theven.' Say that five times!

It's a fact that Lester was the 'Village Drunk' of those days, as well as having other widely varying traits including kindness, being an excellent gardener, a Buyer of Booze for locals, a profuse slobberer and a survivor, but he never hurt a soul. Lester definitely added color to the local community in the '40s and '50s, and in return, the village watched over him for decades.

Bob Eldred, Sr.

Robert C. Eldred, Sr. started his East Dennis-based estate auction business in the '50s at 1483 Route 6A. He soon earned the reputation as a highly knowledgeable antique auctioneer as well as an intelligent and charismatic man. He retired in 1978 after having established his auction house as a center of excellence, with buyers from the U.S., Europe and the Far East. His son, Robert, Jr., was much like his father, in personality and auctioneering skills. He joined the business in 1969, became president upon his father's retirement and continued to lead the auction house until 2014; a highly successful run of nearly sixty years by the father-son team.

Everyone remembers Bob Sr. from his limp, caused by a gunshot to his leg in World War II. His walking stick became another one of his trademarks, in addition to the large, straight-brimmed hat he wore while doing his 'calling' from the auction block. When he slammed the gavel down for each sale, everyone in the house knew Bob Sr. meant business.

His charisma dazzled most ladies in town but his intellect was even more captivating. He once had the opportunity to demonstrate his mental prowess to a group of townsfolk at Carleton Hall. From the many persons in attendance, he selected thirty individuals at random then asked for their name, profession and other personal information from each. A short while later, he was able to identify each person and recite all the personal details they had provided, with perfect accuracy. Surely, he was able to recognize the many active bidders (and recall how deep their pockets were) during each sale at his auction house.

As the Eldred auction business grew, it employed more local residents each year. Adults helped with the summer auctions as well as with incoming shipments year-round. Children also had minor jobs on

site and at the concession stand for food and drinks. Overall, everyone enjoyed working for Bob and his family.

***

Dickie was a few years older than Bob Jr. and occasionally spent time during his early teens at their large home on Route 6A. The house was originally built and owned by Colonel Argo. His daughter, Ellen (Mimi) Argo is a successful author who published three fiction novels, from 1977 to 1980, about Cape Cod and world sailing during the Clipper Ship days.

In the early '50s, Dickie helped Bob Sr. construct an extensive O-gauge electric train set in the attic of their home. And Bob Sr. certainly enjoyed the latest technologies of the day. He had an impressive acoustic sound system installed throughout his house, activated by push buttons to provide music to individual rooms; very modern for the '60s.

When Dickie and Judy got married in 1965, Eldred's Auction House gave them a wedding present of two large, Staffordshire dog figurines as a generous gift, which they cherished for years.

Johnny Rose

The Dennis Highlands Golf Course was constructed within a large parcel of town land, situated west of Old Bass River Road, extending south to Setucket Road and westward to the Yarmouth town line. Much of the overall parcel was and still is controlled by the Dennis Water District.

During the golf course planning in the early '80s, the town acquired a small, privately owned parcel of land adjacent to Old Bass River Road that would become the public entrance to the golf course. This was necessary because all other boundaries of the course perimeter had no access to public roads. As recently as fifteen years earlier, that private parcel was used as a 'junk yard' for old cars; definitely 'pre-owned' vehicles using today's jargon. Visualize hundreds of autos in varying degrees of disassembly and rust, spread over a couple acres of open land. Not a pretty sight but it represented someone's livelihood.

Until 1965, the facility was operated by Johnny Rose; nicknamed 'Cozy Rosey' by his friends. Prior to Johnny's proprietorship, Edgar Bearse III ran the junk car operation.

Johnny was a black man of medium height with bald head and he certainly was strong. He'd pay $10 for each car delivered to his facility, from which he would extract useable parts for resale to townsfolk that needed cheap replacements. If you needed a starter from a 1948 Ford, he'd point you in the direction of the old hulk and it'd be your responsibility to go find the car and remove the part.

Sometimes he'd extract the entire engine from a car and stories have been told that Johnny could lift the large engines out from the chassis with his own might. Most of his time was spent using a torch to cut each chassis into pieces for sale as scrap metal. And there were times when he'd catch his shirt or pants on fire but it was all part of the job.

Finding Johnny in the vast junk yard was often a challenge but a little smoke would often lead you to his torch. He was a good, hardworking man who made a meager living.

Like most people in those days, he'd stoop to pick up any spare coin lying on the ground. Dickie remembers seeing Cozy Rosey bending over in front of Bucky Beaver's Magic Garage. Looking up with his bald head and big eyes, Johnny was quick to comment. 'Don't be telling anybody that Johnny Rose be picking up pennies!' Neither Dickie nor anyone else wanted to be on the wrong side of Johnny.

Mig Maher

Margaret (Mig) Maher was the sister of Dan Walker and J. P. Walker. She was the wife of Fred Maher (the Dennis Postmaster), mother of two boys and teacher in the Dennis elementary school. In 1942, Dickie was a student in Mig's second grade class. He recalls one day during World War II, when 'Miss Mig' invited her brother J. P. into the classroom wearing his full Air Force uniform with helmet and aviator glasses. It was thrilling for Dickie and his classmates to see a real aviator from the war. Joe's active duty was aboard the large B-17 Flying Fortress or B-24 Liberator Bombers.

Mig was a very kind soul and rode the school bus to assist the children to and from school. One day her bus was in a terrible accident at the intersection of Airline Road and Route 6A in East Dennis. Although seriously injured,

Mig helped many of the children off the bus during the perilous situation. She was hailed as a heroine by the local newspapers. Sadly, her back remained seriously damaged for the rest of her life.

In pain, Mig returned to her teaching each day of school for many years. Dickie remembers that at reading time, Miss Mig would have the children gather their chairs in a circle around her. Whoever had been the best student of the day would be rewarded with the opportunity to stand behind her and massage her sore back during her reading session. This was an honor for the chosen student.

In today's world, a teacher would be prosecuted for allowing (or especially, directing) a student to place their hands on the teacher's body. But Mig's students loved her and genuinely wanted her to feel better. It would have been a major loss to the school and the children if Mig had been unable to return to her classroom.

***

It is noteworthy that the famous screen actor Gregory Peck once stayed in a Guest House operated by Mig's parents (Ben Walker, the Harbormaster of Nobscusset Harbor) while he was acting at the Cape Playhouse[5]. It was customary in those days for townsfolk to rent rooms to actors because the Willows Inn was the only large Inn in operation during the '40s and '50s, and the income was 'good money' for the locals. Furthermore, the actors received very small wages which prevented their stay at upscale accommodations.

Similarly, Richard Crenna stayed at my grandmother's home on Whig Street during his acting at the Playhouse. Art Carney and many others also enjoyed stays in the village during the '40s and '50s. Ms. Carolyn St. John was the lead housing coordinator for visiting actors in those days.

Gerard 'Life Jacket' Lowther

Gerard Lowther was born in 1916, the year after his father, William, became the Lighthouse Keeper at Race Point in Provincetown. William and his wife, Rose, 'manned' the lighthouse for twenty years, until 1935. Fortunately, they had departed the light house prior to the Great Massachusetts Hurricane of 1938 which had wind gusts to 186 miles per hour in Boston.

Race Point Lighthouse, the third lighthouse on Cape Cod, first went into service in 1816, shortly after the U.S. Lighthouse Service (USLHS) was created in 1812. Over the 126 years that Race Point Light was in operation, fourteen 'Principal Keepers' were sequentially stationed there, until 1942 when the light was automated. While the average duration for Keepers at the Lighthouse was nine years, William and his wife endured and enjoyed twenty years at the extreme northern tip of Cape Cod. Only one Keeper lasted longer – twenty-five years.[28]

William's wife Rose also had an illustrious career serving in the U.S. Armed Forces. During World War I, she held the position of Ships Cook Fourth Class for the U.S. Navy. Later, she was an Observer for Zeppelins and German submarines at Race Point Lighthouse from 1917 to 1919.

Gerard grew up in the house adjacent to the Lighthouse for his entire childhood and teen years. This required a two-mile trek along the beach and sand dunes to reach school each day. You can be sure Gerard's children heard their Dad's stories if they complained about walking a short distance to the school bus in East Dennis, many years later.

Gerard and his wife Catherine (Kay) purchased a house at 12 Bridge Street[29] and raised a family of three sons and two daughters. The house had previously been owned by Dickie's Aunt Thelma and her husband Bob Jacobs. Kay was well known in East Dennis as she was the Post Master in the early '60s.

Like his father before him, Gerard chose a career with the U.S. Coast Guard, achieving the grade of Chief. During World War II he served in the Battle of Okinawa in the South Pacific. After the war he was assigned to the USCGC (Coast Guard Cutter) *Eastwind* (WAGB-279) which operated off the northeast U.S. coast.

The *Eastwind* was a 269-ft icebreaker having unprecedented structural integrity for winter operations at high latitudes. On January 19, 1949, when 33-year-old Gerard was aboard with the rank of Chief Petty Officer, the *Eastwind* collided with the large oil tanker, *Gulfstream*, while underway in fog sixty miles off the coast of New Jersey.[30] Fifteen Coast Guardsmen perished from the collision and subsequent fires onboard. Gerard experienced severe burns over much of his body but was fortunate to survive. His wife Kay was a Registered Nurse

so she was very involved in his initial care. Prior to Gerard's return home for final stages of convalescence, Kay would spend nights at his bedside in the hospital. Dickie's mother, Ellie, stayed with the five Lowther children each night, as the Buck home was just up the street from the Lowther's Bridge Street home. After a full recovery, Gerard placed an antique fire wagon with large bell on the front lawn of his property to signify his experience with fire aboard the *Eastwind*.

In the latter years of his Coast Guard career, Gerard served as Chief at Race Point Station in Provincetown, the town he grew up in. His friends in East Dennis fondly nicknamed him 'Life Jacket' Lowther for his long association with the Coast Guard, while others called him 'Red'.

Because the Lowther home was located close to Players Plaza of the '50s, their children were very involved in the Pharmacy and adjacent Sinclair gas station, including summer employment and shenanigans during their teen years. Joe, the youngest of the three Lowther sons, recalls having assisted with preparation of medical prescriptions in the pharmacy – imagine that today. He and another friend also pumped gas at Bucky Beaver's Magic Garage when Dickie was off doing 'other business'.

Most of the Lowther children interacted with Dickie although he was much older than the two youngest. One winter, Kay had to scold Dickie for hurting young Joe by throwing ice balls. Boys were boys in those days, especially Dickie!

***

Gerard was a good mentor for village boys. At the time of the Vietnam war, Jonathan Thatcher received the Number 15 from the Draft Lottery, which was a quick ticket to Southeast Asia. He considered enlisting in the Army but Gerard strongly encouraged him to enlist in the Coast Guard. Fortunately, Jonathan was accepted into this branch of the Armed Forces and was forever grateful, admitting that if he'd joined the Army, 'I'd probably have been the first one to come home in a box.' In appreciation, Jonathan gave a bottle of Canadian Club whiskey to Gerard after having been discharged from the Coast Guard on a medical disability, three and one-half years after enlisting.

Jonathan remembers when Buckie Beaver shaved his head before entering Boot Camp in 1970. The 'Beave' assured him that 'You'll receive a lot of grief if you show up with long hair.'

***

When William and Rose Lowther were stationed at the Race Point Lighthouse, their primary means of transportation was via horse and carriage as there were no passable roads through the Provincetown dunes for automobile travel. Young Gerard grew up loving horses and later kept his own horse, 'Billy Boy', behind their house on Bridge Street. Eventually the horse died in the barn, standing up – honestly. Plan A was to bury the horse in the back yard but the frozen ground in winter prevented burial. Gerard's Plan B was to cremate the

horse by burning up the barn, horse and all, but the barn wouldn't conveniently burn. Plan C was to enlist Dickie to get rid of the horse, which entailed using a Ford 9N Tractor to transport the carcass south along Route 134 to the town dump. It was quite a sight with the large, stiff, dead horse being transported with the tractor but Dickie got the job done for his friend Gerard.

The youngest son, Joe, still remembers his Dad getting angry when Dickie would frequently play the trumpet loudly as he stood on the northern, marsh side of the Sinclair service station. Gerard's opinion was that Dickie's trumpeting was more noise than music.

Clarabelle and Mort Sears

Memories of particular village characters remain with us for decades, whether it be from their odd behavior or their peculiar names. In the case of Clarabelle Sears, it was both. The name Clarabelle means bright and beautiful, a name that first appeared in the U.S. around 1910. Who am I to judge whether she was both?

She was a small, energetic woman with little legs and long red hair who lived in East Dennis with her husband Mort. He worked at Hinkley's Lumber in Hyannis and would make the round-trip drive each weekday. Townsfolk saw Clarabelle often because she would walk to Hyannis to purchase specific items. She'd be seen in the morning, hiking westward on Route 6A then returning in late afternoon with numerous bags in hand. It was an extraordinary routine, having carried her purchases all the way from Hyannis, about ten miles on foot.

Apparently, if Clarabelle was not already in the car when Mort was ready to leave for his morning commute to Hyannis, he would leave without her. More surprising is that if she had begun her walk to Hyannis before his departure, he would pass her on the road and drive by without picking her up. It is not known whether she would decline his offer, if he made one. There was no doubt that one or both of them was obstinate.

Her matter-of-fact temperament was obvious on another occasion, when she was leaving a grocery store. As she passed though the swinging screen door, her underpants fell down to her shoes. Nonchalantly, she stepped out of them and kept walking, unfazed.

Mort was a character as well, retaining a strong feeling of civic duty even in his later years. In summer he'd be hired as a Special Policeman, assigned to various duties when the population of the town was high compared to the small number of winter residents.

Many days and nights, Mort would sit in his parked car near Players Plaza waiting for something exceptional to occur at the intersection of Routes 6A and 134. Back in the '50s, this was not a bustling location, as most people know. Nevertheless, when a few cars would arrive at the same time, Mort would leap from his car and rush to the center of the intersection to direct the traffic. There might have been a stop sign for northbound traffic on Route 134 but Route 6A had the right-of-way without much ambiguity. In other words, Mort

was rarely needed but he didn't give a damn, he was there to help, even if he was off-duty.

People recall Mort being somewhat busy on summer nights when the Drive-In Theater emptied out after the second feature and cars drove down the Route 134 hill returning home. There'd be Mort waving his hands to direct the traffic flow. It's noteworthy the town wouldn't justify the need for an automated traffic light at that intersection for another sixty years. Maybe Mort was just a bit eager; like Barney Fife, the Deputy Sheriff in the original Andy Griffith television show of the '60s about police in the fictional small town of Mayberry.[31]

***

For income, Clarabelle cleaned houses in East Dennis and Dickie hired her to do his cleaning before he was married. Around the same time, he and a friend made their own dark beer in frequent batches. During summer the capped bottles would occasionally explode from the intense heat while stored in the attic but the supply was always sufficient. Of course, the smell of the dark beer permeated the house but the guys didn't give a damn.

When Clarabelle was in Dickie's house for cleaning, she'd often help herself to the brew. 'Stout ain't it? Oh that Stout!' she said to Dickie after having consumed a fair volume during her first encounter. She certainly liked the brew. The result was always the same at the end of each cleaning session, with Clarabelle getting quite drunk, walking a few hundred yards up Route 134 and sleeping-it-off in the trees. She was a good worker but not while 'on the sauce'.

***

We mustn't move on without mentioning another 'special' woman of those days, affectionately called the 'Goat Lady'. She lived in the Punkhorn region of West Brewster and had a significant herd of goats that she led around the area. Each day the Goat Lady would direct her flock to the Brewster town dump where they'd forage through the new trash and swill. Regardless of the season, she'd wear her long coat over very old clothes. Old timers warned to never get downwind of the Goat Lady due to her horrific odor; likely worse than the goats.

Bernard Eldridge

Few men were characterized as fashionable but Bernard Eldridge was the exception. He and his wife would often drive through town dressed in dapper clothing of the early 1900s. Bernard wore a tailored three-piece suit and topped it off with a derby hat. Over his dress shoes he wore spats, which were fashionable and made to protect shoes and socks from rain, mud, etc. They certainly exemplified stylish dress of that period which was Bernard's goal.

He projected quite an image, as did his lovely wife who would sit beside him in their open-top Brush motorcar, she in a bright yellow, chiffon dress and a large colorful hat. This couple projected a fine look of yesteryear and the women of Dennis certainly noticed Bernard's stylish attire – very different from their husbands'.

The Brush Runabout was a light, two-passenger, open-style touring car manufactured by the Brush Motor Car Company of Detroit, Michigan. Their production was limited to only six years, from 1907 to 1913. The Runabout was a light car with wooden chassis and iron cross-members. Not a durable car for regular duty but it was ideal for the Eldridges to present themselves 'about town' in good weather.

Bernard also owned Packard automobiles. The Packard Motor Car Company produced luxury automobiles, beginning in 1899 and extending through 1959, shortly after it merged with the Studebaker Automobile Company. Bernard owned two of the shorter, roadster models, one having a convertible top for touring in good weather.

Bernard came from a wealthy family that owned a very large house opposite from where Grumpy's restaurant is located today. The property was the Hall Homestead, located at 1421 Route 6A and built in 1735. When he inherited the house, he divided it into five sections and had them moved to various locations. The Sesuit Motel (opened in 1964 and recently renamed the Sesuit Harbor House) was comprised of the original large building and a newly built motel-style building.

The main structure of Ross Coppelman Goldsmith, Inc., at 1439 Route 6A, also was part of the original Eldridge property. Another piece was moved west on Route 6A to a location near the Indian Burial Ground.

The 'Gentleman' from East Dennis certainly was more of a developer than someone who got his hands dirty. He purchased the home of Gerard Chapman after he passed away in 1963. Some remember the proper Mr. Chapman who was Dennis Town Clerk and Treasurer from 1945 to 1961. His original home at 799 Route 6A was significantly remodeled and expanded to accommodate Mrs. O'Leary's County Fair restaurant that was moved from 905 Route 6A. Some years later, the property was sold again and the Scargo Café was established in 1987.

Although Bernard was known to have 'deep pockets', he was careful with his money. For instance, although he owned multiple Packards, he registered only one vehicle and would move the number plate to the auto he intended to drive that day. Wisely frugal, albeit bending the law.

When Bernard passed away, he was buried in the Dennis Cemetery. Those who participated in the burial service recall an oddity in the procedure, with his coffin being interred on its side. This was necessary because there was a large boulder in the ground at that specific plot which restricted the size of the grave for the casket. Village trivia.

Wilber Gibbs

On the other end of the financial spectrum was a Dennis character named Wilber Gibbs. He and his family lived on the east side of Corporation Road, a few lots north of Route 6A. Wilber was the brother of Francis Gibbs, one of the early lobstermen from Nobscusset Harbor.

Wilber was infamous for his hobby of collecting, everything. It has been said that many items entered his yard but nothing ever left, whether it be vehicles, mowers in disrepair or junk. Unused items were perpetually added to the growing piles of steel and rust in his yard. Around town, he earned the nickname 'Swill-ber', pronounced with an intentional pause. When the man died, it was a massive community project to help clean the plot of land and rid the village of a major eyesore.

Those who knew Wilber best remember him as a friendly, slight man with remarkable optimism, especially given his life status. He had high energy and was always busy - going places and acquiring. Wilber often visited the Dennis Garage, needing assistance to repair some item of machinery that just became 'his property'. Dan Walker and Paul McDowell, proprietors of the Garage, got a kick out of Wilber because he could perform a few feats that no one else could match or care to attempt. For instance, he could put his fingers between a car's spark plug and the plug wire of a running engine, with the current running through his hand with no consequences (that were visible).

To demonstrate his upper-body strength (of all his 130 pounds), Wilber would grab an overhead rafter and pull himself up, doing repeated pull-ups. What was most extraordinary is the he'd grasp the narrow edge of the two-by-ten-inch rafter between the fingers of one hand, put his second hand around the wrist of the first, then lift himself using just his thumb and four fingers on the beam - an impressive feat of strength. Wilber certainly was one-of-a-kind.

Edgar Bearse, III

Edgar was another unforgettable character of the time. Although he was not a 'distinguished' individual, nearly everyone called him by his full name: 'Edgar Bearse the Third'. He served in the U.S. Marine Corps during World War II.

Edgar worked hard until he got married. This was no accident, as Edgar chose Nancy Pomeroy for his wife. She had substantial wealth from her family, who were not Cape Codders.

One rumor is that Ms. Pomeroy's wealth was derived from the London-based Mrs. Pomeroy Ltd. company that developed a highly successful line of beauty and skin-care products. Beginning in 1895, the Mrs. Pomeroy line became a leader in the British cosmetic industry, until the late 1940's. The founder of Mrs. Pomeroy, Ltd. was however, a woman named Jeannette Scale who simply used the name Pomeroy for marketing purposes. The surname was borrowed from her mother's side of the family, having been related to General Pomeroy, an American Revolutionary War hero. It is unknown whether the American Pomeroys tapped into the wealth of the British Scales. And the irony is most amusing, with a British business founder using the surname of an American General who fought in the war to gain independence from the Brits.

Regardless of Nancy's financial ties, Edgar lived a comfortable life, well supported by her pocketbook. Without need to work, he maintained an odd schedule, sleeping all day and driving around the village all night. He claimed he was keeping an eye on what was going on in the Village (not much, typically). It was not uncommon for Edgar to drive into a friend's yard at 5 a.m. and knock on the front door because he wanted to talk with the person over a cup of coffee. Most people did not appreciate the timing of such house calls but they understood it was just Edgar's way.

Albeit a minor issue, it was noticeable that Edgar's hair never grayed. He had a full head of dark brown hair right up to his death, in his seventies. This was likely because he had no stress in his everyday life, absent employment.

Edgar was quick to make purchases of the newest appliances, toys and cars as money was no object. He invited many townsfolk to watch his new, colored television, likely the first one purchased in the village. And when Henry Ford introduced the new line of Edsel automobiles in 1953, of course Edgar was the first owner on Cape Cod. On 'E-day', September 4, 1957, Ford dealers unveiled the new design but it turned out to be a marketing flop. Nevertheless, Edgar and Nancy drove around in the sportiest new American-made vehicle.

Nancy's image was a bit out of the ordinary for Dennis, as she had very short, curly hair that seemed mismatched with her plump stature. Her presence was hard to overlook because she often wore brightly colored dresses, often pink.

Dan Walker at the Dennis Garage often complimented Nancy's 'piano legs', but his words were shared only with his friends.

Nancy and Edgar certainly were a peculiar pair. Like most couples in the '50s, they birthed two children, Russell and Theo. Unfortunately, Russell developed friendships with a few teen boys who were big trouble in the town. One night they came to his house to shoot him on his own front lawn. Russell rushed into the house to get his shotgun in defense but he proceeded to load it with the wrong-sized shell. As he went outside to do battle with his enemies, the 16-gauge shell went directly through the barrel of the 12-gauge shotgun when he pulled the trigger. Consequently, no shot was fired.

Simultaneously, a sawed-off shotgun was pointed out of the car window and immediately shot Russell in the chest at close range. They had previously been in a fight at the sandpit on Old Bass River Road so the boys in the car decided to visit Russell to get even.

Dickie had just ended his night shift tending bar at the Lower Deck on Route 134 and was driving on Pilgrim Road to return home. As he passed the Bearse house, Theo ran into the street yelling, 'Dickie Buck. Dickie Buck Stop! Russell's been hurt. Russell's been hurt real baaaad.' Dickie got out of his car and quickly went to Russell but the boy was already in the process of dying from the massive blast to his chest.

At that time, there was a group of boys who were serious 'trouble makers' that put fear in many of the residents. The boy who shot Russell was convicted

and sent to jail but others remained on the streets. There was a rash of fires, including the large barn adjacent to the Willows Inn on Seaside Avenue, a house fire on Shore Road and attempted arson at the box office of the Cape Playhouse. Eventually, the problems ended and the village returned to its quiet lifestyle but none of the suspected arsons were ever convicted.

Adam Fletcher

While Dickie was proprietor of Bucky Beaver's Magic Garage (see Chapter on Landmarks), Phil Dubin, owner of the Garage building and the entire Players Plaza, would purchase gasoline for the station from a regional wholesaler in Hyannis named David Lavender. David's company had provided fuel to Phil's station for many years, while Ralph Richardson and Chris Myland had run the operation prior to Dickie.

David was a friendly and energetic character whom Dickie befriended. Additionally, David was an amorous man who enjoyed womanizing outside of his marriage. To maintain the covert, adulterous lifestyle, he created an alias of 'Adam Fletcher' and had business cards printed with the profession of 'Structural Component Engineer'. He had no experience in this fictitious line of business but it didn't make a difference as no one else knew what an SC Engineer was either.

David certainly enjoyed his dual lifestyle, until one night when his wife answered his phone and discovered he was having an affair. She proceeded to follow him around town, eventually finding him with a girl in a Cotuit motel. Next, she lit the motel on fire with both of them still in the room. Fortunately, no one died from the fire but consequences followed for all involved.

The Berrien Sisters and Other Village Artists

The village was graced with a variety of active artists and sculptors such as the Berriens[32] and Geissbuhlers; potters - Harry Holl and family; and painters such as David Gross. Harry and Mitzi Berrien Peterson created the original creche for the nativity scene that was assembled in front of the Dennis Union Church each Christmas season. From plaster of Paris they built Mary, Joseph and the Christ child. Subsequently, Mitzi created additional figures including the three Wise Men, a goat, sheep, donkey and even a camel.

The original figures were heavy yet fragile, having been constructed using wooden inner frames, chicken-wire webbing to form the first semblance of the figures, then various types of cloth, bedspread material and other textures to finalize the statues' bodies and clothing. Plaster of Paris was then used to add rigidity to each figure, then numerous coatings of paint were applied for color and weatherproofing. The end products looked garish up-close because they were intended to look best from a distance, primarily from cars driving past on Route 6A. Some people felt the figures

looked more like a carnival exhibit but they were very much appreciated for a first creche in the village.

The harsh weather during many Christmas seasons took its toll on the figures constructed by Harry and Mitzi. They (the figures) gradually fell apart which posed a major problem during activities of transport, assembly and storage.

Prior to Halloween in 1982, the figures were destroyed by a fire in the storage wing of Carleton Hall. It was almost a blessing as the old figures had to be replaced.

New nativity figures were commissioned by the Village Improvement Society of Dennis and created by wood sculptor Walter Horak. The existing creche is one-of-a-kind and cannot be duplicated. The new figures are true works of art and insured to a substantial value.

***

Note that the Cape Museum of Art was founded by the same group of artists who graced the village in the '50s.

Air Force Duty

Which Direction for a Career?

During his senior year in High School in North Carolina, Dickie's academic performance was very good. As described earlier, his Principal, Mr. Claude Hunter Moore, had gotten to know him well, having first met him in Dennis during summers. In hopes of expanding Dickie's life opportunities after High School, Mr. Moore successfully negotiated Dickie's enrollment at the Kentucky Military Institute (KMI) with a full scholarship, starting the next fall. KMI was a fine preparatory school established in 1847 and located in Lyndon, KY. Similar to the Virginia Military Institute, all of its students were classified as Cadets. Mr. Moore knew this prep school would provide disciplinary training and social guidance which Dickie had not received during his upbringing on Cape Cod. An understatement!

The news of this terrific offer both surprised and pleased Dickie but the military school direction wasn't what he wanted. Although his personal advancement and career opportunities surely would be limited back in Dennis, he was drawn to his home town. With maturity that exceeded most eighteen-year-olds, he was confident he could find a job and support himself, as had been the case since he left home at sixteen. And he knew he could find enjoyment, especially in summer with boating and many tourist girls. Dennis was a strong magnet drawing him back with no opposing forces. It was right, in his mind.

To this day, Dickie admits that his life has paralleled that depicted by Thornton Wilder in his classic American play *Our Town*. Set during the period from 1901 to 1913, Grover's Corners, NH was a small, fictional town where its citizens lived a routine existence and that normalcy pacified everyone. Howie Newsome's daily milk delivery typified the mundane patterns that made people comfortable. Everyday life was enough.

George Gibbs, the son of the town Doctor, decided not to attend college, choosing to stay locally and run the farm of his aging uncle. In Dennis, Dickie had seen examples of George all around him, with sons (his friends) taking over pharmacy, oil delivery, carpentry, landscaping, and many other trades as life-long vocations. Inheriting a bank was certainly a windfall for a few, but the other careers sufficed for many and their lives have proven to be comfortable. Dickie could have enjoyed living in Grover's Corners. Dennis was his comfortable equivalent.

Dickie's heritage was not aligned for financial inheritance but he learned at an early age that an energetic personality can attract persons of all ilks. Some are drawn to his energy and optimism while others may be repelled by his risky actions and behavior. Every day in his life has been a test, learning who his true friends are and which persons view him negatively. His perception of people is refined from these thousands of interactions. I doubt that another Cape Codder has dared behave as bold and defiant as Dickie, whether in the presence of police, angry opponents with their fists drawn high or even husbands of women he had befriended.

Dickie is alive and energetic in his ninth decade. Nearly all of his early friends and enemies have passed away, with most entombed in the Dennis Cemetery or their ashes spread over Cape Cod Bay. He lives on, happily, and still provides the everyday fabric which was Dennis in the mid-1900s. The local community has grown but he provides continuity that is loved by some and despised by a few. He makes his rounds in his numerous vehicles, keeping his finger on the pulse of the village and always ready to provide a solution to a needy person's shortfall.

In *Our Town,* Emily passed away but returned to view her family and friends. It was painful for her to see that people do not appreciate the simple joys in life – that every moment should be treasured. Dickie thinks exactly in these terms, especially when he visits the Indian Burial Ground on Scargo Lake. He knows Mashantampaine and the Nobscussets appreciated the land now called Dennis more than most of today's residents. Dickie makes a conscious effort to appreciate every day.

***

After high-school graduation, Dickie worked various local jobs. In the summer of 1953, while eighteen years old, he worked at the Woods Hole

Oceanographic Institution (WHOI) as a steward aboard large oceanographic ships that went to sea for multi-week research cruises. His older brother, Lee, had worked aboard ships at WHOI for many years, travelling the world's oceans, so it seemed logical for Dickie to investigate his brother's career tracks.

Dickie's first assignment aboard ship entailed washing dishes and changing bedlinen in staterooms of the Captain and Mates. Soon he moved up to a Seaman position with on-deck duties that he much preferred. He was initially stationed aboard the R/V Atlantis, a large steel-hulled, two-masted sailing vessel which made frequent cruises to Bermuda and the Sargasso Sea in the western North Atlantic. This vessel was 142 ft long and operated by WHOI from 1931 to 1964.

Dickie worked on the Atlantis briefly then transferred to the R/V Bear, an old troop carrier and minesweeper from World War II. The Bear was 103 ft long and operated by WHOI from 1951 to 1963.

Most of the cruises Dickie participated in were for the U.S. Navy, conducting acoustic testing of sound emitted by distant vessels. This required 'Silent Ship' operations which meant that all machinery (propulsion, electrical generation, air conditioning, etc.) had to be shut down for nearly the entire day. Generators would be run only when batteries had to be recharged.

During Silent operations, the ship would be 'dead in the water', drifting and rocking broadside in the trough of the waves, no matter how large. This was uncomfortable for everyone aboard and Dickie was often seasick. Any smell of exhaust from the diesel engines only made it worse.

From those many days at sea, he realized that a career in the U.S. Navy was not for him.

Air Force Basic Training

When nineteen years old, Dickie made the decision to enlist in the U.S. Air Force. All of his friends and other village men had signed up to do their service in the Armed Forces and he was no less of a Patriot.

On December 20, 1954, Dickie's mother and his best friend, Roger Goodell drove Dickie to the Air Force recruiting office in Boston. From there he was driven to the airport and boarded a flight aboard a twin-propeller Convair aircraft operated by Mohawk Airlines. The destination was Geneva, NY, the site of Sampson Air Force Base and home of the Air Force's Air Training Command. This was the first day of Dickie's four-year enlistment period.

Stepping from the propeller aircraft onto the tarmac was a shock because the air temperature was -20° F and the wind was howling. Young Dickie was wearing a gaberdine coat but this was grossly insufficient to face the elements of upstate New York in December. He and the other enlistees were quickly directed into the barracks and processed, thereafter wearing long underwear and fatigues beneath their big winter GI coats.

***

Right from the start of Basic Military Training (BMT) Dickie was smart enough to do as told and he rose rank quickly. His Training Instructor (TI), Airman Brill, enjoyed Dickie because he took orders readily. Within a few weeks, Dickie became a Basic Assistant (BA) to the TI and he admits that he 'shined' in the military training environment. Some of us wouldn't have guessed that he'd be so obedient.

On-base when Airmen had to walk somewhere in a group of three or more, they had to march and be led by an Airman of higher rank. This meant that Dickie, as BA to the TI, led the marches and other formation activities of his Company. Picture him leading the other men to dinner, a movie, or anywhere else. Dickie has confessed that he was a bit of a 'brown-noser' but the small increase in rank had its benefits.

I immediately have flashbacks of the

movie character Forrest Gump when I picture Dickie answering 'Yes Sir!' to his TI. Hard to imagine.

***

On a few occasions during the seven-week BMT period, Airmen could obtain 36-hour passes to go off-base for whatever reason they chose. Prior to departure, Airman Brill made Dickie pass a basket among the Airmen to obtain monetary donations for the March of Dimes charity. One morning Airman Brill barked that there was insufficient donation money in the basket so he made Dickie pass it around a second time, before the Airmen could head out on Leave. This collection procedure had apparently existed for years.

Everyone noticed when Airman Brill had a new Ford on base but within a few weeks, he was no longer seen on the Base.

When Dickie and other Airmen had completed their Basic Training, each was assigned to another Air Force facility for technical training; Radar Training in Biloxi, MS for Dickie. All were excited when they boarded their departure flight but suddenly the flight was 'red lined', which meant that it was grounded and all the Airmen were ordered to return to their barracks indefinitely. The reason for this strict procedure was that an investigation was being conducted by the Air Force's Office of Special Investigation (OSI) in association with Airman Brill's misuse of charity funds. This was a serious criminal investigation and the Airmen were held for potential questioning.

COMPLETES BASIC

RICHARD BUCK, son of Mr. and Mrs. Herbert Buck of Florida and East Dennis is spending a ten-day leave at the home of James Howes. He has finished his basic training and will

Apparently, Airman Brill had been stealing money from the donation basket and using it for payment of his new car. Rumors speculated that he was shipped out to Leavenworth Federal Penitentiary for stealing.

Radar Training and Operations - Stateside

Following Basic Training in New York, Dickie was transferred to Keesler Air Force Base in Biloxi, MS, which is located about 75 mi east of New Orleans. First, he flew from New York to Cape Cod to pick up his 1934 Ford Hot Rod then drove to Sarasota, FL to spend time with his parents. Events during his drive south are described in the Chapter on Vehicles he owned. From Sarasota, with duffle bag in hand, Dickie took a bus to Keesler.

Keesler was an excellent facility for training to become a Radar Technician. He also recalls that his schedule was considerably more flexible than during Basic Training, with adequate time for enjoyment, renting cottages on the seashore and partying with cute, southern girls.

Next, he was transferred to Edwards Air Force Base in Southern California where he would work as a Radar Technician. Edwards was well known as the Flight Test Center of the World. And living in California sounded exciting to Dickie, a small-town boy from Cape Cod. He envisioned many blonde girls on Malibu Beach and throughout the Hollywood area. Certainly, close by and only a short drive from the Base.

Not the case for Edwards. Dickie quickly learned the large Base was located in the Mohave Desert about 90 mi northeast of the Pacific shore at Malibu. This was brown desert, the likes of which he had never seen. The 'city' of Barstow is 40 mi to the east, while the town of Boron coincides with the northern perimeter of the Base. Unfortunately, off-duty Airmen were not enthralled with Boron as it was

a backward little town with a population of about 1,000. Its greatest notoriety was based upon having the world's largest borax mine, as well as being the site of the original Twenty Mule Team Borax Wagons that were used to transport the dry ore out of the vast open-pit mines. Those of us who recall television from the '50s can still picture the Mule Teams shown in advertisements for Borax scrubbing powder.

Regardless of the remote location of the Edwards Base, Dickie always found ways to raise hell and hook up with girls, near or far. More importantly, he continued to advance his rank.

When in High School, Dickie had become a proficient typist. This was a distinguishing factor when Officers at his Base were evaluating Airmen candidates for a Clerk position. Dickie 'shined' during the testing and earned the new responsibility, with access to secret information of a high security level. He was wise about this, taking care not to breach protocols during the handling and distribution of new information. Additionally, he was privy to details of all new Regulations sent from above. This became extremely useful when the time came for his evaluation for promotion to the level of Airman First Class.

The evaluation entailed questioning by a panel of Officers and Dickie did very well, especially when questioned about Regulations. The Code of the U.S. Fighting Force (the Military Code of Conduct) had been established by President Eisenhower very recently, on August 17, 1955. Dickie could already recite the Code verbatim which impressed the panel of Officers, some of whom were less conversant with the new guidelines than Dickie. He received the promotion and obtained his three stripes.

Of course when off duty, Dickie was his active and mischievous self. To earn extra cash, he worked part-time at a gas station in Boron. One night, two pretty girls in their mid-twenties drove into the station in a nice truck and proceeded to flirt with the nineteen-year-old Airman. Within a few minutes they convinced Dickie to join them for a drive to Las Vegas.

His recollection is that they 'taught him much', staying in a motel room with one king bed for a night. He was just a toy (albeit very cooperative) for these experienced girls. They were done with him by the next morning and drove away, leaving Dickie to hitch-hike back to the Base, a distance of 200 miles. The experience was enlightening for Dickie and he'd certainly do it again if given the opportunity, even today I'll bet.

The next day, the Police caught up with Dickie at the Boron gas station and interrogated him about the girls and the truck. Apparently, they had stolen the new truck but the Police quickly concluded that young Dickie was not part of the girls' plan for driving east and evading the law.

Following a Girl to Japan

As the months passed during his assignment at Edwards, Dickie developed a relationship with a girl named Vera Johnson. She lived in San Bernardino with her two children and mother. He would often drive 72 miles across the desert in the middle of the night just to have a cup of coffee with Vera.

Vera's father was a civilian fireman who worked on Johnson Air Force Base but it happened to be quite distant, in Japan actually. What seemed to be an impulsive move, she packed her bags and took the children to Japan to live with her father. Dickie learned this news when he went to Vera's house one day for a visit. He was shocked, as was the mother who spoke little English. He consoled her as best he could, given his own bewildered state.

One thing led to another and the consoling smoothly transitioned to spontaneous intimacy for the comfort of both. This was his first consensual relationship with daughter and mother.

Dickie still cared a great deal for Vera and wanted to see her again. Being twenty, it was easy for his heart (spelled: penis) to get ahead of his mind. Quickly he developed a plan to follow her to

Japan; he had no reason not to.

He started searching for Radar Technician positions in Japan. Eventually, a position became available at Sado Gashima so he applied for the transfer and it was granted. Again, Dickie's typing and clerical experience got him the job, over other candidates with radar qualifications.

From a quick look at a map of Japan he assessed that it would only be a 'hop, skip and a jump' to get from his new location to Johnson Air Force Base where Vera was located. Only a few hours? Actually, more like two days if he were to make the journey.

Radar Technician on a Remote Japanese Mountain Top

His Radar Technician assignment was inside an isolated building atop a mountain on a small island off the coast from Niigata. Remote for sure! After the 30-mile ferry ride from Niigata to Sado island, it was a slow, 10-mi drive up the mountainside in the 6 x 6 (six-wheel, all-wheel drive) weapons and personnel carrier. Dickie still remembers the sound of the whining gears of the truck's transmission during the long ride uphill. A Base Camp was situated half way up the mountainside. Eventually, Dickie's good rank allowed him to drive the truck, rather than be in the back with all the other Airmen and soldiers.

The peak's altitude and low temperature allowed snow to persist until July 4th. In winter, snow accumulated to 36-ft thickness so only the tops of the evergreen trees were visible. Airmen could slide downhill to the Base Camp by lying on their large winter parkas. Water from melted snow was the only source for showers in winter.

Dickie was stationed in the radar building for 10-day periods then allowed to go down to the Base Camp and obtain Passes to Sado's village at sea level.

Although the Korean War had ended two years prior, his Radar Technician responsibility was to monitor for aircraft that may be inbound across the Sea of Japan from North Korea and possibly Russia.

Dickie learned to speak Japanese from the many months of uninterrupted time with Japanese soldiers and civilians on Sado. Until he understood the calm temperament of the Japanese culture, he was surprised that no swear words exist in their vocabulary. 'Much different from Cape Codders' often-forked tongues.

Radio Operator on the Northern Tip of Honshu Island

A position opened that could possibly facilitate Dickie's transfer back to civilization. The position was located at the northern tip of Honshu Island. Compared to the remote, mountaintop assignment on Sado, any position on the mainland of Japan's largest island sounded ideal.

There were however, two obstacles: First, the position was for a Radio Operator which Dickie had no experience. Second, it required a minimum rank of Staff Sergeant or better (a Non-Commissioned Officer) due to the sensitivity of information that would be handled via radio communications.

He first requested the transfer upon the (untrue) grounds that he had a cousin stationed at Komatsu Air Base but that got him nowhere.

Dickie petitioned for a waiver and promotion for an increase in rank from his present position of Airman First Class to Staff Sergeant. With minimal delay, it was granted for excellent performance and past duty at a remote base (Sado).

His new responsibility was to communicate with aircraft that were passing over the tip of Honshu. At this strategic checkpoint, he verified all aircraft and provided the distance and bearing to Tokyo and other destinations.

When his promotion became effective, Dickie became the officer in charge of the radio station. When on duty, he was in the radio room alone and had his own machine gun at his side in the event the station would be overrun by the enemy. This occurrence was highly unlikely because the Korean War had been over for two years but Base Operations specified this armed protocol.

This extreme northern base was not large but it had lovely grounds near a large mountain. The runway was one mile long and known historically as one of the key Kamikaze departure points in Japan. The Japanese continually acknowledged the spirits of the lost pilots from the past.

When Dickie moved into the radio position, he acquired a dog from the prior officer. The dog became his pet for the duration of his assignment. When aircraft flew low overhead in the night, the dog would bark to awaken Dickie.

When it was time for Dickie to leave the Base, he had to sell the dog at a high price. If he hadn't, it was likely that a new owner would eat the dog. But if a buyer paid a high price, the dog would be too valuable to consume. Japanese tradition.

UFO on the Radar Screen

When Dickie was on duty in the Radar Room, he was normally the Supervisor with responsibility for overseeing at least four Radar Technicians sitting at scanning scopes. During one shift that he still remembers vividly, two Technicians announced they each had an unidentified object coming inbound from the north. Dickie went to the scopes and agreed with their observations. The object was approaching at a relatively slow speed. Unable to validate identification, U.S. fighter jets were quickly scrambled to make contact with the aircraft.

As soon as the fighters made distant, visual contact, the object immediately turned and departed at a speed that was incomprehensible. Whereas typical jet fighters of the '50s could travel at 400-500 mph, the object seemed to travel at four times that speed. The departure-streak left on the radar screens demonstrated speed characteristics that had never before been seen.

Dickie summoned his Supervisor, the Officer on Duty, who immediately gave an order to everyone: 'Forget what you saw. It was just a fluke.' All hands knew this sighting was real but they couldn't buck the orders. The rapidity of the standard order in the absence of any investigation proved it was standard procedure to deny UFOs.

Dickie never tried to contact the Airmen who were on duty with him that day but he remains confident that the sighting was a UFO and that the Air Force will deny all such observations.

Transfer to Otis Air Base on Cape Cod

After his two-year, overseas commitment had been met, Dickie decided it was time to return to the U.S. mainland for his final year of enlistment. He never met with Vera but his time in Japan was enlightening and unforgettable. He still speaks Japanese; his dining table is always set with Japanese tableware and classic Japanese artwork is prominent throughout his home.

When he started planning a transfer from Japan, he knew that his rank of Staff Sergeant would be insufficient for him to specify the Base of his choice for his next assignment. However, his Active Duty on remote bases would give him a choice and he immediately selected Otis Air Base on Cape Cod for his final radar assignment. The next challenge he faced was that the radar position open at Otis was a flying position and he lacked this training and experience. No problem; Dickie made the long-range transfer, obtained the necessary in-flight training and became a radar technician aboard the fleet of large C-121 Constellation aircraft stationed at Otis. This was 1957.

Otis and the Air Force Base in Boron, CA were elements of the twenty-eight radar stations comprising the Air Defense Command that was established at the start of the Korean War in 1950. Both facilities were associated with the 750th Aircraft Control and Warning Squadron. The squadron's role was to guide interceptor aircraft toward unidentified intruders that were detected on the unit's radar scopes.

For the Otis Base, radar reconnaissance was accomplished via three elements: aircraft; a large balloon anchored at Truro containing radar equipment; and lastly, radar systems mounted on fixed platforms positioned on the continental shelf south of New England. These were tall structures called Texas Towers because their design was modeled after the offshore oil drilling platforms in the Gulf of Mexico. Each tower consisted of a large triangular platform, 200 ft on each side, standing on three caisson legs. The structures were built on land, towed to the site and jacked up to clear the sea surface by 67 feet. Radar and other equipment were installed on location.

Three towers were built at the following locations: on Georges Bank, on Nantucket Shoals and south of Long Island. They were in operation from 1958 to 1963 and proved effective for extending radar surveillance several-hundred miles offshore, giving 30 minutes of additional warning of a potential aircraft attack.

Dickie made a big leap from monitoring radar within a small building on a mountaintop in Japan, to the inside of the Air Force's largest aircraft. The C-121 Constellation was an ideal aircraft for military transport and reconnaissance. With its 123-ft wingspan, 4,000 mi range and 330 mph maximum speed, the C-121 could make long hauls better than any plane of its day. Four propellers and a triple-tail configuration made 'Connie' easily distinguishable from all other aircraft. Over 800 were built from 1943 to 1958 and used for military and civilian airlines until the early '60s.

The radar reconnaissance flights consisted of triangular flight patterns, from Otis to Montauk Point, NY, then out over the Atlantic and back to Otis, with 150 mi on each of the three legs. The mission purpose was to search for enemy submarines and unidentified aircraft. Dickie was Crew Chief on the aircraft, responsible for everything from the wings back, including radio operations and everyone on the radar scopes.

Ball Lightning Inside the Aircraft

Another vivid memory from Dickie's flying days were times when ball lightning struck inside the big Constellation planes. The large flash would illuminate the inside of the fuselage and seem to roll down the broad aisle from front to back in the plane. Within a couple seconds, the ball of light would be gone, apparently out the back of the plane. He experienced this phenomenon four or five times during a single year, while aloft offshore New England. None of the airmen were injured but the experience was unforgettable.

For those who wish to learn more about ball lightning and its impact on aircraft, an excellent, quantitative study was published in 2009[33]. During the period from 1938 to 2007, a total of 87 impacts of ball-lightning with aircraft were reported, worldwide. It is likely that reported sightings greatly underrepresent actual occurrences.

Forty-three percent of the reported occurrences were observed inside aircraft. Major damage to the aircraft occurred from 13% of those incidents. There was only one occurrence of a major injury to a crewmember.

The typical size of a lightning ball ranges from ten inches to three feet in diameter. Yellow-red is the most common color and their duration is typically around ten seconds but some persist for over one minute – very long compared to typical bolt lightning having durations of fractions of seconds. One-third of ball-lightning events end with an explosion. Structural damage inside an aircraft is extremely rare, as is serious injury to crew and passengers. Nevertheless, ball lightning is an extraordinary phenomenon to encounter.

Engine Fire Aloft – A Hero in the Making?

During one of Dickie's routine three-legged, 'round robin' flights to New York and back, a fire developed in one of the four large Constellation engines. Each have magnesium engine castings which burn at very high temperatures once ignited. Because the engines were positioned out on the wings, this prevented the flight crew from attacking the fire directly. The only solution was to use the automatic fire extinguishing system, but this method was not solving the urgent problem.

One of the Crew Chief's pre-flight responsibilities was to assure there were enough parachutes aboard the flight; actually, ten-percent more chutes than men aboard. As soon as the reality of the fire registered in Dickie's mind, he immediately shifted to the issue of the parachutes. 'Oh shit'. He knew that not only was there no surplus of chutes aboard, there was one too few. He couldn't inform Captain Holtgrew as the consequences would be severe IF they landed.

At 23 years old, Dickie wasn't highly religious but he felt it was definitely time to talk to God, again. His first time was aboard his small duck boat as it was sinking in Cape Cod Bay while he was a Boy Scout. This time, aboard a doomed aircraft, was direr. 'God, I know I fooled you the first time, but this time I'm serious. I'm going to die. Help me.'

Not waiting for an answer, he remembered that as Crew Chief, he was required to be the last Airman to jump out of the plane as it was descending for the crash. Even the Captain had to leap out before him, according to protocol. The only good news was that no one would know that he didn't have a chute for himself. Doubling up with another man would have made it obvious and he didn't want to do that.

With Dickie's NCO rank, he did have some experience with his hands on the controls of the big Connie. At least he could steer and mind the compass. Noticing that the plane was over Cape Cod Bay, he thought his chances of living were best if he could fly the plane down rather than let it crash on its own guidance, with him aboard.

His mind immediately shifted to a best-case scenario. 'Maybe I can be the hero!' He envisioned gliding the massive plane down onto the shallow waters at Corporation Beach. The plane would come to rest on the sand bars and he'd jump out safely, having singlehandedly saved the big Air Force plane. Everyone from town would be there to cheer him on. Yes, he'd be a hero forever. The Mayor would be there and the band would be playing - hooray! Dickie was delusional, temporarily.

Reality set in, as all the Airmen donned their chutes and lined up at the escape door. Each would jump out, the Captain would follow then Dickie would be the last Airman aboard. He'd have to hurry forward and turn the big plane toward Corporation Beach.

Just then, the voice of the Captain came over the loud speaker. 'Fire is out. Return to your stations.' For a few seconds, Dickie vacillated between the euphoria of the fire being extinguished versus the disappointment of not having the opportunity to be the Hero of Dennis.

Final Duty at Otis

Dickie's final year at Otis was routine, with radar reconnaissance flights aboard the C-121 Constellations. His rank allowed him to live off-base and he made housing arrangements with his long-term friend Hudson Eldridge. When off duty, he quickly drove back to Dennis to party in his familiar stomping grounds.

For extra cash, he worked for Chris Myland at the Sinclair gas station at Players Plaza. But most of the time he was drinking. When he had to return to Otis, he often took pills to keep awake. He has confessed that on one trip westward on the mid-Cape highway, he was so high from the drugs that he hallucinated the image of a large freight train approaching him head-on at full speed. The train proceeded to plow into him and out the back of the car. Quite startling to say the least. Dickie hasn't forgotten this image.

When he returned to Otis, he was exhausted from all the partying in Dennis. His subordinate Airmen covered for him while he was on-duty, as he recalls having slept for many hours in the bunks of the Constellations.

Honorable Discharge and Life in Grover's Corners

Dickie was discharged in December of 1958 at age 23. He felt proud, having traveled across the Pacific, lived on mountaintops, learned Japanese and was an experienced Technician and Instructor for radar and radio operations. He didn't have a long-term career plan nor did he give a damn. He was just happy to be home with his friends. He liked being a big fish in the small pond of East Dennis. Some people might have differed with his assessment, saying that in his mid-twenties, Dickie was a wild, hyperactive, electric eel in a small fishbowl. You couldn't help but know when he was around.

Although Dickie had done well in the Air Force and advanced his rank numerous times over his four-year enlistment, choosing to return to Cape Cod was probably a big mistake because of the life-style he settled into. Drinking and partying became his vocation at that point in his life.

***

In the final days before discharge, Dickie started planning what he'd do when out of the Air Force. He decided it'd be best to make a trip to Florida to spend time with his family who lived in Sarasota during winter months. It was December and the weather on Cape Cod was frigid.

Eager to bask in the sun of Florida, he chose to get an artificial base-tan. He had his own tanning lamp at the Base, so on the night before he was to be discharged, he sat under the lamp. He figured that 'If a little tanning is good, a lot will be better.' Foolishly, he spent way-too-much time under the tanning lamp with the result that his entire face became terribly blistered. He couldn't open his eyes for many days.

His friends Hudson and Shirley Eldridge, who he had been living with during his off-base time, were keen on spending a few weeks in warm Florida so they decided to ride south with Dickie. Hudson helped him fabricate a metal frame so he could tow his motorcycle behind his car, with intentions of giving the cycle to his brother Bertie in Sarasota.

The long drive south was relatively uneventful. Dickie could open his eyes by the time they reached Virginia and he helped drive the rest of the way south. As planned, he visited his family and gave the motorcycle to his brother but after one week with family, he decided he didn't want to live there – Dennis was the place for him. I can almost hear Dickie singing a rendition of the theme song of the mid-60s television show *Green Acres*: 'Dennis is the place to be; Coastal living is the life for me...' Happy as a clam in his small town.

By coincidence, Hudson and Shirley called him from Miami the same day. They wanted him to come back home with them to Dennis rather than have him stay in Florida. The three were good friends and Hudson felt confident he could find some type of employment for Dickie. Shirley spoke from her heart. 'If we starve, you'll starve. If you starve, we'll starve.' This may sound drastic but it was a very caring offer to young Dickie.

Hudson and Shirley were staying with a friend of theirs who lived in Miami. Dickie accepted their offer and drove across southern Florida, arriving early the next morning. The man they were staying with got pissed off because Dickie was drinking beer at six in the morning. Being no stranger to morning drinking, Hudson stuck up for Dickie and told his friend off. 'Well, you don't have to worry about that because you won't be seeing us anymore.' They had been having a bad time with this old friend and were ready to leave, regardless.

Dickie, Hudson and Shirley jumped in the car that night and headed north from Miami. They drove for many hours then stopped to get a motel when exhausted. After all that driving they had only reached Hollywood, FL which was 15 mi north of their starting point in Miami. Both Hudson and Dickie were so buzzed they didn't realize they'd been driving around and around in circles.

Farther north on their journey, they had another incident coming off the George Washington Bridge in New York. Somehow, they got in the lane of oncoming traffic. Hudson yelled 'We're going to get killed!' Dickie was driving and quickly jumped the curb to avoid a head-on collision. Eventually they made it to Dennis alive, but not sober.

***

Upon returning to Dennis, Hudson helped Dickie establish a small landscaping business. Dickie had accumulated a good amount of flight pay from his year aboard the Constellations. Additionally, he was able to obtain a loan from the Brocton Savings Bank under the Veterans' First-Time Home Buyer program. With this $9,500, he and Hudson were able to buy a plot of land in East Dennis and build a small Cape-style house. The sale of that property jump-started a business partnership between Dickie and Hudson.

Dickie was enterprising right from the start, selling the extra loam that resulted from excavation for the house's foundation. $20 per truckload was good money for 24-year-old Dickie. He wasn't keen on house construction but landscaping became one of his long-term jobs later in life, and still today at 83.

Vehicles by Land, Sea and Air

When Dennis boys returned home in the fall of 1945 at the end of WW II, the priorities of most were: cars, drinking, girls and fighting. They were brave, young veterans with lots of testosterone and fear of nothing. Cars and drinking were a preferred mix in those days, with frequent tickets and arrests from speeding. Fortunately, cars were cheap compared to present day prices and if they rolled their car or totaled it, another could be found for a few hundred dollars. Most boys were mechanically inclined and learned to repair or 'soup-up'[34] their own Straight-6 or V-8 engines.

When girls were not available, the next common pastime was fighting, always fueled by alcohol and lots of it. I'll say it again – these boys feared nothing. This was such a significant trait of the young veterans that an entire Chapter is given later, addressing fighting and run-ins with the police. And Dickie was one of the toughest 'scrappers' on Cape Cod in his day. Many of his personal stories are worth documenting, for readers who enjoy that sport.

The situation in the village wasn't much different when boys came home at the end of the Korean War in 1953. This was Dickie Buck's era, having returned home in 1958, at age 23, from his Air Force active duty in Japan.

First Bicycle

Of course, all boys begin their vehicular days with a bicycle. Dickie was no different, learning to ride on the new two-wheeler that his parents purchased from Sears, Roebuck and Company in 1945. Sears sold the J. C. Higgins brand of bicycle which was built strong, having been manufactured since 1908.

The bicycle arrived in a large box, disassembled and Dickie was eager to get his built. He had only a pair of pliers rather than all the tools that were recommended for assembling the bike correctly and safely. Nevertheless, he put it together and immediately rode it to the top of 'Charley Hallett's hill' located at the north end of Old Bass River Road.

Proudly, Dickie raced his friends down the hill on his new cycle but hit a rock in a patch of dirt in front of Carleton Hall. This caused the front wheel to come out of the front fork as the bike went in the air. Dickie flew over the handlebars and the bike came down on top of his head making a large cut across the ten-year-old's skull.

Dickie's friend John Trenholm quickly contacted his father, Julian, to drive Dickie to Dr. Hunt in Yarmouth Port, as his head was bleeding severely. Stitches eventually solved the problem but the scar is still visible today. (I suspect that Dickie has let very few people look down on him!)

Model Airplane

Throughout his life, Dickie has been drawn to anything with an engine, whether it be on the road, afloat or in the air. The first sign was his curiosity for model (miniaturized and motorized) airplanes that could be assembled from kits. Seth Crowell of East Dennis, who grew up with Dickie and was the same age, shared a story of he and Dickie flying a model airplane that Dickie had built. It had a six-foot wingspan but a very small engine, Seth recalls. On the first test flight, the boys got the plane aloft in an open field near Seth's house on Sesuit Neck Road. It flew around the house a couple times then bounced off the ground and headed due north, out of sight toward Cape Cod Bay. The boys ran in that direction and saw Seth's uncle who was tending his cranberry bog, situated just south of the shoreline bluff. He hollered that he'd seen the plane and pointed in the direction of the Bay.

Dickie and Seth ran to the beach and spotted the plane floating offshore. It was December and the water was very cold but Dickie jumped in and tried to reach the plane. Seth said he 'pretty near got to it' but was freezing so he came ashore. Next, they ran to the harbor, borrowed a rowboat and used two boards to paddle out of the harbor and along the shore to the west. A couple seals popped up next to their boat with curiosity. The boys eventually spotted the plane still floating about a mile offshore. It was constructed of balsa wood and covered with cloth so it trapped air and floated like a cork. They retrieved the plane and paddled back to the harbor safely. A typical day for two adventurous Dennis teens.

A Desire for the Unique

As described below, Dickie started driving cars well before he obtained his official Driver's License. Not surprisingly, this corresponded with his first arrest by the Dennis Police. Over the next seven decades, Dickie purchased and operated more types of mechanized vehicles than anyone in town, possibly the State. He surely had an 'attraction for contraptions'.

J. P. Walker, for whom Dickie drove the company's truck for home deliveries of heating oil, accurately characterized Dickie's affinity for vehicles. When someone asked about Dickie's financial status, he replied: 'I don't know where he gets his money but he can certainly buy anything he wants.'

Dickie later confirmed this, 'Every time there was something interesting or exciting, I'd buy it.' And he always did, throughout his life.

Motorcycles

When Dickie was sixteen, he had his first ride on the back of Sonny Black's motorcycle. Sonny owned a big Chief, manufactured by the Indian Motorcycle Company[35]. The early Chiefs had wide saddle seats made primarily for a single rider, versus the long, slender seats on today's cycles, made to accommodate both the driver and a passenger. A passenger on the Chief would normally hold onto a steel rod that was attached to the back of the seat.

Sonny had a long heritage on Cape Cod and was one of thirteen children. His father was a barber in Brewster who cut Dickie's hair for fifty cents. And Sonny's mother, Grace Black (later Cash), was famous for making the best meat or fruit pies in town.

Sonny took Dickie for a ride to the south side to see the Dennis Clippers baseball team[5] whose roster included J. P. Walker, Ralph Richardson, the Hodsdon brothers and other fine athletes from the village. Dickie never forgot that first experience on the Indian motorcycle. Soon after, he bought his first Indian and owned motorcycles continuously until 2017.

Indian Bonneville Chief Special

Chris Myland, Sr, who operated the Sinclair gas station at Players Plaza before Dickie took over, had a 1947 Indian Bonneville Chief Special motorcycle built in Middleboro. It was large, powerful and made specifically to beat the latest Harley motorcycle of its day. And it succeeded. Dickie said the cycle was a horror to keep running right but when you cranked the throttle it would catapult you forward with incredible acceleration.

The Chief Special had a stick-shift gear box and a tall vertical windshield with rounded top, like police motorcycles looked for decades after. Definitely a man's bike! Dickie bought this as his first (i.e., 'starter') bike, which says a lot about his daring nature.

A few years later he sold The Chief Special to Billy Brister, Sr. During an evening ride on Route 6A in Brewster, Billy was making a turn at an unlit stretch of road and proceeded to drive into the side of an oncoming car. He and his cycle drove through the rear, side door and out the back window. Nearly dead but still conscious, he was approached by a priest from the nearby La Salette Seminary. Billy's critical condition didn't soften his typical negative attitude. 'I'm not dying and I'm not Catholic, so get the fuck out of here.' Last Rites may have been in order, but silent prayers likely followed, as the priest walked back to the Seminary.

Billy was in the Air Force at the time of the accident, which was very fortunate as a helicopter was dispatched to bring him back to the Otis base and begin to put him back together as best they could. He was in the hospital for nearly a year but never fully recovered from the terrible motorcycle accident.

Dickie also sadly remembers another motorcycle accident when he, Roger Neal and William Lowther were returning home on their motorcycles, along Route 134, from a High School party at Bobby Churchill's house. William started to pass Rogers cycle but tragically, William's front wheel hit Roger's back wheel and William was thrown from his cycle and off the road. Dickie saw William flying end-over-end in the air and knew he'd be seriously injured from the crash. Arriving at William's side, Dickie was shocked when William jumped up and started saying 'I'm okay, I'm okay.' Dickie told him 'Lay down Billy, you're dead.' From watching him tumbling over and over in the air, he figured William must be dead. 'You've got to be hurt, bad.' Fortunately, William lived on but Dickie's mental images of his friend's accident have never gone away.

Honda CB750

One of Dickie's favorite motorcycles was his candy-apple red Honda CB750. This model was the first 'modern' four-cylinder motorcycle produced by a major manufacturer and designed for the American 'street racer' market. With its transverse, four-cylinder engine, disc brakes, 120 mph top speed and comfortable ride, the CB750 was acclaimed as the most sophisticated production motorcycle of its time. Of course, Dickie had to own one.

The CB750 was first produced in 1969 and it became extremely popular. Because the initial demand for the CB750s had been uncertain, Honda used a temporary mold-casting technique (erroneously called 'sandcasting') for the engine blocks of the initial runs, prior to August of 1969. These early CB750s (called 'sandcasted models') became collector's items and recently, one of the low serial number cycles sold in auction for $148,000. Experts can easily recognize the early models from a distinctive rough finish on the engine cases, as well as other design characteristics.

In 1976, Honda introduced the CB750A model, with the 'A' suffix designating its new automatic transmission; another very popular model.

Everyone knew that Dickie loved racing his CB750. Local competition arose from brothers Ross and Larry Riley (who later took ownership of Gina's restaurant). They purchased a new 500-cc, two-stroke Kawasaki motorcycle which was supposed to be the fastest, standard-production, street-bike on the road, until Dickie beat them. He even beat their next cycle, a 750-cc Kawasaki which proved to be a very fast cycle. Ross Riley promised that he'd throw his cycle into Sesuit Creek if it didn't beat Dickie's CB750 four-stroke. Dickie was kind after he won the race; not forcing the Kawasaki to a salty grave.

For clarification, Ross did beat Dickie's Honda, once, during their last race, but Dickie is emphatic that this occurred after young Bobby Sears had damaged the CB750 and the cycle's compression was limited; its horsepower too. Do you think these guys were competitive?

Larry still remembers Dickie's skills on motorcycles. 'Dickie was always the guy you wanted to beat. He was amazing on a motorcycle and would put on a show for you.

Dickie always bought the newest model that came on the market. He had to have the fastest.'

Owning Two-Strokes

Dickie's CB750 had a sad ending. While loaned to Bobby Sears, Jr. the drive chain flew off and ruptured the crankcase. Ernie Holmes was able to do a quick fix with some metal tape to prevent oil leakage but she was never the same, likely losing pressure at high speeds.

Soon after, Dickie purchased a 500-cc, two-stroke, three-cylinder Kawasaki. It was one of the fastest production (out of the box) motorcycles on Cape Cod.

Next was a brand new two-stroke, twin-cylinder Suzuki X6 Hustler, also called the T20 Super Six as it had the first six-speed transmission used in a production motorcycle. It was very popular as it had high performance with 247-cc and a lightweight design. This model was manufactured only between 1965 and 1967.

Unfortunately, Dickie took a bad spill on this cycle heading up the sand grade as he left Corporation Beach returning to the paved parking lot. While motoring at a moderate speed, he hit a large bump and was tossed straight up in the air. His female passenger landed on top of him and was unhurt. Dickie went unconscious but she managed to get him into her car and to the local doctor. All Dickie could remember was telling her to 'Have the doctor cut my shirt off so I don't need to move my bones!'

The doctor gave Dickie a shot of morphine and directed her to quickly drive him to the Cape Cod Hospital in Hyannis as he definitely had broken bones. 'He's as comfortable as he's ever going to be.' said the doctor, seeing that Dickie was in a relaxed, painless state at least temporarily.

Having broken his collar bone and wrist, a large cast was put on one arm and he was kept in the hospital for a couple days' observation. When discharged, he wore a sling to immobilize the arm and shoulder. The next day he got back on the Suzuki and took a ride. Motorcycle riders know full-well that accidents are not the bike's fault.

Harley Davidson Softtail

Dickie last owned and rode a motorcycle in 2017 when he was eighty-two years old; a sixty-six-year run! The

cycle was a 1350-cc Harley Davidson Softtail; a big, fast and heavy cycle which he rode for about six years before selling it.

His wife Judy was very pleased when his motorcycling days were over, especially as many of Dickie's friends were either crippled or killed from accidents. Dickie even admitted that his big Harley was getting difficult to pick up at his considerable age. 'If I 'dropped it' (had it fall over) I'd be in serious trouble, especially if I had a girl on the back.' – and he always did.

Motorcycle Acrobatics

Dickie's closest friends know that although he typically rode the fastest motorcycles, he was very careful. 'He knew when to be crazy and when not to be.' His only accident was leaving the sand incline coming ashore from Corporation Beach.

Dozens of people have seen him perform outrageous stunts on his motorcycles. No, he hasn't tried competing with daredevil Evel Knievel, jumping dozens of parked cars nor catapulting over the Grand Canyon. And he doesn't view himself as a 'risk taker' but he certainly enjoys entertaining.

Over the past fifty years, there have been numerous, first-hand reports of Dickie performing the following stunts:

- Riding down Route 6A while standing on the seat of his motorcycle; also, standing on his seat while motoring down Shiverick Road, just to impress the children of the neighborhood.
- Another friend of Dickie's saw him riding down Route 6A in East Dennis doing 75 mph while standing on the seat.
- Doing a hand-stand on the seat, while the cycle was moving through the intersection of Routes 6A and 134, and
- While riding, he turned around on the seat of his cycle to face backward at friends in a following car, balancing with his weight and no hands on the handlebars.

Returning to seated antics, Billy King recalls that one day in 1967 he was driving his car down Route 6A on his way to work at Louie's when he heard knocking on the passenger-side window. He rolled down the window and there was Dickie riding alongside on his motorcycle. He hollered to Billy, "What'd ya' think of my chick?"

Billy slowed and expected to see a good-looking girlfriend on the back of Dickie's motorcycle. Wrong - it was a live chicken sitting in a milkcrate on the back of the cycle. Another practical 'yolk'.

Over the years, Dickie had many dogs that became his best friend and passenger on his cycles. 'Auto' the Dachshund, was a frequent rider for the enjoyment of all.

Automobiles

Teen Car Racing in East Dennis

Back in the '40s and '50s, many boys learned to drive cars well before they were eligible for a driver's license, at age sixteen. The most adventurous would purchase a car for $20 and drive it off-road wherever open space was available. Racing against their friends' jalopies was the most fun.

Dickie and a group of his friends, including Tommy Dexter, Bobby Sears and 'Sethy' Crowell all had cars and would meet at a location in East Dennis – five or six cars ready to race. Because they couldn't take their cars on the road to buy gas at a 'filling station', they went out at night and siphoned gas from nearby cars. All the boys would add to the common supply: three or four fifty-gallon drums all lined in a row. This was behind Roger Goodell's house on Sea Street, which had lots of open space in those days. 'Today, the area is littered with 'mega-mansions'.' Dickie complains.

As a side comment, Dickie used to mow the large lawn of elderly Ms. Lisa Goodell. Using the push-style reel mower was enough of a challenge but she would give him strict orders to steer around each lovely buttercup! And the job wasn't done until after he used a long-handle sickle scythe to cut the blackheads that would evade the blades of the reel mower. Some boys pretended they were swinging a golf club when trimming with the manual sickles.

Picture these East Dennis boys, aged thirteen to fifteen, driving big, old cars with heavy bodies, large bumpers and big rounded fenders. These cars were built in the mid- to late '30s and most had crank handles to manually start the engines. This was a physical challenge for the young boys. Often, they'd go to school with injured arms from the cranks kicking back during the car-starting process. Of course, they couldn't tell their parents they were injured nor how it happened. Their cars would be taken away and they'd be 'grounded'− forced to stay in their own yard after school; a fate worse than death for these energetic teens.

One day, an adult discovered what was going on; likely from hearing the big cars driving around in the neighborhood after school. Whoever it was 'lit up' the big barrels of gas because almost nothing was left when the boys arrived one day for more car racing.

Land Rover Named 'Mooncusser'

Not surprisingly, Dickie was attracted to the versatility of the all-terrain Land Rover which offered four-wheel-drive capability, a useful power-take-off (PTO) as well as more passenger seating and a longer wheel-base than standard Jeeps. The early British models used military surplus, aircraft cockpit paint which was limited to shades of light green – this became a trademark of Land Rover vehicles.

Dickie liked the vehicle because it was different from all others on the road – consistent with his extroverted, trail-blazing personality. The vehicle looked 'rigged out' for safari. A bit of a stretch for Cape Cod.

Dickie appropriately named his vehicle *Mooncusser* following the lore of land-based pirates of Cape Cod from the 1800s who would intentionally use lights to signal passing vessels to steer toward shore at locations where they would unsuspectingly run aground. The pirates would loot the foundering vessels for personal gain. These scoundrels would cuss at the moon on nights when it was sufficiently bright that vessel captains could see the shoreline and prevent grounding.

Some individuals from Provincetown have recently promoted a contradictory perspective of Mooncussers, viewing them as a resourceful, innovative group. This opinion is less fear-based and focused on positive traits, whereby citizens were rightfully taking advantage of local resources of opportunity. Those who promote this characterization likely are descendants of the original Cape Cod Mooncussers.

Dickie's Land Rover certainly spent many hundreds of hours on Cape beaches. Likely a successful Mooncusser of his day although his prey may have taken a female form.

As a final comment, some locals still remember Dickie driving into the parking lot of the Hamburger Galley aboard *Mooncusser*. The Land Rover had a very loud horn that made the sound of a wild animal calling in the night. So appropriate for Dickie! When the horn blared, everyone knew who had just arrived. Good thing Bill Stone didn't have access to one of these for his Cadillac. One of these horns was enough in the village.

Ford Fairlane 500 Skyliner Retractable Hardtop

Dickie had a close friend named Peter Tufts who worked for the Ford automobile dealership in Hyannis. Peter always had access to the latest Ford models and Dickie was crazy about a new, 1959 candy-apple red Fairlane 500 Skyliner which had a retractable, hard-top roof (which rarely worked properly). It was the first of this model on the Cape. The roof sections and closing mechanisms were substantial which required the rear trunk to be very large and mostly unusable for other purposes. Regardless, it was a very sporty looking car.

Dickie often borrowed this special model from Peter so he could impress his friends on joy rides around town. One day, Dickie was driving the Fairlane on a stretch of Airline Road nicknamed the 'sexy road' because it had lots of curves. His friend Jimmy Drake was riding in the front seat. As Jimmy was leaning over to reach for something in the back seat, Dickie started skidding at the sharp curve and hollered 'Brace yourself!' Jimmy

did, by accidentally pushing his foot on Dickie's right foot which happened to be on the gas pedal. The car accelerated and spun around but fortunately stayed on the road. Dickie got the car to stop but it was a close call for sure.

Jeep FC-150 Snub-nosed Truck

From 1956 to 1965, the Willys Motors company manufactured short 'snub-nosed' utility trucks as part of their Jeep product line. The FC-150 featured a forward cab (FC meaning Forward Control) and a six-foot rear bed and options for extension. The four-wheel-drive feature of Jeeps made this model very popular over standard two-wheel-drive pickup trucks of their day. Its short wheelbase translated to a small turning radius and advertisements claimed the FC-150 could climb a 60-degree grade. Because this was a unique design for a small utility vehicle, of course Dickie had to acquire one. And he likely tested all the features including mountain climbing.

One day, Dickie decided he'd be the first person to drive a vehicle around the perimeter of Scargo Lake, and his FC-150 was well suited to the task. Not quite - Jon Thatcher encountered Dickie trying to get his vehicle 'unstuck' from the trees at waters' edge. Although Dickie achieved only a partial circumnavigation, 'Jon Boy' helped tow him out and later bought the vehicle from Dickie. Its distinct, snub-nosed profile was seen driving around for years.

Jaguar XK120 Roadster Convertibles

For two decades, Dickie enjoyed investing in preowned Jaguars. Most of his purchases were made through an experienced auto-body specialist, midget-car racer and friend named Al Neves, of Hyannis. Whenever Al spotted a Jag that could be refurbished and made street-ready with only modest effort, he'd call Dickie to come take a quick look. In all, Dickie owned eight jags over his car-trading days.

The Jaguar XK120 series was manufactured between 1948 and 1954. It was a stylish two-seat roadster that became instantly popular. The '120' designation referred to its top speed of 120 mph which made the XK120 the world's fastest standard production car in 1948. It was available in two convertible versions: The Roadster (designated OTS, for open two-seater) and a closed coupe (designated FHC, for fixed-head coupe).

The roadster version was popular with Hollywood stars such as Humphrey Bogart, Ingrid Bergman, Clark Gable and Lauren Bacall. Of course, Dickie drove around the Cape Playhouse in summer, wishing to be mistaken for Hollywood talent. He owned two XK120s.

Jaguar XK140 Roadster Convertibles

Dickie also owned two XK140 roadsters, which were manufactured only between 1954 and 1957. This model (which actually started in 1955) included a number of mechanical improvements as well as 140 hp top speed, substantial front and rear bumpers, and flashing turn indicators. The interior was more comfortable for taller occupants with the addition of three inches in height.

In 1956, the XK140 was the first Jaguar sports car to be offered with an automatic transmission. The convertible Roadster model had a light canvas top assembly that fit behind the seats and disappeared into the body. The interior of the Roadster had no wood embellishments but a leather dashboard.

Jaguar MK V and MK VII Sedans

Dickie loved owning classy sports cars and the Jaguar Mark V and VII Sedans were impressive, top-of-the-line models; generally viewed as higher-class vehicles than the Roadster convertibles. The Jaguar Mark V was a saloon-type (extended salon) sedan, sometimes called the "Gestapo" model.

The Mark V was introduced the same year as the XK120 but outsold the Roadster by more than a factor of two. The styling of this sedan was traditional Jaguar with upright chrome grill and a hint of the most recent Bentley. Rear wheel spats (fender skirts) were standard. The Mark V had a top speed of 90.7 mph; considerably less than the convertible Roadsters.

***

In 1951 the Mark V was replaced by the Mark VII Sports Saloon model. The Mark VII had the same ten-foot wheel base as the Mark V, but a longer and more streamlined body. This four-door model was manufactured only between

1951 and 1956. It could exceed 100 mph and was available with automatic transmission. Its integrated headlights added to the classy presence, similar to a Rolls Royce of that period.

Dickie loved driving his Sports Saloon around the village. But he does recall another ride in his big Jaguar that was not so regal. Each year he'd volunteer to be Santa Claus to present a small gift to each of the local children as they sat on Santa's lap during Christmas Eve at the East Dennis Hall. He'd arrive early in his Jaguar sedan so the local organizers could help with his costume and make-up. Being a joyous occasion, the Committee members always provided a generous supply of alcohol for the pre-event preparations.

One year, there was a snowstorm on Christmas Eve but it was decided 'the show must go on'. Dickie's arrival was perilous because his Jaguar Sedan had no breaks other than the emergency brake attached to one wheel. As always, the alcohol flowed, possibly more than normal because of the storm excitement. Consequently, Dickie got inebriated before the gift-giving ceremonies even started and it was obvious to everyone in attendance. So bad that he recalls having trouble finding his big chair after making the initial 'Ho, Ho, Ho's'.

After all the presents had been given to the children, he intended to make a fast departure to avoid any curious onlookers. Although he did manage to get into his Jaguar and make a quick escape, the snow and lack of good brakes nearly resulted in an accident.

That was the end of Dickie's Santa Clause career in East Dennis. Everyone knew the Committee had supplied the alcohol for the festivities but all fingers pointed to Dickie when the gavel came down. Dickie looks back at that evening with regret.

Rolling the Jag

Most people who owned a classy MK VII Sports Saloon were careful to prevent accidents, especially on slippery roads during winter months on Cape Cod. Not Dickie!

On a routine day when Dickie was drinking with his friend Kenny Adams, they decided to go ice skating on Simmons Pond, north of Setucket Road, midway between Route 134 and Old Bass River Road. The two men jumped in Dickie's Jag, plus two of Kenny's children and off they went. When Dickie was driving on Setucket Road, he wanted to show Kenny how easy it was to turn corners using just the rear brake which worked only on the right side. They made it around the sharp corner but the car tipped on its side and they kept sliding. Dickie could see dirt and rocks passing by, as his driver's side window was nearly touching the road. They came to a stop and no one was injured, fortunately, as that was well before seat belts. They all climbed out of the sliding roof including Dickie's dog.

Dickie and Kenny went to borrow a tractor from Hudson Eldridge in order to get the car back on all four wheels. By the time they returned, the car was upright, thanks to Arthur Franklin and Tom Judge who had driven by and seen Dickie's well-known Jag. The friends were able to tip it right-side-up with assistance from another motorist.

Just another day of joy-riding with Dickie.

Jaguar XK-E Convertibles

And he owned two Jaguar XK-E convertibles that projected the image of sport and style. This model, manufactured between 1961 and 1975, offered a sleek chassis and high performance, with a top speed of 150 mph and acceleration to 60 mph in less than seven seconds.

Picture Dickie riding in his low, white Jag with the convertible top down, wearing a full-head white helmet. All he lacked was a large number '666' on the side of the car and everyone would imagine he was competing in the Grand Prix of Monaco. 666 has always been Dickie's favorite number for its association with the Devil. To this day, his cell phone number ends in 6666 following negotiation with the cute girl at the cell phone office.

The rear trunk of the XK-E could be opened by the driver while sitting in the front seat. Dickie would activate the lever then tell his dog to jump in the trunk and they'd go for a ride.

Oddly enough, Dickie didn't have any outlandish or dangerous experiences with either of his XK-E convertibles. There was, however, one occasion when he was about to leave Bucky Beaver's Magic Garage on Route 6A when a car ran into the front of his stationary Jag as the other driver was passing through the intersection heading westbound. The collision was definitely not Dickie's fault but the police officer tried to ticket him for Driving to Endanger, although Dickie's car was off the road and stationary. Dickie wasn't about to accept this accusation. His insurance company covered the body repairs as he was not at fault.

1934 Ford Roadster

Dickie's friend Jerry Evans (of Hyannis Elks hockey fame) worked at Mid-Cape Ford in the '40s. Back in those days, Dealerships sold standard automobiles but the on-site mechanics also enjoyed building specialized vehicles with high-performance engine components from a variety of manufacturers. One example is a 1934 Ford Roadster which Jerry and his team constructed. It fit the image of a 'Hot Rod' perfectly, with a large engine compartment forward, a small passenger area and a convertible top (at least initially). The original Ford engine was replaced with a 1948 Mercury engine and Edelbrock high-performance, manual choke, dual-chamber carburetors paired with dual exhaust pipes.

For the power train, the Roadster was outfitted with a Lincoln-Zephyr transmission and rear-end differential. The Zephyr was manufactured by the Lincoln-Ford company from 1936 to 1940, as a mid-size luxury vehicle. A perfect source for high-quality drive components.

Jerry and his team had built a very fast car, able to accelerate from 0 to 60 mph in nine seconds. Today's fast cars can achieve that speed in four seconds but this Roadster was constructed nearly seventy years ago!

One night as Dickie was leaving

Gina's restaurant in Little Taunton, he noticed Jerry leaving in his Roadster. Dickie said to himself, 'I've got t'have that car!' Not long after, he bought it from Mid-Cape Ford. To this day he's still not sure how he came up with the money but at the moment, it was not an obstacle to Dickie. 'Seems that was the case when he set his aim on any exceptional vehicle or motorized contraption.

New Jersey Cop

Dickie owned the Ford Roadster when he enlisted in the Air Force at age nineteen but had to leave it in storage when he reported for duty. Following Basic Training, he briefly returned to Dennis to see his friends then drive to Sarasota to visit his parents before heading to radar training school in Biloxi, MS.

Patricia Walker and Dicky Sears remember the day when Dickie drove down Nobscussett Road in his Hot Rod

then pulled into J. P. Walker's driveway. It was the day before Dickie would drive to Florida. He was dressed in his fatigues and long underwear as it was March and rainy, as typical of Cape Cod spring. Worse yet, the car had no top. Who would be crazy enough to drive the 1,400 miles from Dennis to Sarasota, FL with no roof?

A few days later as Dickie was driving south on the New Jersey Turnpike, he noticed the gas tank was nearly empty. Rather than risking the substantial drive to the next exit, he slowed, turned left and drove over the grassy median to exit via the nearby off-ramp of the northbound lane. He filled up the tank then noticed that his only access to the Turnpike was to head north. Shortly after getting on the main road in the wrong direction, he slowed and prepared to again cross the median strip to head southward. As he was about to make the turn, he noticed in the rear mirror that a police car was about to pull him over. It was fortunate that Dickie was not caught in the act of changing directions on the highway, which might have meant a quick 'Go directly to Jail' ticket for the kid from Massachusetts.

After requesting Dickie's License and Registration, the assertive (read: Redneck) Cop made it clear he didn't like the looks of young Dickie nor his Roadster. 'You think that's a Hot Rod. You think it's a beautiful machine. Let me tell you somethin' - it's a piece of shit. Get it off my highway. If I see it on my road again, you're under arrest.'

Now Dickie had to turn off at the next exit of this northbound segment and pay the full price for the toll from the distant,

Delaware border because he didn't have a northbound ticket. Then he got back on the Turnpike heading south, with fear he'd again be seen by the angry Cop and end up in the local Jail. Having to pay the equivalent of double tolls was also a problem because he was "piss poor".

Dickie got Lucky and the remainder of the trip went smoothly, arriving in Sarasota in less than two days. He generously gave the Roadster to his younger brother Bertie before taking the bus to radar training in Biloxi.

1995 Cadillac

As of October 2018, Dickie was driving a 1995 Cadillac as his primary, family vehicle. He loves this car albeit a large, 23-year-old Detroit machine. What is more significant is how it became his property.

Back when Dickie was Harbormaster of Sesuit Harbor, he met many people who were new to Dennis; some just passing through for a day, others making a brief fishing trip aboard the *Albatross*. With his outgoing personality, he'd always engage with strangers, welcoming the person and offering tips on where to go, what to do and who to befriend in the village. Some of Dickie's closest friends called him the 'Mayor of the Northside'. He was helpful and inquisitive, keen on learning what brings people to his backyard.

One day he met a man and his wife from Canada who were searching for interesting shoreline properties for potential purchase. In his helpful manner, Dickie offered to take the couple for a boat ride along the shoreline

so they could view properties from the Bay. This vantage proved very helpful to the newcomers and they eventually purchased a number of properties near the shore at Crocker's Point. One thing led to another and Dickie became a caretaker of their 1995 Cadillac which they would leave at their Dennis home during winter months. They paid Dickie well because he was very reliable, starting the car and driving it on the property twice per week. If a repair was needed, he'd take care of it so the vehicle would always run well when they were in town. They appreciated his reliability and trustworthiness for the twelve years he provided this assistance.

During the warm season when they spent time at their Dennis property, Dickie was their part-time chauffeur, for rides to Boston, Logan Airport and occasional Red Sox games at Fenway Park.

As the ultimate sign of appreciation when they no longer needed the low-mileage Cadillac, they generously changed the title of ownership to Dickie so he could thereafter enjoy the car he had become attached to. To this day, Dickie views them as friends and Benefactors of sort, rather than an employer or client. Another example of how Dickie helps to promote Dennis via his kind and friendly nature, even to persons from the far north.

Car Races on Scargo Lake

Back in the '40s and '50s, thick winter ice on Scargo Lake offered another sport for village boys and men. Many would take their oldest cars out on the ice for short races across the lake. Chains and other means of traction were disallowed. Whereas land-based car races focus on maximum speed, races on the ice were won or lost by how soon a car could get moving from a stationary position. If the tires spun, there'd be no movement; just melting of the ice under the rear tires. It was amusing to see no cars move after the starting flag was waved.

There have been claims that one or two cars fell through ice while racing in areas where the ice was too thin to support the heavy old cars.

Limousines

During World War II, Dickie's father "Buckie" operated a fleet of cabs at Otis Air Force Base. This was a successful business as hundreds of airmen needed transportation to Hyannis or 'over the bridge' when off duty. The celebrated end of the war unfortunately resulted in the immediate demise of Buckie's cab business as the Base population reduced to pre-war levels.

Independently and with no linkages with his deceased father, Dickie developed a limousine business of his own in the village. He had been working as the Project Manager for construction of Jamie Cashman's large home on the bluff west of Corporation Beach. The Cashman family had a limousine and full-time driver that would transport family members near and far. Dickie had loved the big limo. When the project ended, Jay Cashman said 'Why don't you buy that car.'

Dickie replied that he'd love to but couldn't afford it. Jay kindly extended his offer, 'No, take the car and pay it off as you can.' They agreed on a price and Dickie worked the limo business hard, to the extent that he had earned funds to pay it off completely by the end of the summer. Additionally, they kept Dickie on the payroll for local trips for family members.

Over the next few years, Dickie developed a very successful livery business with two limos and two Lincoln Town Cars in his fleet. With an insatiable craving for vehicles of all types, he also owned two Corvettes, two Mercedes Benz and other autos, eighteen in all at one point.

His limo services included relatively long trips to Boston, Newport, regional airports and concerts at the popular Foxwoods venue. He was a favorite chauffeur for local events including weddings, proms and other galas. People got to know him from his extroverted personality and word spread that Dickie's drives was as much fun as the main events. He'd predictably start another party in his limo for the return home.

Additionally, Dickie's daughter would sometimes hear friends talking about their wild limo driver who performed outlandish acts – Too Much Information for a daughter's ears!

Limo Stolen

Early in Dickie's limousine business, he was proud to drive his new 'stretch' wheels. Everyone knew Dickie was close when the long limo was on display.

Another reality is that Dickie loved to play practical jokes on people; friends and foes, alike. However, few had the opportunity (or dared to) pull a joke on Dickie.

One night, Billy King stopped at the Stagedoor Restaurant in the days when Pam McMurtry was the proprietor. He noticed Dickie's shining limo in the adjacent parking lot. Upon entering the bar, he saw Dickie seated at a distant table and 'shooting the breeze' with some friends. Unable to pass up this fine opportunity for a prank, Billy went outside to the limo, found it unlocked with the keys in the ignition and proceeded to drive it away then park it out of sight, behind the Cape Cinema.

Calmly he walked back inside, took a stool at the bar and had a beer, feeling proud of his prank on Dickie – the best joker of the village. All of a sudden there was lots of noise and commotion. He heard someone yell that Dickie's limo had been stolen. The bartender was preparing to call the police to report the car stolen. Billy didn't say a word but had difficulty keeping a straight face. When a friend came and sat beside him, Billy expressed his surprise. 'Jesus, that's terrible. I can't believe they did that.'

Dickie had quickly borrowed a friend's car and drove frantically around the village to no avail. Within a half hour he returned to Pam's restaurant in a sad state, expressing that the limo was his only source of income for the summer, with no other prospects for a job.

Just then, Dickie noticed Billy sitting at the other end of the bar. Dickie didn't say anything but he knew that if anyone local was going to pull a prank on him, it'd likely be Billy. Putting 'two and two' together he walked over to Billy and said 'You son of a bitch. I can't believe you stole my limo.'

With a big 'Billy King smile', he proudly replied, 'People have trouble pulling jokes on you but I got you this time! Ya, I took it. It's behind the Cinema.'

***

Dickie's limo business was going well until September 11, 2001. As a direct result of the '911' terrorist acts, people were not happy any more. They stopped booking trips and going to concerts and gambling casinos. Money tightened up and people were no longer comfortable traveling in style aboard Dickie's limos. Furthermore, vehicle insurance costs and registration for the Livery plate skyrocketed. Dickie was forced to sell his vehicles and pursue other business opportunities.

Boats

Some people say that Dickie likes his women fast and his dogs well trained, not to be confused. He also likes fast motor boats, as proven by dozens he's owned over seven decades. Below are examples of pleasure craft that delivered much pleasure, sometimes at considerable risk.

Near-Death in a Tiny Duck Boat

Dickie's nautical genes likely originated from his Grandfather, Elmer Newell, the Bootlegger of the Bass Hole. The type and shine of the vessel were not important to Elmer; it was all about having the right boat for the job. This seems to have been the case for Dickie as well, starting at an early age. One day he chose to use a boat for travel to a Boy Scout event at Little Taunton beach (now called Chapin). It was 1946 and he was only eleven years old but asking his parents for a ride to something as 'insignificant' as a local Scout gathering was out of the question.

Living a short distance up the road from Sesuit Creek, Dickie had been 'hanging around' boats from a young age. By the time he was a seventh grader, he had his own 8-ft long 'duck boat' that he bought from a friend, Tommy Dexter. This was a low-sided boat designed for hiding in the marsh while duck hunting. Dickie jury-rigged a small mast and sail for propulsion, as he had no outboard engine to mount on the transom.

The boat had a small wooden rudder he had made in his school's Wood Shop class but it wasn't very strong. Beneath the boat was a small, hinged center-board, tethered vertically beneath the hull for use as a keel while sailing. When not needed, the center-board would lay flat against the hull with the tether cleated off.

Dickie decided to use his duck boat to make the trip to Little Taunton for the Scouting event. Why not, it was only about three-and-a-half miles along the shore from the Sesuit jetty to Horsefoot Path where the Scouts would be gathering?

The trip started fine with Dickie in his little sailboat leaving Bridge Street, sailing north along the sinuous creek then out through the jetties. He turned left and aimed his bow toward Corporation Beach to the west. The wind was increasing and he started having trouble keeping his course near the shoreline. Soon he realized that his center-board had broken because despite using the rudder to keep his boat aimed correctly, the little craft was sliding sideways through the water and farther offshore.

Eventually he was as far west as Corporation Beach but getting very scared because waves were splashing over the eight-inch sides of the boat. No matter how fast he wagged the rudder back and forth, he couldn't get his boat to move toward shore. When near Jackass Rock he started screaming with hopes someone on shore would hear his distress calls and send a boat to tow him in. He kept drifting farther offshore with each half hour and started to cry as he thought he would not be saved. Sobbing, the young boy spoke, 'God, I'll never do anything bad again, if you don't let me die.'

Continuing to sail/drift toward the northwest, he could smell the Scout's camp fire on the beach. Maybe they had spotted him and called for help? He was probably more than a half-mile offshore at that point and the sun was going down. Fortunately, the wind dropped and the waves decreased so he could stop bailing. He leaned against the transom and somehow fell asleep.

After a while, he awoke from the sound of his center-board banging on the sandbar where he had just run aground. Knowing that he had probably gone too far west, he got out of the boat and pulled it toward shore to the southeast, in the direction of Gina's restaurant. It was dark but there were many cars in the beach parking lot, with all headlights headed north to aid the search for little Dickie. Many townspeople were there because of the news of the lost boy. Additionally, the town-owned, amphibious vehicle (DUKW) was preparing to drive into the Bay water with fireman aboard to begin their search.

All of a sudden, Dickie appeared in the lights, pulling his little duck boat ashore, to the relief of all. He couldn't believe that he was saved.

It certainly was a frightening Scouting adventure for an eleven-year-old. He views it as the first near-death experience of his life. Others followed, as identified in a later Chapter.

Speedboats

To Dickie, it's all about speed and performance; size doesn't always matter. And when it came to purchasing boats, he was always an opportunist, ready to snatch a good deal that presented itself. If a boat was high performance and/or a bit out of the ordinary, Dickie would always make an offer and frequently close the deal with a cash sale. Some people joked that he was 'Mr. ATM' (automatic teller machine), with more cash in his pocket than anyone around. This allowed him to act on opportunities that arose, before any competition could develop.

Returning to the topic of fast boats, here are a few that he 'played hard' in.

17-ft Checkmate Speedboats

Dickie owned two small, deep-V, Checkmate speed boats with 50 hp Mercury outboard engines. One was dark brown while the other was glass-flaked red, a popular coating in the '70s.

Since 1963, Checkmates have been known as one of the fastest small-boats of conventional style, versus hydroplane hulls that only could race in flat-calm water. Dickie's Checkmates were ideal for speeding in Cape Cod Bay when winds were light or from a southerly direction.

He and his friends often waterskied from his Checkmates at the Bass Hole near high tide when there was calm water and a good lee from any wind. One afternoon skiing with Eddie Whittemore and friends, he injured his leg by jump-starting off from the vertical edge of the marsh. His anguish was distracted by the approach of the Coast Guard who spotted Dickie's second boat anchored a short distance offshore and thought it had been abandoned. Next, they insisted on conducting an inspection and life jacket check on both of his speedboats. With some quick 'Presto Chango' action by his daughter Linda, he convinced the Guardsmen that each speedboat had the required number of personal flotation devices. Nevertheless, Dickie's boating antics nearly got him written up with a slew of boating violations. Having been directed to follow the Coast Guard back to Sesuit Harbor, Dickie felt they were cruising too slow so he proceeded to speed in circles around the Coast Guard launch. They weren't happy with his 'donuts'. Dickie certainly was a 'wise guy' toying with the law!

19-ft Chris-Craft Runabouts

Chris-Craft boats have been synonymous with top-quality wooden design for 144 years. Chris Smith & Sons Boat Company was founded in 1874 and still holds a tradition of excellence. One of their most popular styles was the 21-ft runabout that had a long foredeck, behind which was the windshield then a broad Captain's seat and large steering wheel. Another seat was positioned near the stern, like a cockpit, for up to four passengers. These were fast, classy boats with a single inboard engine.

Dickie owned two 19-ft runabouts. One had the exposed-teak construction but this was difficult to maintain both from a visual perspective as well as maintaining its structural integrity with screws that often came adrift. The other runabout was a classy boat in Bristol condition because the prior owner had applied a mirror-like fiberglass coating over the exterior surfaces.

In 1952, 'Blue Tango' was the song of the year, an instrumental composition that swept the country and Europe too. Of course, that was the name originally given to Dickie's Chris-Craft runabout at the time of construction and he chose to keep the name on the boat. He still can hum the melody, with fond memories of that classy 19-ft runabout.

***

During the time when Dickie owned the 'Blue Tango' runabout, he had been hired as a part-time Counselor for the Youth Fellowship of the Dennis Union Church. This role required Dickie to accompany the teen boys on various events and chaperone their camping outings at Nickerson State Park in Brewster. One evening when the boys were returning from Brewster in Dickie's car, they persuaded him to take them all for a ride in Cape Cod Bay aboard 'Blue Tango'. It was dark but Dickie had no qualms about riding around in the Bay on a calm summer night.

After a couple hours with no sign of their teen sons, the parents became very concerned of their whereabouts. Eventually, Dickie brought them all back to Sesuit Harbor safely but the parents were angry that he had taken them out boating after dark without their prior consent. That was the end of Dickie's Counselor position. He learned a lesson about responsibility, with regret.

21-ft 'Lemon Drop' Speedboat

Dickie's next speedboat was named the 'Lemon Drop' because of its bright yellow hull color. This was a trailored boat with a large 350-hp, Chevrolet V-8 engine. It was well known in the area because it could achieve speeds of 80 mph on flat water. 'Lemon Drop' sounded like a suped-up Hot Rod as it streaked across the lake or Bay.

31-ft Huckins Fairform Flyer

When Dickie was in his mid-20s, he was part-owner of a 31-foot motor yacht that was moored in Sesuit Harbor during summer months. His partner was Hudson Eldridge, for whom Dickie had worked many years in 'Huddy's' local construction business. The handsome vessel was named *Shirley* after Huddy's wife, who became a partner with Dickie in the Real Estate business.

Dickie said that the preowned vessel was purchased in Falmouth, MA, from Robert Ballard or one of his relatives but this has not been confirmed.

The M/V *Shirley* was a Fairform Flyer model, constructed by the Huckins Yacht Corporation in Florida. Huckins yachts have been highly-respected since the company was founded in 1928. Their wooden vessels are well known for being fast, with planing hulls, narrow beam, shallow draft and excellent maneuverability. The company still constructs pleasure yachts as a family run business in its third generation.

Huckins gained notoriety from the war movie 'PT-109' which portrayed John F. Kennedy as a young Navy officer in command of his Patrol Torpedo platform boat on Pacific duty during World War II. In 1943, the Navy commissioned Huckins Yacht Corporation to build eighteen boats and Kennedy was in command of number 109. Huckins PT boats were well-regarded by the sailors who manned them. They were 78-ft long with 19-ft beam, crew of 11 and cruised at 40 knots.

M/V *Shirley* had the profile and characteristic length-beam ratio of all Huckins yachts and she was fast for boats of that size, in the '50s. She was double-planked with Honduras mahogany.

Dickie would often take his friends out for short pleasure cruises in the Bay, by day or night. One of his favorite guests of those days was Leah O'Leary who operated Mrs. O'Leary's County Fair restaurant with her mother. The restaurant was originally situated where the Pheasant restaurant is located today; the County Fair was later moved to the present site of the Scargo Café. Leah would often bring a large, baked roast beef and her restaurant's chef to assure proper presentation of the meal for Dickie. A real treat for any boater, compared to normal at-sea cuisine.

On one memorable cruise offshore Dennis, Dickie asked Leah to take the helm because he needed to attend to matters below. After a few minutes, he came topside and immediately realized they were about to run aground on the rocks.

Apparently, Leah didn't like the heading which Dickie had chosen for the vessel because the waves were making her uncomfortable. Instinctively yet with nautical naiveite, she changed course with no concern about what lie ahead. When Dickie noticed the situation, the *Shirley* was west of the Sesuit jetty but inshore of the jetty's tip where large rocks were strewn everywhere. Running aground was imminent, within seconds, but Dickie averted the catastrophe.

He recalls other amusing activities on the *Shirley* when it was moored in Sesuit Harbor. That was back in the days when many boat owners didn't have nice launches or dinghies for transport from the town pier to their moored boats a few hundred yards away. They'd normally holler to a friend who was motoring by and ask for a lift to shore.

Quite often, Dickie and his close friend Jimmy Drake spent nights on the *Shirley*, with the result they'd still be buzzed when morning came and they needed to head to work. Normal procedure was to strip naked, stuff their dry work clothes in a five-gallon bucket, swim to the pier then get dressed for work. No problem when you're in your twenties and immodest. Those were the good 'ole days for Dickie.

***

I too have fond memories of cruising on a Huckins Fairform Flyer, in 1960 before I was a teen. My father had been invited on a fishing trip to the south side of Nantucket by two friends who owned a large power boat berthed on the south side of the Cape; maybe Osterville. My father woke me early that morning and spoke few words but I knew the drill: 'We're going fishing. Bring your boots and foul weather gear.'

His two friends were brothers, Buck and Ray Schofield, who owned a large construction business off-Cape. Their fine craft was a 44-ft Huckins with a flybridge and characteristic Fairform Flyer lines. At the time, it was the biggest boat I had ever stepped aboard. All I knew was that we were going bass fishing and that was fine with me.

Although very young, I had enough experience on the water to notice it was blowing 'like stink' (over 20 knots) when we boarded the boat. I asked my father whether we should be going offshore because the seas were likely over four feet and worse on the back side of Nantucket. His answer to my youthful inquiry was to not worry, son, but spoken in words that were less politically correct.

Buck and Ray were 'men's men' as proven when Buck headed the boat out of the jetties and on a course for Nantucket. There was no discussion about weather nor sea state – it was definitely a 'go' although the wind was strong in our face and the seas were over four feet already. At slow speed, the bow of the big, narrow boat was pitching about six to eight feet vertically on each wave. Buck was on the helm, standing on the flybridge, and In Charge! I still remember him hollering, 'Hang On!'

We did, as he put the throttle of the Huckins Full-Ahead. Within seconds, the engines roared and the Fairform Flyer leapt on top of the oncoming wave crests. Buck knew that at 30-plus knots, his boat would ride the wave-tops finely. He certainly was right and we were fishing on Old Man Shoal south of Nantucket in less than an hour. We caught many fat bass that had obviously been overeating on herring between the shallow rips which threw white spray ten feet upward with the passage of every wave.

These were men, fishing like men., on a boat that was made to go fast on rough seas. Late afternoon, Buck headed his Fairform Flyer north, full speed of course, as that was his only speed. It was a great ride home as she skimmed over the wave crests like a day on Scargo Lake. And not a breath of wind in the cockpit because we were 'running before the wind'.

38-ft Novi Fishing Boats

Dickie also purchased fishing boats in partnership with Danny Schadt of East Dennis. Together they owned two different boats of the conventional Novi (Nova Scotia) fishing design with high bow, large wheelhouse, fly bridge, large cockpit for fishing or handling of lobster gear and a low transom. They named the first Novi, 'Danny Boy' because of Danny's name which also happens to be Dickie's middle name. The second boat was named 'Dream' but that vessel proved to be a bad purchase. Apparently,

their pre-purchase inspection of the vessel was conducted in the dark but they liked the looks of her and made the purchase. After taking ownership, they soon realized the boat was anything but a 'Dream' and in much poorer condition than they originally thought. Thereafter, their unofficial name for the boat was 'Wet Dream' but the first word wasn't added to the transom.

'Danny Boy' made many fishing trips in Cape Cod Bay and around Provincetown but it also was a popular venue for many parties with friends. On one occasion when most of the partygoers were below, Danny's sister was running the boat in the vicinity of Sesuit jetties when she ran the boat on top of Tautog Rock north of Stone's Point. The rock was not visible because it was near the time of high tide and the rock was submerged by a couple feet of water. Regardless, whoever was on the wheel should have known their proximity to this famous rock that has been stationary since glacial times.

Fortunately, the Novi settled gently on top of the rock without damaging the hull, shaft or running gear. Dickie quickly radioed his friend Jimmy Manning (founder of Grumpy's restaurant) who came out in his lobster boat and slowly pulled 'Danny Boy' off the rock.

40-ft Chris-Craft Constellation – House Boat

The most handsome large boat Dickie ever purchased was a 40-ft wooden Chris-Craft Constellation that was built in 1954. Everyone recalls the *Sand Castle* being in perfect condition in

1972 when Dickie and his family lived aboard for one summer. This included he, his wife, two young daughters and his mother.

Charming *Sand Castle* was a conventional, 'snub-nosed', triple-cabin motor yacht with sleeping quarters located forward, amidships and at the stern of the vessel. Dickie affectionately called the aft cabin the 'mother-in-law apartment'.

After the summer of 1972, Dickie and his family rented a home near the harbor until they could take occupancy of their new home in the village. Thereafter, *Sand Castle* became a favorite party site for Dickie and many of his friends, including Jon Gordon who spent many nights aboard. If only those planks could talk!

***

Dickie's daughter Alesia fondly recalls living aboard *Sand Castle* when she was a mere three years old. She was very fond of her 'Grandma' who lived in the aft cabin.

One afternoon, Grandma was taking a nap with Alesia aboard and playing close by. Faintly, the young girl's voice could be heard saying: 'Goodbye Grandma's glasses. Goodbye Grandma's keys. Goodbye Grandma's lipstick. Goodbye Grandma's teeth.' Immediately, it occurred that her little granddaughter might be doing something with her most important possessions. Just as Ellie opened her eyes, she saw little Alesia throwing her false teeth out through the open port hole and into the harbor water.

Later in the afternoon, father Dickie was able to dive beneath the boat and locate most of his mother's possessions on the muddy harbor bottom. Fatherly duties when you live aboard a boat.

40-ft Commercial Clamming Dragger

Being the optimist that he is and a lover of all things that float, Dickie seized the opportunity to buy a 40-foot, 'preowned', steel clamming dragger. It had the required Commercial Fishing Licenses and he knew there was an abundance of sea clams in the Bay so why not invest?

Dickie's personal interest in running the boat full-time for commercial fishing was marginal so he hired a few local men to run the boat for commercial clamming. That proved to be a fruitless venture as the hired help focused more on alcohol or drugs, and less on clamming. They quit suddenly and disappeared without telling Dickie that they had hung thirty bushel-bags of live sea clams on lines beneath the boat in the harbor. A week passed before Dickie made this discovery. Anyone who knows how bad a dead sea clam smells after rotting in the harbor for a week, can multiply that by 1,500. He had to idle offshore and dump the bags, to the delight of the local lobster population. I wonder if Dickie dove at that location the next day to reap a big harvest of clawed crawlers?

Thereafter, Dickie's primary use of the dragger was for pleasure cruises in the Bay. His wife, Judy, fondly remembers taking evening dinner cruises in the big metal boat. Not lavish affairs; typically, just a couple large buckets of fried chicken and drinks for the kids. Dickie's mother also loved coming along for the ride and she always had her bottle of Scotch whiskey clenched in her fist. The young kids most vividly remember when 'Nana' had to pee, as there was no bathroom nor toilet onboard. Nana would nonchalantly go to the stern, lift her dress and pee in the old, five-gallon pickle barrel (which everyone knew was no longer used for its original purpose).

Dickie also enlisted his dragger for occasional at-sea ceremonies for spreading of cremation ashes. This wasn't a business venture for Dickie; rather, he welcomed the opportunity to take close friends out on his big boat for a respectful affair and farewell toast to their loved one. Dickie would often be 'decked-out' in his black tuxedo and top hat to enhance the visual effect.

As frosting on the celebratory cake, he'd select the most opportune time to stand on the bow and loudly play *Amazing Grace* on his old trumpet. Often, people on the beach could hear the horn, and likely say "That's Dickie Buck again. Up to something!"

These nearshore cruises always turned into lively parties. If they didn't, there's no way Dickie would have been willing to conduct this type of activity frequently. A more accurate way of saying this – Dickie was there, so parties happened!

In addition to the ash-spreading ceremonies in Cape Cod Bay for friends, Dickie and his family spread the ashes of his wonderful mother, Ellie, and his elder brother, Lee. Both ceremonies were conducted off Chapin Beach near the Bass Hole as that is where their family

originated, back in the days of Dickie's grandfather, Elmer Newell. Not even the family ceremonies were somber affairs.

One of Dickie's daughters vividly remembers tossing Dickie's mother's ashes into the water. No sooner had they landed on the surface when a school of fish arose around the boat. Without hesitation, the family rigged up their fishing lines to take advantage of this great opportunity for a fresh dinner. No one can (or wish to) remember whether this was the same ceremony when the wind blew most of the ashes back aboard, immediately after they had been thrown over the side. Never mind.

As a fact that will likely surprise everyone except those persons closest to Dickie, he has not drunk a drop of liquor since he was 29 years old. Not a single drop, at any of the hundreds (thousands?) of parties he has attended over the past 54 years! More discussion on this later.

***

By far, Dickie's fondest memory of an ash-spreading ceremony for which he presided was that for a close friend, Nathan Greenberg, Esq. 'Nate' was a long-term, summer resident who owned a law practice in Boston. He and his wife Ellie were known as active Partygoers, with a deserved capital 'P'. As a couple, they had sharp contrasts which seemed to work for them: he being Jewish and an obvious businessman while she was an Irish Catholic girl – a very energetic, attractive, outspoken, strong-minded, passionate, flirtatious and fun-loving woman! Everyone loved Ellie, even those with whom she argued, over politics or any other topic she might choose at the moment.

Her closest friends cannot forget the diverse types of people she befriended. On more than one occasion, Ellie convened a group of Black Panthers at her home. This was the radical political group founded in 1966 to protest police brutality in Oakland, CA. Community social programs became the Panther's primary focus but their core practice of inciting armed, urban citizen patrols is most remembered when people talk about the Black Panthers. Who knows, maybe Ellie had Bobby Seale and Huey Newton at her home on Beach Street. If so, Nate certainly wouldn't have had much 'say' in the matter – Ellie likely made most (all?) of the family decisions.

It's hard to deny that she was a Revolutionary but most people didn't want to know the depth to which she pursued her convictions, nor was it our business. Regardless, we all cherish our memories of Ellie Greenberg.

Returning to the topic of Dickie's ash-spreading ceremonies for Nate, it was a fun affair, more so than somber. They conducted the activity off Nobscussett highlands where Nate's family had spent many years of enjoyment. When it was time to return to Sesuit Harbor, Dickie tried to impress the onboard group with the speed his old clam dragger could achieve. Not such a good idea. The valve providing the supply of 'raw water' (seawater) for cooling his diesel engine failed. Within seconds, his engine overheated and without coolant water, the asbestos insulation wrapped around the engine's exhaust pipes overheated and started to catch fire. Furthermore,

old lubrication oil that had accumulated on top of the engine manifold and injector pump had already ignited. This was a small fire but it could spread to the overhead deck supports within the engine room.

Dickie instantly knew that his best course of action was to activate the large cylinder of Halon gas he had aboard for that exact purpose. If he didn't fill the engine compartment with Halon, the small fire would spread rapidly. Dickie knew that as soon as the Halon cylinder was placed in the hot engine room, its temperature-activated, bimetallic fuse would open and discharge the entire contents of the cylinder in the engine compartment.

Thinking fast, for the safety of his family and friends, Dickie slowly and carefully drove the bow of his steel dragger up on the top of Tautog Rock which was partially exposed because the tide was low. Captain Dickie ordered 'all hands' to muster on the bow to keep the boat's weight on the rock so it would remain anchored there, at least temporarily. Next, he called a friend in the harbor to summon for help and Jim Manning headed out immediately with his large lobster trawler.

Most of the passengers were in shock as they watched Dickie toss the large Halon cylinder into the engine room but Dickie knew what he was doing. This wasn't the typical household situation where you aim a small extinguisher nozzle at the fire and squeeze the trigger handle. The Halon cylinder was designed to open automatically and its denser-than-air gaseous contents would displace all the oxygen in the engine room, preventing further fire spread. He did toss the cylinder onto the low deck in the engine room and he heard the valve open automatically – a big relief.

Lastly, he had two men help with a hand-powered bucket brigade so Dickie could douse the small oil fire that persisted on top of the engine.

Within minutes, Dickie had 'saved the day', all fire had been extinguished and Jim Manning's boat was alongside offloading everyone from the party. With only a couple men remaining aboard, Dickie was able to bring his dragger back into the harbor idling on its own power as the diesel engine was not ruined.

When everything had settled down, Ellie was pleased with the entire day's event. Her final comment was that it '…was very appropriate to have a fire and big commotion during Nate's final ceremony. He would have wanted it that way.'

Someone from afar might have thought that Dickie had accidentally (or stupidly) run his boat onto Tautog Rock at mid-tide and panicked during the fire, throwing his fire apparatus into the engine compartment angrily. Not so – Dickie knew exactly what to do and all hands were saved. He was after all, one of the competent men on the North Dennis Volunteer Fire Department.

Iceboats

Another popular winter activity on ice-covered Scargo Lake was iceboat racing. This was a fairly crude competition back in the '50s, with local men spending a few hours each constructing their unique craft from spare planks, angle iron and a big piece of canvas with a masted sail. Most used one-foot sections of two-inch, steel angle-iron as runners, attached to the underside of the wooden frame. Occasionally a pair of old, metal-framed ice skates was bastardized and bolted on for runners. Whatever steel was used, the bottom edge was put on a grinding wheel to make it sharp to maximize boat speed.

The rear runner and hand tiller were constructed to accommodate 360-degree turns as this was the only method for avoiding catastrophe at the downwind end of the lake. Even the crudest iceboats could reach speeds up to 40 mph in a good wind and over the half-mile distance along the lake, this translated to only 45 secs for the race to be over; sooner if the jury-rigged mast and sail 'came adrift'.

As teens, Dickie and his friend Seth Crowell took their iceboat to Funn Pond in East Dennis to seek better wind than could be found on Scargo Lake. This proved to be a mistake as Funn was situated in a depression amidst the trees, greatly limiting the local wind at ground level. The small pond between the tenth and eleventh holes at Dennis Pines is Funn; definitely too short for serious iceboating. They remember abandoning the iceboat in the woods adjacent to the pond; likely removed when the golf course was constructed in 1965.

Dan Walker and a couple other men from the village tried to construct an iceboat from parts of an airplane that had crashed recently. They brought the engine and fuselage to the lake but they had to make a propeller. Their fabrication was not well balanced and it flew apart as they were motoring across the lake.

No one was hurt but the plane hit a wall at the edge of the lake and no further attempts were made.

Jet Skis

Like most Cape Cod sportsmen, Dickie owned two jet skis which he used on occasion, mostly in the Bay. It's likely that he didn't favor this watersport because it was too conventional for his personality; 'seemed like everyone owned one. And when sea conditions were favorable during times of good weather, dozens of 'yahoos' would be streaking around the near-shore waters of Dennis. Many property owners on the Bay, and boaters as well, hated the jet skis because of their loud engine noises and erratic weaving around all other craft.

Probably his most memorable jet ski ride was with one of his employees, John Elland, on a cold January day. Dickie loaned John one of his old wet suits that fit "very poorly"; a visual that added to the fun of the day. They each rode one of Dickie's jet skis from Sesuit Harbor to Corporation Beach and back. Nothing extraordinary, other than the fun from surprising many people parked in their cars while viewing the cold waters of the bay.

'Hey, isn't that Dickie Buck out there? Damn fool, riding in the Bay in January.'

Amphibious Car

The most successful amphibious pleasure automobiles (called Amphicars) were manufactured in Germany from 1961 to 1968. Because of their popularity on the U.S. market, the Amphicar Corporation of America in Orange, NJ, became the U.S. based representative for the German manufacturer. Sales of these multi-purpose vehicles accelerated, even with hundreds of purchases from Red Cross organizations in Europe and the U.S. due to the vehicle's capability for reaching victims trapped in flood waters and other near-shore marine disasters. The eventual decline from popularity was driven by the poor reliability of the vehicle's mechanical systems.

As mentioned in the earlier Chapter about notorious Lester Hallett, Dickie was likely the first Cape Codder to purchase an Amphicar, in 1967. His was bright red, not surprisingly, considering Dickie's penchant for being noticed. In those days, spirits were high and colors were bright, even on cars, especially Dickie's no matter what design.

Mechanically, the vehicle was a four-seat convertible with a 43-hp, Triumph four-cylinder engine and four-speed, two-wheel-drive transmission. Two small propellers mounted near the rear bumper provided propulsion when immersed; one speed forward and one speed in reverse. The separate transmissions for wheel-drive versus propellers added to the complexity and cost of the vehicle. Steel was used for the frame and body construction because the cost of rust-free aluminum was prohibitive in the '60s. Cape Codders know that a single ride in the salty Bay would likely initiate rust in unreachable places, despite thorough rinsing. Would this result in a much shorter lifespan than of on-road vehicles? Dickie probably had no concern, knowing that within a few years of the Amphicar purchase, he'd be driving or flying some other type of new contraption.

Dickie's Amphicar was legally registered for road driving as well as motoring on Scargo Lake and Cape Cod Bay (when seas were minimal). Its side doors shut tightly to keep water from coming aboard but overall, the car didn't have much freeboard. Consequently, if water came to the door tops, it would enter the window openings and wreak havoc with the internal mechanisms, especially if it was saltwater.

Dickie was proud of his newfangled, land/sea vehicle and he sought opportunities to shock unsuspecting passengers when he took a sharp turn into Scargo Lake or into the Bay. As long as he had firmly locked the special door-seals before he suddenly turned into the water, there'd be no wet feet, or worse.

When Dickie worked winters for J. P. Walker, delivering home heating oil, he knew that his boss loved fresh trout for breakfast. He would drive his Amphicar down Dr. Lords Road - South, enter the water of Scargo Lake at the swimming beach and troll his fishing lure behind his car as he putted along at one knot. Often, he'd catch a couple trout on his small, collapsible rod as he drove toward Fisherman's Landing at Route 6A. No concern for fishing season dates, fish size, limits nor anything else for that matter. It was a cold December morning and a warm donut from Mrs. Harriman would solve all problems; maybe two donuts.

And there was another rumored adventure when Dickie offered to take his friends Hall Machon and Percival Sears sea clamming in his Amphicar. Dickie's proposal sounded advantageous to the two men as they'd be able to motor out to an ebbing sandflat, dig their clams and motor back into Sesuit Harbor with minimal walking and lugging of burlap bags full of heavy clams. George, Hall's son, recalls hearing his father cussing for years about that damned day when Dickie took him clamming in his 'water car'. It started off fine, leaving Sesuit channel and reaching Chapin Beach. As they were clamming, the fog came in so thick that they couldn't see the shoreline. They quickly lost their bearings and the seas picked up as well. Given that the Amphicar had minimal freeboard, the two passengers were worried that the car would take on too much water to stay afloat.

Hall sat under the canvas convertible top and used a cigarette lighter to see the compass. Dickie was worried they'd reach Provincetown that night rather than returning to Sesuit Harbor. "We all were very concerned." which is a strong statement from Dickie's mouth.

Somehow, they found the flashing-red jetty light amidst the fog and managed to motor into the harbor before the Amphicar flooded and sank. With essentially no flotation built into the Amphicar, they'd have gone down like a stone, possibly out in the Bay.

The bottom line is that Dickie has lived his entire life without worrying that he was going to die. Certainly, there were dozens (maybe hundreds) of times when his friends, family, lovers and enemies thought they were going to die in his presence or from his actions or miscalculations, but not he.

When I asked him to comment on his mortality, his reply was simply, 'I never worried because I knew I wasn't going to die! This premise is revisited later in the book, but obviously he's still with us, likely for many years to come. Impressive control of destiny? Some may have another answer.

Submarine

The British rock group *The Beatles* premiered their animated film *Yellow Submarine* in July 1968, followed six months later by the release of their highly popular record album of the same name. Everyone in the late sixties had yellow submarines on the brain so what did Dickie do? He went out and bought one; not the record album – a real yellow submarine.

He admits not being sure what he was going to do with the new full-submergence vehicle but it wouldn't take much time for outlandish activities to come to Dickie's mind. Maybe transport it to Bermuda or The Bahamas and slither into the lucrative drug transport market? He wisely decided to avoid that career path.

Stealth trips across Scargo Lake under darkness of night – missions he cannot reveal?

As with all of his newly acquired contraptions, Dickie devised unique pranks that had previously been impossible before acquiring his new submersible.

We must acknowledge that Dickie's yellow submarine was a small craft, capable of transporting only a single (brave) passenger/pilot. It had a small internal motor and propeller driven by a 36-volt bank of batteries. The pilot could adjust the sub's ballast to accomplish dives and return to the surface. The manufacturer's specification boasted horizontal speeds reaching 10 mph but it's unlikely the sub ever exceeded 5 mph, even with a tail current.

Additionally, the sub was configured with a glass dome at the top that allowed Dickie to view his surroundings from inside but if the seas were more than a foot or two high, motion in the sub was unbearable. An onboard compass was used to maintain a heading when motoring beneath the waves. The sub rode so low in the water that only the glass dome could be seen bobbing above the surface. From a distance, the sub was nearly indistinguishable from the sea.

Perry Submarine Builders, Inc. of Florida was the manufacturer of the Cubmarine model which Dickie owned and on the side was the name 'Shark Hunter'. Perry began construction in the early '60s and produced many models over the next few decades for military applications and recreation. Additionally, Perry subs were used around the world for scientific, exploratory and commercial ventures. Dickie's adventures were a bit more modest, surprisingly.

An exact replica of the Cubmarine model that Dickie owned hung in the New England Aquarium in Boston for more than 30 years. Another appeared in the underwater chase scene in the 1977 James Bond movie, *The Spy Who Loved Me*. If only the Director knew of Dickie Buck, he surely would have been one of the stuntmen.

The Woods Hole Oceanographic Institution used a two-person Cubmarine to photograph whales in Cape Cod Bay in 1962 and later conduct an underwater survey of Woods Hole Passage.

Dickie was Harbormaster of Sesuit Harbor in the mid-60s which overlapped with his submariner days. When search and rescue operations exceeded those of himself and other local divers, he volunteered to find the object or body with his yellow submarine. But, there was no doubt that Dickie's favorite activity was pranks.

***

During late afternoon of a winter day in 1974, a number of villagers saw a meteor streak low across the Dennis sky, with presumed impact in Scargo Lake. A group ran to the edge of the lake and saw a distinct wake of disturbed surface water, a couple hundred feet long and oriented in the same direction as the supposed meteor had traveled. Some of the witnesses reported that water in the surface wake was frothing but they couldn't be sure if it was due to gas rising from the meteorite that had sunk in the depths or just air bubbles from turbulence upon impact.

Of course, Dickie was recruited to solve the mystery. The following April, he transported his yellow submarine to the lake and conducted an underwater visual survey of the lake floor in the vicinity of the supposed meteorite crash. He found no large object but spotted some small rock-like matter on the bottom. Returning with his dive gear, he recovered a number of these brittle clumps and had them analyzed in a geological laboratory at Massachusetts Institute of Technology. They concluded that the clumps were not natural material typically found on Cape Cod. It was possible they were cinders or slag from a metal foundry and with the Lake's close proximity to Prue Foundry on Paddock's Path, that might have been the source of the material found. No relationship to the suspected meteor or UFO.

On another submarine dive in Scargo, Dickie found an old wooden skiff lying on the bottom immediately north of what is today called Princess Beach. He didn't attempt to recover it because of its fragile condition but guessed it was well over one-hundred years old.

***

In the early '70s there was a small gang of village boys who were causing many problems around town. One day it was discovered that a fine Chevrolet Corvette had been stolen from someone's yard. These same boys were known to take stolen cars to Scargo Lake when frozen over, race around wildly in circles on the ice, then ditch the car as it was sliding toward one of the open-water patches that always occurred on the frozen Lake. Rumors all pointed to the Corvette likely being on the bottom of Scargo. Dickie was enlisted again but no car was found.

***

As a last submarine story: one fine summer day when hundreds of bathers were on Corporation and Howes Beaches,

Dickie had his friend David Sears use Percival Sears' small, motorized punt, named *Beach Plum*, to tow the yellow submarine from the harbor jetties to a point half way to Corporation point. After being disconnected from the tow line, Dickie was free to maneuver as he wished.

With his clever (read: devious) mind, he mounted one of his large, black-rubber swim flippers beside the top dome so it stood vertically above the sea surface. He succeeded in making the flipper resemble the dorsal fin of a large shark, especially when the sub was moving forward at a knot or two. You can imagine the continual smile on Dickie's mischievous face as he cruised parallel to shore, back and forth along the crowded stretch of Corporation Beach, instilling fear in the hearts of parents and children alike.

'Shark! Shark! There's a big shark out there!' Dickie couldn't hear the loud screams nor frantic calls to the police, but he surely got his chuckles inside his quiet, little sub beneath the waves. After a while he peacefully motored back to the harbor.

Upon arrival he was confronted by frantic Dennis Policemen insisting that he, the esteemed Harbormaster, must get rid of the school of big sharks at Corporation Beach and calm the fears of hundreds of beachgoers. 'At least go there and make people get out of the unsafe waters.'

Bravely and without hesitation, Dickie jumped into his boat and headed west to Corporation Beach to slay every shark he could find. He knew he could get the job done. His stature and confidence were nothing less than demonstrated by

Captain Quint of the movie *Jaws*. Even the Police were relieved Dickie was going to perform this perilous task.

Within ten minutes, everyone on the beach was relieved and happy to see the brave Harbormaster steaming around in the nearshore waters of Corporation Beach. Their hopes of seeing their hero hoist up a bleeding, fifteen-foot shark didn't materialize but they felt safe that brave Dickie had again saved the day!

Hovercraft

Everyone has heard of hovercrafts, mainly as an alternative configuration for large maritime ferries. Additionally, Navies worldwide have fabricated large hovercraft for transport of personnel and equipment. However, few persons realize that small hovercrafts have been manufactured for personal use and recreation since the '60s. Dickie is the only person I know who has ever owned one. No surprise to J. P. Walker, rest his soul.

A hovercraft, or air-cushion vehicle (ACV), is a multi-terrain vehicle that is capable of travelling over land, water, ice and other surfaces. Their engines (blowers) generate a large volume of air that is blown under the hull to provide lift. The engines also are used to turn large propellers (fans) at the rear of the vehicle which propel the craft horizontally, similar to propellers on an airplane or Everglades airboat. A small, flexible 'skirt' is attached around the lower perimeter of the craft to cushion the hull from small obstacles. The unique design of the hovercraft

also offers lift without forward motion, unlike hydrofoils that require substantial forward motion before the vessel can be lifted up on a fixed wing (foil) beneath the water surface.

Small hovercraft are convenient and relatively affordable for light-duty transport tasks and recreational use. Additionally, they're easy to operate, maintain and transport to various locations. Physical size, horsepower, carrying capacity and speed vary greatly among manufactured options.

Dickie sometimes rode his hovercraft on Scargo Lake in winter, when it was covered with ice and vertical lift of the hovercraft was optimum (in the absence of waves). A major advantage of the hovercraft is that it could travel over ice that was as thin as one inch. Additionally, the hovercraft could travel much faster over smooth ice than it could over waves of any size.

Even cautious William Ernest Crowell dared ride in Dickie's hovercraft across Scargo (albeit when very thick ice was proven). The craft could achieve speeds of 60- to 70 mph over the frozen lake which was impressive, even compared to the fastest homemade iceboats. The only caution was that the hovercraft engine would have to be shut down when it reached only a quarter of the distance across the lake because there was no way to stop at the end. Apparently, towed drag elements were not yet devised at that time.

Dickie had fewer winter riders when the ice cover on Scargo Lake was marginal. This was understandable as most people didn't trust that the craft would skim over the open water segments of the Lake. The consequences could have been disastrous in the cold lake waters.

One winter day a man approached Dickie to buy his hovercraft so he transported it to Corporation Beach for a demonstration. He wanted to show how it ran on the Bay, running parallel to the beach. Unfortunately, recent wave action during high tide caused a berm of ice to accumulate on the beach. After starting the hovercraft, Dickie rode over the low berm to reach the Bay water but the stationary ice ripped off a section of the craft's flotation collar. As Dickie continued offshore, he could see the flotation on the surface, trailing behind him. He knew it wouldn't hamper the air cushion that kept him above the water. But he had to keep the craft horizontal in any waves so the 3- to 4-inch air lift cushion would not be compromised; if it were, he'd quickly settle into the water and go down like a rock because the craft was not buoyant in the absence of the flotation collar. If Lester Hallett were accompanying Dickie, he'd surely have yelled "It's not the day, boys!", meaning, I'm not ready to die today.

Dickie continued to run the hovercraft at a high engine speed to maximize the air cushion. He stood up the entire time to keep watch on his precarious situation and show no panic to the prospective buyer. With considerable effort, Dickie managed to turn the craft toward shore and make it to safety on high ground.

The man ended up buying the hovercraft after Dickie's Cape Cod Bay demo, even though the flotation needed repair. Dickie was happy to see it leave because the ending could have been more severe.

Powered Paraglider

When Powered Paragliders (sometimes called Powered Parachutes) became commercially available in the mid-80s, of course Dickie had to own one (two actually). Paragliders are configured with a tethered, inflated, parachute wing overhead and a two-cycle, gas powered motor for thrust. The vehicle's ground frame is triangular shaped with three small wheels and a single seat forward. Steering was accomplished with foot pedals. A wire, safety-basket structure was fixed around the large propeller blades like airboats are equipped for the Florida Everglades.

Note that 'Ultralight' is the correct term for a one- or two-seat, light-weight aircraft with a fixed, overhead wing and motor. That configuration is made for higher speed and altitudes than a paraglider possessing only a flexible wing (parachute) overhead.

Dickie owned the single-seat version of a paraglider that could achieve altitudes of many hundreds of feet; ideal for flying over Dennis' coastal waters and shorelines. The power-off glide ratio was 5:1 which meant that if the motor died while aloft, he could glide 1,000 ft to reach shore if he was originally at an altitude of 200 ft over the Bay. Great for spotting white sharks.

Fortunately, Dickie never crashed into the Bay but did have one near-death experience on his paraglider, crashing on Corporation Beach. He had purchased the paraglider from someone who had a Cape family member killed from crashing that specific paraglider near the Cape Cod Airport at Marston's Mills. Additionally, it was the same configuration of paraglider that John F. Kennedy, Jr. had crashed several weeks before his fateful flight on July 16, 1999. In his paraglider accident, John broke his ankle when his foot was caught under the metal-wheel frame during a rough landing; not unlike Dickie's accident. John's leg cast was removed just a few days before his airplane crash, although not believed to be the cause of the deadly event.

To get aloft, Dickie would drive the paraglider for roughly a hundred yards across the low-tide sand flats at a speed of 10 mph. When a wind was available, he would head toward it to gain lift quickly. On the day of his accident there

was no wind at Corporation Beach so Dickie figured he wouldn't need a long 'runway' to take off. Rather, he headed north toward the low water mark. The flight started well, quickly achieving an altitude of ten feet and the parasail opened directly overhead but suddenly, a tailwind flipped his glider wing upside down and the wheeled frame flipped as well. Immediately, he ended upside down on the sand flat with the motor still running loudly. He landed on his shoulder and couldn't get his seat belt undone nor his feet free – essentially trapped by the motor carriage and unable to escape. Dickie suspected his shoulder was broken but his biggest fear was that of being trapped with a leaking gas tank overhead and enough heat from the engine to ignite the entire tank. Fortunately, Hudson Eldridge and four other friends saw the accident and came to Dickie' rescue, freeing him from the paraglider before a fire ignited. Considering that only his rotator cuff was torn, the ending could have been much worse, possibly Dickie's ending.

Skills and Experience

Most people develop a handful of skills for employment and/or enjoyment. Dickie's experience is broader than most, including this long list of talents which is still growing. Those gained during his childhood years have been discussed previously and thus, not repeated here.

Throughout this book, stories are told that involved many of these skills. Other stories that are too lewd to have been included herein are omitted, as well as his areas of associated 'proficiency'.

It mustn't be overlooked that Dickie once made a run for public office. In 1972 he ran for Selectman of Dennis against Joseph Merchant who 'owned' the South Side, almost literally. His business connections were strong also which prevented Dickie from winning many votes in Dennis Port, West Dennis and South Dennis. Despite a strong showing in North and East Dennis, Dickie lost the contest.

Appliance Installer

Auto Mechanic

Auto Salesman

Ballroom Dancer

Bartender

Boat Salvager

Boxer   Brew Master

Carpenter   Chauffeur

Chef   Church Usher

Clammer   Corpse Retriever

Dog Trainer   Fight Referee

Tuna Fisherman   Forklift Operator

Funeral Director   Harbormaster

Heating Oil Deliverer

Heavy Equipment Operator

Impersonator   Japanese Translator

JUDY, DAUGHTER LISA, RICHARD D. BUCK AND DAUGHTER LINDA.

TOWN OF DENNIS
ELECT
RICHARD D. BUCK
your SELECTMAN
MONDAY, MARCH 6, 1972

Landscaper Marine

Mammal Rescuer

Motorcycle Acrobat

Paraglider Pilot

Property Manager

Radar Technician

Radio Operator

Real Estate Broker

Roofer

Santa Claus Impersonator

Scout Counselor   Scuba Instructor

Seaman   Sharpshooter

Submarine Pilot   Theater Usher

Trumpeter   Yacht Captain

Antics and Adventures

This Chapter presents only a fraction of the antics and adventures Dickie has 'performed' during his life in the village. From discussion with dozens of persons who have known him over his eighty-plus years, more than one-hundred stories were conveyed to me, with smiles and sometimes raised eyebrows and shaken heads. Furthermore, these friends each admitted there were other crazy feats he performed that have either escaped their memory or were too lewd to describe.

Below is provided a subset of his stories, some amusing others shocking. And these don't include stories in categories such as stolen cars, stick-ups, fistfights, arrests and (which may surprise some) generosity, that are given in later Chapters.

To prepare you for what lies ahead, here are a few introductory statements about Dickie's personality, especially during his younger, wild years.

- Some villagers have summed up Dickie's early years as 'Misspent youth!' Stressing that his time was spent foolishly or on frivolous things. Just their opinion, of course. It is not overlooked that he was a hard worker, through which he gained much independence.

- From his late teens to age twenty-nine, alcohol fueled his craziest antics and misbehavior.

- When something out of the ordinary occurred, everyone assumed Dickie was involved. The worse the act, the quicker he was blamed. If he wasn't involved, he still enjoyed the notoriety.

- Taking risks and performing dangerous stunts were of no concern to Dickie because he was confident 'he would never die'.

- Some residents of North Dennis were quick to say he wasn't a local boy. 'Yes, that's crazy Dickie Buck; he's not from here.' They were pleased he lived 'far away', in East Dennis.

- Parents warned their children, 'Stay away from that Dickie Buck, he's trouble.' And fathers were advised to lock up their daughters.

- 'Like a race horse, he ran hard and was put away wet.'

Amusing Activities

Dr. Ajax Fennelletti

Decades ago, Building Security and Visitor Access within hospitals were very lax compared to today's procedures and protocols. As another prank, Dickie decided it would be amusing to impersonate a doctor to gain access in the local hospital. He dressed the part, wearing a white lab coat, black glasses and carrying the typical black-leather doctor's bag.

As he approached the main desk, the nurse asked his name and he rapidly said "Doctor Fennellitti, Ajax Fennelletti!" and kept walking. She stopped him and asked him to spell his name, as it was not on her Shift Roster.

Flippantly, like a doctor may reply, he barked at the nurse: "F E double-N E double-L E double-T I. FENNELLETTI! Can't anybody spell?"

"What do you do Doctor?"

"I'm a Brain Surgeon." he replied, knowing that no one wants anything to do with a Brain Surgeon. But if he said 'Internal Medicine', everyone would ask for advice for their illness.

Dickie's plan was to visit a lady friend from the village who had been admitted with a leg injury. When he entered her hospital room and they recovered from their initial laughter, she got up on crutches and they walked next door to the Maternity ward. She was only a Junior in High School at the time but Dickie and she pretended that one of the newborns behind the viewing glass was theirs. Fortunately, they knew better than to interact with the babies and the prank ended with many laughs and no harm done. Dickie could pull anything off!

Dickie had no trepidations while attempting such a bold prank because if resistance was met with one of the hospital employees, he'd just start pouring on his charm to accomplish what he set out to do. Hospital security procedures certainly were different back in those days.

'666' Cell Phone Number

Dickie strives to be unlike others and he succeeds. This applies even with regard to his phone number. When he needed an initial cell phone number, he visited the phone company's office in Hyannis. He didn't wait in line and accept any random number given to him. No, that's not Dickie's style.

He spotted a pretty girl behind an office desk and approached her without delay. In a few minutes, they were friends and he had negotiated a number that suits his personality: xxx-xxx-6666. The devil would have been proud of his newest recruit.

And do you suppose his post box at the U.S. Post Office was assigned randomly? It is '69', really!

Dancing Performances

Dickie's reputation of being wild and sometimes dangerous is matched by his excellent dancing skills when on public display. Showmanship and the element of surprise are Dickie's premeditated methods of maximizing a public opportunity.

One afternoon, a few girls were planning an evening of dance at a south-shore venue. Dickie happened to see Patricia Walker and lightly asked what she was doing that night.

"A group of us are going out dancing."

"Have a good time." Dickie replied.

"I don't expect it to be that great because most guys nowadays are not good dancers."

As the conversation was ending, he asked where they were going then went on his way. Patricia never thought anything important of his question.

Later that evening, the girls were having a decent time dancing but not terrific. Then Dickie arrived and things got much better. Her recollection:

"Without delay or spoken words, he grasped my hand and we were instantly on the floor, dancing like 'Fred and Ginger'. People were moving back to watch as we quickly took over the entire dance floor.

Mid-dance, he said 'When the music is over, just turn and walk away. Don't look back.'

I did as told; when the music ended, I turned and walked away. He did the same and walked right out the door with no return.

Everyone in the dance hall was wondering, 'What the hell was that?'"

Patricia also was startled, equally with Dickie's unexpected entrance and his grand exit. Regardless, the dance experience was one she has cherished ever since.

And Dickie had succeeded as always: Shock and Awe, with a ballroom twist.

***

At a wedding reception in the village, one of his lady friends walked up to Dickie and asked him to dance, knowing of his terrific skills on the dance floor. It started off fine but his dance moves soon switched to lewd, 'dirty-dancing' gyrations, certainly intended to grasp the attention of everyone nearby. She quickly realized that she should have anticipated this behavior from Dickie, as he is the attention-getter extraordinaire. Her embarrassment was the least of his concern, possibly a secondary goal. No matter, as she and everyone knew that Dickie is harmless and always has good intentions.

Bacon Fat in a Boy's Hair

When Dickie was in his early teens, he was hired by a family to babysit for their young son. He was given money and told to take the son to the Cape Cinema for the afternoon movie. Before they left the home, Dickie decided the boy needed to have his hair combed to look proper in the public setting. The boy had a big cowlick in the back and looked disheveled. To solve the problem, Dickie found a pot of lotion that he assumed was hair oil and smeared a liberal dose on the boy's hair to make it lay flat. After careful combing, the boy looked presentable and they headed off to the movie. Dickie felt proud of his role as the mature babysitter.

Being summer, the theater was warm inside because this predated air conditioning. Soon a strong odor blossomed in the immediate vicinity of the two boys. Nearby patrons were leaving their seats to escape the awful stench. Dickie noticed goo dripping down the side of the young boy's face and it was in fact, the source of the odor. With minimal analysis, Dickie realized that he had applied bacon grease to the boy's hair.

Heating Oil Delivery

Beginning in 1966, Dickie made winter deliveries of heating oil to houses in the village while employed for seventeen years by J. P. Walker and Sons, Inc. The customer list was relatively short and changed minimally from year to year. And the business office knew which houses were receiving oil on any given day according to a well-planned schedule.

Before cell phones were common, the office occasionally needed to contact Dickie during his route. The village's small area made it easy for J. P. Walker or his son to drive to the ten or so houses planned for delivery that day to find Dickie. The large delivery truck could easily be spotted from the road so a quick drive-by could confirm his whereabouts.

Another day, Dickie was unreachable for a few hours. J. P. was frustrated and started bitching to his guy friend, 'Jesus, I can't believe it. Dickie got the truck stuck in her yard.'

'Well Joe, the ground is wet and muddy so that's going to happen.'

'She doesn't use oil to heat her house. That's the problem.'

J. P. learned that if he couldn't find Dickie, there were a few houses that he'd check first to locate his truck.

The only problem that Dickie caused was during oil delivery at a home on Beach Street. He had put the hose nozzle into the fill pipe behind Tom King's house and was pumping at a normal rate but he got distracted by a flock of chickens in a nearby coop. By the time he returned to the hose, the basement oil tank had overfilled and a large volume of oil had already been spilled. The owner was not a happy customer.

***

When Dickie recalls his job as an oil delivery man, he has only positive things to say. Initially, he told J. P. that he'd try it for one day and decide whether he'd continue. Seventeen years proved that it was good employment for Dickie when the weather was too harsh for his Harbormaster job.

The only time Dickie pushed back on J. P. was when asked to help repair some fence posts in his yard.

'You're not paying me to fix posts. You hired me to deliver oil and that's what I'll do.'

Quitting Coffee and Salt

"I haven't had a cup of coffee in a long time; nearly fifty years. Back in the early '70s, I was on my way to Florida, traveling with my mother. We were having breakfast in a restaurant before boarding the flight. I was sitting at the table drinking coffee – back then I was drinking three or four cups every day. As I was pouring salt on my eggs, they started flashing in the sunlight…like crystals, like diamonds all over my eggs. I said, 'That's it! I'm drinking too much coffee, eating too much salt.' I knew it wasn't good for me so I quit 'em both."

To this day, Dickie hasn't drunk another cup of coffee! And he abstained from salt for fifteen years as well.

"I'm a great quitter. When I quit drinking liquor and smoking cigarettes, it was both on the same day, Labor Day in 1965, when I was twenty-nine." That was fifty-four years ago.

Poor Howard's Post

A fine example of the summer eccentricity and journalistic fabric that graced Cape Cod years ago was a newspaper called *Poor Howard's Wednesday Afternoon Post*[36]. The first issue of the paper was distributed in June 19, 1966 at a price of one penny!

Co-Editors-in-Chief Carol Rubright and Howard Schneider created a 16-page regional newspaper about interesting human-interest topics in Provincetown and throughout the Cape. Howard was a longtime Provincetown resident, artist and cartoonist and he enlisted a number of bright and eager Journalism majors from his alma mater, Syracuse University in New York, to roam the Cape looking for peculiar news topics.

Dedicated to 'imagination and responsibility', the paper was about real people and freedom of speech, rather than providing an income for 'Poor Howard'. As stated in Issue No. 1, 'We are here to provide the Cape with a vehicle for its own expression. …to provide the residents of Cape Cod with something they can call their own and the tourists with something that will help them to understand what the Cape is all about.'

When two young journalists from the Post were exploring the cultural richness of Route 6A, they encountered Dickie. Immediately they recognized their rich discovery of an unpolished gem; a crude exterior with a sparkling core and energy that would blind most conservatives. They enjoyed his eclectic personality, his motorcycles, his odd lifestyle, his Magic Garage, his yellow submarine and the houseboat he lived on – truly an Unforgettable Character as later mentioned in the Post.

One issue was dedicated to the interesting toilets and bathrooms the journalists had discovered while 'scouring' the Cape. The issue's cover was a photo collage of twelve toilets; most were not pretty but all were unique. When Dickie saw the issue, he was proud that two of his 'thrones' were now infamous. With trepidation he quickly scanned the article to see if they printed his stories about the sexual antics that occurred in the tiny bathroom of Bucky Beaver's Magic Garage. Most likely, the Editor deleted the draft text as the truth was too lewd to print.

***

There were additional authors and journalists that were 'taken aback' upon first meeting Dickie. Joe Hurley, author of *Ten Million Steps on Route 6*[37], met Dickie on his first visit to the Indian Burial Ground at Scargo Lake. He was eager to learn the history of Mashantampaine and the local Indians who lived by the lake before the settlers arrived. Dickie proudly drove him around the village to show points of interest such as Scargo Tower and what had been Nobscusset Harbor.

Also, it was important to Dickie that he demonstrate the unfortunate changes that had occurred over the past twenty years, specifically the razing of quaint, ivy-covered cottages along the shore, only to be replaced with mansions such as the monolith built at the north end of Bridge Street.

Dickie vehemently described how wealthy, off-Cape people ('wash-ashores' they're sometimes called) had moved into his village and constructed these mansions '…to show us how to live. Their twenty-bedroom structures look like hotels – terrible!'

No doubt the traveling author remembered Dickie's passion for maintaining local consistency, probably stronger than a physical image of Dennis.

Ping Pong with a Tea Bag

Teens would often play ping pong in the basement of Carleton Hall and Dickie would frequently stop by to share wisdom and collect local gossip. He was in his twenties and the kids would speak candidly with him because they thought he was 'cool', always riding a motorcycle or driving a flashy car.

These kids are middle-aged or older now but they still remember Dickie being an excellent ping pong player, a skill acquired during his two years of Air Force duty in Japan. The image that's most vivid in people's mind is Dickie playing with a Tetley tea bag in his mouth with the string and small cardboard square hanging out. Very unnerving for his opponents.

And who can forget the Tetley slogan, 'Time out for *tiny little tea leaves* in Tetley Tea'.

Giant Tuna in a Station Wagon

Dickie occasionally caught giant bluefin tuna in Cape Cod Bay and around Race Point in Provincetown. Some fish were landed by rod and reel; others via harpooning. All were between 400 and 1,000 pounds. In the '80s when the Japanese sushi market began tapping into the U.S. Atlantic fishing industry, prices for fresh bluefin skyrocketed. Sushi buyers sometimes paid in excess of $30,000 for a single fish.

The price per pound for bluefin varied greatly depending upon the quality of the raw meat and the time in the buying season, with fish caught early in the summer bringing very high prices due to basic supply-and-demand economics. Age (hours) since catch and keeping the raw tuna cool were the most important factors affecting quality and thus price.

One afternoon after landing a huge tuna, Dickie negotiated an acceptable price per pound for his fish but the wholesale buyer was deducting a ridiculous cost for commercial transport of the fish from Sesuit Harbor to the Fresh Water Fish Company in Boston, where the tuna would be packed with ice inside a 'tuna coffin' for rapid shipment to Japan.

Dickie insisted that he'd make the delivery in his own station wagon to eliminate the major shipping cost. His first challenge was to get the large tuna in the back of his car. With a bit of persuasion, Dickie enlisted a group of strong men to lift the fish head-first into the back of his station wagon. The initial lift was accomplished but most of the eight-foot-long fish was still hanging out of the vehicle. Pushing the fish forward by its tail was not feasible.

Clever Dickie looked at his friends with a smile and said, 'I'll do the rest.' He climbed into the front seat and started driving across the harbor parking lot at about fifteen miles per hour. Everyone watched then suddenly saw him hit the brakes abruptly. The tuna slid forward just as Dickie had planned but the huge beast slammed into the back of his seat, pinning him between the seat and the steering wheel. Unfazed, he had the guys yank the fish backward so he had room to drive the car, then he gave the thumbs-up sign and headed for Boston.

Attempted Sting on Dickie

One summer afternoon Dickie was sitting on his boat with his friend Jon Gordon when a Hippie kind of guy walked down the dock toward them. He came up to the gunnel and said, "Which one of you Cats, hey, which one of you Cats is Dickie Buck?"

"I am. What's up? What can I do for ya?" Dickie replied.

"My name is Sonny Boy. Sonny Boy Decalashero. And I got your name and number from a couple of colored dudes over at a party in Hyannis."

"What, what are you talking about? A couple colored dudes? What are you here for?"

"I want some grass, you know, whatever kind of drugs you have, whatever I can get."

"How'd you get my name?" Dickie was getting annoyed with the apparent nonsense.

"I got your name from a couple colored dudes."

"Ya? When was this?"

"Uh, I don't know. What's the deal, can you help me out? What's the deal?"

"What's your name? What's your name?" Dickie started pressing.

"Sonny Boy. Sonny Boy."

"Sonny Boy. What's your last name?"

"Decalashero."

"Decalashero? Spell your last name, Mother Fucker!" Dickie was heated at this point.

"I don't have to prove myself to anyone. I'm not spelling my name in front of any witnesses."

Dickie snapped back. "Not in front of any witnesses? Then take me for a ride. And I'll pay for the gas." Dickie was ready to take this kid out of sight and beat the shit out of him.

Sonny Boy shook his head and walked away.

Dickie hollered, "And you go back and tell Bill Kelly and Pat Patton they're a couple of fucking assholes."

Sure enough, policeman Bill Kelly called Dickie the next day... "Hey Buckie. We got your message, we got your message."

They were laughing about their attempted 'sting' but certainly were trying to set Dickie up, suspecting he was selling some kind of contraband drugs, which was not the case. They wanted his ass but Dickie was both not-guilty and smarter than their plan.

Inverted Cigarettes

Dickie quit smoking at age twenty-nine and wisely, never lit up again. But this didn't stop him from keeping an unlit cigarette in his mouth. To gain the attention of anyone standing nearby, he'd insert the wrong end of his unlit Marlboro cigarette into his mouth with the filter visible. Secretly, he was sucking on the tobacco in his mouth.

They'd be alarmed and say 'Hey, you've got that cigarette backward in your mouth!'

His reply, 'I know it. You should try it, it's great this way...I love it, they all should be this way.'

Most people found this behavior strange; thus, Dickie had succeeded with his intended shock factor.

The added truth is that when Dickie stopped smoking, cold-turkey, he had to fight off his nicotine addiction. Placing an unlit cigarette in his mouth with the non-filtered end under his tongue actually provided access to the ground tobacco leaves and nicotine. A clever solution.

The Fruit Fly

Extensive entomological research has proven that common fruit flies (Drosophila melanogaster) are attracted by alcohol emitted by decaying fruit left in the open. They can sense the smell for miles, seemingly to appear out of thin air.

Many people have likened Dickie with the common fruit fly because of his uncanny ability to arrive wherever pretty girls have just appeared, sometimes with no delay. Do girls give off a scent that only he can detect for great distances; their equivalent of alcohol emitted by the fruit? Possibly so. Dickie would certainly enjoy conducting such an experiment.

Or maybe his omnipresent lifestyle is the key. He often hangs out at the Northside Marina or Sesuit Café talking with friends and watching the many boats pass through the narrow channel. During warm summer months, boats often have music playing loudly and pretty, bikini-clad girls dancing and singing on deck. Who wouldn't notice? And Dickie is smart enough to know that if a boat is heading south in the channel, it'll only be a few minutes before it arrives at the town dock and needs assistance with lines. And the tipsy girls could use a helping hand as they step off the boat; some might even need to be lifted up and carried ashore. Chivalrous Dickie is always there to help, with a big smile. He's provided this assistance for decades, to the humor of many jealous men standing on shore. 'Damned Dickie Buck!'

***

'Johnny on the spot' – another description of Dickie, by many who know him well. He's always there to help people. And if there's fun anywhere or a party brewing, he'll be there in a flash with uncanny skill for premonitions.

'If there's a good piece of ass somewhere, he'll show up.'

'He must have a periscope on his boat. He'd always show up when there were pretty girls around.'

Dog on Top of the Oil Truck

While Dickie was working for the oil company doing home deliveries, a competitor oil company initiated an advertising campaign showing a dog standing guard over its clients. Without speaking to his boss, Dickie decided it would be fun to compete with the dog advertisement and drive around with his own dog on top of the tank truck. He had to out-do his competitor and get some laughs.

His advertising campaign lasted for only a short while and he was very careful to drive slowly as he loved his dog and would never have put him in harm's way. Double leashes on his pooch added full protection.

Girls Skinny Dipping at Corporation Beach

Another one of the village boys was

Nate Howes, Jimmy's son and nephew of Anson. Nate's life was fairly simple and he hadn't had much luck with girls in his early years. After High School he joined the Army and when discharged, he bought a nice new Chevrolet convertible; a small coup.

Dickie would ride around with Nate in his new car, sometimes driving down to Corporation Beach at night because he knew that girls that worked at the Cape Playhouse would sometimes go skinny dipping at the beach. Of course, Dickie knew these types of things.

They'd drive down onto the sand bars at low tide, grab the girls' clothes when they were in the water, then drive up to the high-water mark and wait. When they saw the girls coming out of the water, searching for their clothes and shrieking, the boys would turn the car's headlights on to see the naked bodies running around. Eventually the boys returned their clothes. Harmless fun.

Water Skiing at Night

Dickie and his friends enjoyed water skiing during summer months and always had cute girls or female lifeguards with them. One night around 2 a.m. they decided to go waterskiing in the Bay. Cleverly, they attached five Ray-O-Vac red floating flashlights on the ski belt around Dickie's waist. The purpose was solely for relocation of Dickie if he fell and lost his grasp of the tow rope.

As a skilled skier, he readily got up and was having a great time. His friends in the boat could see him well as they motored near the jetties and Tautog Rock. The driver dumped him a couple times for laughs, as is standard procedure.

Next, Dickie said 'Take me wide open through the harbor and drop me in front of the *Albatross* fishing boat.' It was unfortunate that lots of people weren't around to see Dickie come whizzing through the harbor wearing his flashing-red ski belt. The storyteller didn't comment on whether Dickie was still wearing a bathing suit.

Clamming with Heavy Equipment

In the old days, men would take their horse and drawn wagon out on the sand flats for clamming. The weight of the horse's hooves and wagon wheels would make nearby clams squirt high. Dickie would walk behind the wagon, dig those that had blown their cover and pitch them onto the back of the wagon. No bucket nor burlap bag needed.

Another time, Dickie was out on Chapin Beach clamming without a wagon. As he dug a dozen clams, he'd make a pile so he could easily spot them when the tide was rising. Along came Anson Howes from behind, who started taking Dickie's clams. 'Hey, don't pick up my clams.' he hollered to the old man.

'Oh, I didn't know those was your clams.' as if the clams had dug themselves out of the sand and gathered in a pile.

Kindly, Dickie replied, 'Go ahead and keep 'em.' knowing he could dig up dozens of others.

***

Years later, Dickie and his friends would drive a farm tractor out on the clam flats to aid the collection procedure. The tractor had a single-bladed farrow plow towed behind. This was very effective for tilling a swath of sand as the tractor was left in low range at idle speed and pointed to the far end of the sand bar. Dickie would walk behind as spotter. When a clam was seen, they'd stop the tractor and dig in the general vicinity for more clams as the original was often broken by the plow's spade.

When they had collected a large number of clams, one of the men drove the tractor to shore but made the mistake of driving directly toward the high-water mark. This route took him through troughs of very deep water that often exist between high sand bars. He should have steered from bar to bar which would have kept the tractor out of deep water.

When the tractor encountered water, the fan blades threw saltwater over the engine distributor, spraying the coil and spark plug wires and immediately stalling the engine. The tide was coming in fast and the tractor was dead. A bad situation and only minutes to spare before the whole tractor would be under water. Four of the men rolled the tractor by hand up onto the nearest sand bar. When they tried restarting the engine, the starter turned over but the engine would not start because of the wet ignition system.

They next dipped a rag into the gas tank, doused gas all over the engine and lit it on fire. This seems like a crazy move but they were easily able to throw water over the engine to extinguish it when they wanted. As intended, the heat of the fire dried out the wires and the engine started right up. So that this problem wouldn't happen again, they cut the fan belt so that when the fan blades turned, they wouldn't splash water all over. By then, the tide had risen considerably and they encountered deep water a few more times, but the clever guys were able to get the tractor to shore.

**

On another occasion when Dickie was using heavy equipment for clamming with friends off the Brewster flats, they encountered a case of Champagne that presumably, had been buried back in the Bootlegging days. That region was notorious for liquor smuggling because there were few houses or roads on the shore for spotters of the illegal activity.

Dickie and his friends decided not to donate the cherished case to the local historical museum.

Echo Chamber in Scargo Tower

Dickie enjoyed playing the trumpet at functions such as at the Church's Sunrise Service, the dedication of Ezra H. Baker School and also at funeral services. But there was added enjoyment for Dickie when he could annoy others with his horn. Quite often, he'd drive up to Scargo Tower at three in the morning and play his trumpet at full volume while standing inside. He loved the sound in the cylindrical rock-and-concrete tower because it was an effective echo chamber.

Selectman Earle Davidson finally put his foot down and prohibited Dickie from playing in the middle of the night.

Telephone Pole Linemen are Good Beer Can Openers

Dickie and his friends had considerable experience drinking and driving but occasionally one of the 'birdbrains' would forget the beer can opener. This was before the invention of screwcaps on beer bottles and flip-tops on beer cans. Someone had to carry a 'church key' to puncture the can's top with the triangular metal tool.

On one joyride to Hyannis, they had a fine stock of full beer cans in the car but were ill-equipped for opening them. Driving down the road, Dickie spotted a lineman climbing a telephone pole at the side of the road. He stopped his car, hopped out and caught the attention of the lineman who was up the pole working on wires. Dickie signaled for him to descend, to the confusion of the worker. When he was nearly at ground level, Dickie grasped the man's boot and used the pole-climbing spike which was attached to the inner side of his boot, as an effective beer can opener. Very resourceful drinkers these boys were! Of course, they opened a good supply of cans before they departed.

Undercover Cop at Scargo Tower

In 1971 a new housing development was proposed upon land immediately to the north of Scargo Tower. This perturbed many locals because they felt it would detract from the pristine hill covered only with bushes and scrub pines. Worse yet, some felt the entire hill was sacred land of the Nobscussets and should not be altered.

When the housing project received approval, the developer installed a large sign indicating the project plans and development map, beside the road to the tower. Thereafter, all people who went to visit the tower encountered the sign and some were angered by the plan.

At 10 p.m. one summer evening, three boys in their early twenties drove up to the tower with a plan to destroy the sign. They decided to vandalize it as an expression of their distaste for the project and representing others who shared their resentment of the development plan.

When they approached, another car was parked by the tower but it soon pulled away when one of the boys started using his double-sided, long-handled axe to destroy the four-by-eight-foot plywood sign.

Bad timing for these boys, however. An off-road motorcycle roared up the hill and caught them in the act of vandalism. The helmeted rider quickly flashed his badge and directed the boys to meet him at the police station where officers would review their act of vandalism.

One of the boys immediately feared his summer employment at the Town Highway Department would be terminated and he'd have no income to support his college tuition. This thought was soon cast aside by his self-righteous fervor and he readily agreed to meet the police and atone for his actions in the spirit of historic preservation.

The biker sped away while the Volkswagen containing the three boys headed toward the police station. They drove along Routes 6A, 134 and 28 to reach the police station in West Dennis. At one point, a motorcycle drove past them but the boys were unsure whether it was their "arresting officer". As they neared the station, the boys discussed the fact that the biker had disappeared. Rather than turn themselves in, unaccompanied by the biker, they opted not to stop at the station.

A few months later, one of the perpetrators was describing the event to a friend and the immediate reply was that the biker was surely Dickie Buck. There was no proof but who other than Dickie would have made this type of Citizen's Arrest?

When Dickie was Harbormaster, he was required to carry a badge identifying himself as a Special Police Officer. Do you suppose?

Perilous Barbershop

During Dickie's heydays, he'd try to stay away from police whenever possible. The local barber, Pete Peterson, remembers one day when Police Chief Earl Whittemore was in the chair getting his regular trim. Dickie walked in, saw the Chief in the Chair, looked at the barber and back at the Chief then quickly bolted out the door without speaking a word. His intuition knew that close proximity with the police could only lead to trouble.

Dickie always referred to the proprietor of the barbershop as 'Ali Barber', making the amusing connection with the famed Arabian Nights tale *Ali Baba and the Forty Thieves* and their familiar command to the stone cave: 'Open Sesame'.

Returning from Mike Dubin's Wedding

Mike Dubin was one of Dickie's closest friends, having spent much time together before, during and after Dickie ran the Sinclair gas station at the Players Plaza. When Mike decided to marry Judy, Dickie was certainly eager to participate in the event. He drove to the Temple in Dorchester for the wedding, danced like a professional and drank up a storm. He was the life of the party, as always. When time came for everyone to depart, Mike's mother noticed that Dickie was too buzzed to drive back to Dennis so she asked one of Mike and Judy's best college-enrolled girl friends to drive him in his Jaguar. She too was a friend (albeit non-intimate) of Dickie and shared the concern about his state of inebriation. Dickie had arrived with his big Jaguar Sports Saloon, a beautiful car by all standards, so it seemed to be a nice trip in the making. And this was before he got married so it was not an adulterous plan.

The trip started off with Dickie explaining that his car was low on fuel but that it had an auxiliary tank that would get them home if the main tank went dry. Likely necessary as it was too late to find an open gas station. And the car had no brakes, except for the hand-operated emergency brake which grabbed on the right rear wheel only. For the ride, Dickie chose to operate the brake as she drove the car and controlled the pedals.

Another complication was that it was snowing hard. About five inches had accumulated on the highway by the time they reached the Cape bridge. Other than that, the drive started off uneventfully.

Driving on the Mid-Cape Highway, they made it to Marstons Mills before the main tank ran out of gas. Dickie was too buzzed to remember the lever for the auxiliary gas tank so he decided they should just spend the night in the car and wait for assistance to arrive in the morning. Immediately, his mind shifted to the goal of 'scoring' with her (a first time) so he said 'Let's get in the back seat. They had run out of gas on the side of the road so why not? It totally made sense to Dickie.

She wanted nothing to do with Dickie pawing at her. Her reply was 'No thank you, Mr. Buck! I'll be walking home.'

Her brother and two of his friends also were returning from the wedding, in route to Dennis in a separate car. They knew she was riding back to the Cape with Dickie and were following, likely a few miles back. When they saw Dickie's Jaguar on the side of the road in Marstons Mills, they all laughed, suspecting Dickie was having his way with her, or at least trying. They decided to leave the two 'lovebirds' alone and drove past.

Meanwhile, back in the Jaguar, Dickie figured his female driver knew where she was and it couldn't have been too far a walk it that's what she proposed to do. He climbed into the back seat, with intentions of sleeping until morning. His chivalry sure was lacking as he watched her step out of the car in the snowstorm, still dressed in high fashion and heels.

A few minutes later, a car stopped to pick her up. She was kind enough to encourage Dickie to ride with them rather than leave him in the car to freeze for the night. The good Samaritan driver took the couple to the taxi stand in Hyannis, from which they obtained a ride to her brother's home in Dennis village. When she and Dickie told their side of the story, the brother felt bad that he had driven right past Dickie's disabled Jaguar on the highway. He and Dickie found a can of gas and returned to the Jaguar to retrieve the car in the storm.

Dickie's late evening was very unsatisfying but the ending could have been much worse. Never the less, his memories of the wedding were grand.

Trumpet for Easter Sunrise Service

The Dennis Union Church had a long tradition of conducting 'Sunrise Service' atop Scargo Hill on Easter Sunday. The Pastor would conduct the service as the sun rose over the eastern Cape. To add to the effect, Dickie played 'Amazing Grace' and other worship songs on his trumpet as the sun first shone above the horizon.

Dickie remembers these mornings fondly, except for one morning when the temperature was well below freezing. The liquid that dripped from the horn's spit tube created three-inch-long icicles. Not a pleasant horn-blowing ceremony.

Winter Siege of Sesuit Harbor

By definition, a siege is a military operation in which forces surround a building or town to cut off essential supplies, forcing the locals to relinquish control.

In the mid-1900s Dennis had adequate roads for transport of food and common goods to supply the local population. Thus, Sesuit Harbor was not an essential supply route nor lifeline for the village. Regardless, Dickie and a best friend decided they would 'Lay Siege' to Sesuit Harbor. This plan must have been concocted with assistance of alcohol because they decided to block the outer channel to Sesuit Harbor during mid-January.

It was frightfully cold as the men sat near the ends of opposite jetties with the large hawser spanning the channel and attached to huge boulders. They cared not whether the single line would prevent passage; rather, it was all about symbolism. Had Hillary Clinton been on-scene, she surely would have proclaimed 'What difference at this point does it make?' And she would have been right, this time, as no boats were planing to enter or leave Sesuit on those January days.

This event was not publicized but it actually occurred, and likely the last time such an operation was conducted at Sesuit.

Ladder to a Girlfriend's Bedroom

When Dickie was in his early twenties, he was in love' with a beautiful girl who lived on Mashantum Road. His recollection: 'Everyone thought she was gorgeous; they'd stop what they were doing to watch her walk by.'

She initially owned a Triumph, then went to a Corvette and another Corvette and more. Dickie was friends with her for a number of years prior to his marriage.

One night he was going to visit her at the house but her parents were to be there so Dickie devised a plan that he'd climb into her second story window. He drove his dump truck to a yard on Whig Street and walked to her house carrying his long ladder. He climbed up and looked into her bedroom but it was totally dark as she was not there so he climbed down to ground level.

When he attempted to take the ladder away, the bottom was stuck in the snow. With a strong yank he freed up the bottom but as it jumped away from the house, the top of the ladder slid rapidly downward and the tips of the ladder made a loud machine-gun-like sound as it crossed each shingle bottom.

Dickie looked at the front of the house and there in the doorway was the father standing, looking back. And out the door came their two dogs. Dickie started running down the road with the ladder on his shoulder and the dogs chasing close behind. He ran all the way to Edgar Bearse III's house on Pilgrim Road.

Dickie's Trained Dogs

The expression Man's Best Friend certainly applies to Dickie. He loves dogs 'But not more than people'. And he's proud that his dogs are always well trained. Everyone knows that Dickie has deep emotions about his dogs.

He's had many, of various sizes and numerous breeds over the years and they all were his best friend. Definitely too many to identify here but his ability to train them is worth mentioning, in some cases downright amusing. And there were times when his dogs misbehaved as well.

Dickie had a red Irish Setter that he took into the Sesuit Café one crowded afternoon. The dog was being rambunctious like most Setters are.

He hollered "Hey, whose dog is that?" and pretended it was not his.

A friend of Dickie spotted him with a new dog one year. "What's the name of your dog?"

"Dog."

Another time he let his dog into a local store but the dog was a mess, all muddy and dripping. Before anyone could say anything, he burst out, 'Who let that dog in here? Damn dog.'

Some people are amazed how well his dogs are trained. Jon Gordon described it, with some humor sprinkled in: 'The dog doesn't blink until he tells him to blink. And the dog will hold his breath for twenty minutes then pass out, unless Dickie tells him to breathe.' A bit of intended exaggeration but the gist is correct; his dogs obey his orders.

Dickie's little dog Maxine would ride around in front of him, sitting on the fuel tank of his motorcycle. If anyone did that now, the driver would be arrested.

On occasion, Dickie would bring his dog into an office waiting room where a friend worked. He'd order his dog to 'Go over and take that woman's purse'. The dog would obey and bring the purse to his side. 'Just another outlandish thing Dickie would do in public. No harm meant; just his way to initiate more shock, then laughs. No one would get mad at outlandish Dickie.

The girls at the local bank loved Dickie's dog and would let him inside the restricted area to visit and have some treats. Another of his dogs would take orders amazingly well, such that Dickie could point across the bank's lobby and the dog would go to the specific chair, sit and wait until called.

More Antics at Local Banks

Over the period of many years, the Office Manager of the Cape Cod Cooperative Bank, Maryann Smithers, got to know Dickie well. She learned that many of his visits were accompanied by amusing antics; definitely not harmful or threatening to the bank. One day, Dickie entered the local Branch wearing wild clothes and hysterical glasses. A relatively new Bank Teller was the first employee to spot Dickie coming through the front door. Her first reaction was that this odd individual was going to be a problem, possibly a bank robber in disguise. 'Of course, no one from the East Dennis area would dress like this during a normal day.' she thought. Fortunately, the Manager noticed that the girl was about to pick up the phone to call the police but she stopped her in time. 'It's only Dickie Buck. He's harmless. Hello Mr. Buck, how are you today?'

Dickie remembers another time when he and his best friend, Peter Alby, were conducting 'pest removal' at Hudson Eldridge's large barn which was located next to the Cooperative Bank in East Dennis. The barn's rafters were littered with pigeons that continually 'painted' everything situated beneath their roosting point. The birds were definitely a menace. The two male problem solvers proceeded to fetch their air rifles and blast puffs of wind at the stubborn pigeons. One by one, the birds reluctantly left their perch and flew out of the barn.

One bird had an injured wing but managed to fly out and land on the roof of the adjacent bank building. Of course, the boys felt it was their duty to rescue the distressed pigeon.

They climbed through the thick bushes then into the garden behind the bank. When they reached a clearing, they were located at the window of the Teller who assists drive-up patrons. She was shocked and instantly screamed as she was preparing to push the Panic Button that calls the police. The bank Manager saw that it was Dickie outside the window and quickly hollered to the Teller, 'No, No, No, don't do it.' She had to plead with the girl Teller not to call the police. The boys were just attempting to get the wounded bird off the bank's roof.

Home Run through DPM's Window

Across the street from the Dennis Public Market, there's a small public playground at the apex between the southern ends of Nobscussett and New Boston Roads. For decades this park has been used as a make-shift baseball field despite its limited width and length. When boys place home plate at the extreme north end of the park, it's possible for teen athletes to hit the ball over the southern fence. But hitting a ball onto Route 6A is another matter.

There's a legend that Dickie was the only boy to hit a ball completely over 6A and through the window of the Dennis Public Market. Maybe other boys will make a similar claim as they read this milestone.

Emergency Diving to Assist Others

There was a summer resident who was an executive of a major, international wristwatch company. He owned a boat, kept it moored at Sesuit and became a friend of Dickie, like everyone does. One day he was showing his own, quite spectacular, watch to a friend and accidently dropped it into the harbor.

Of course, he contacted Dickie immediately and asked if he could attempt to find his watch on the bottom. Always cooperative Dickie jumped in the water right away and made a few attempts, but no luck. He complained that it was dark at the bottom and there was no visibility. A few more dives and still no luck.

"Sorry, I just can't find it. The damn mud is so horrible down there."

Two more dives and he came to the surface exasperated. But when he lifted his hand out of the water, the man's watch was shining brightly on Dickie's wrist. Dickie had actually found it on his first dive but he wanted to make it look like he worked very hard to make the discovery.

That was Dickie's kind of humor. He'd go out of his way to help someone, often at his own physical expense, but he always added the element of surprise and end the escapade on a humorous note. The consummate showman.

***

A similar diving request arose, for Dickie to recover the false teeth of an old man who had a boat moored at the south end of the harbor. Not a valuable prize nor was there money involved, but Dickie saved the day regardless.

***

A wealthy East Dennis resident had a sailboat in the harbor. One day he had an executive on board, from the nation's largest soft-drink manufacturer. The guest accidently dropped his watch in the harbor. The resident contacted Dickie and begged for him to recover the watch of his important friend. 'It doesn't matter what it costs. If you can find that watch, we'll pay you.' The expensive watch had been given to his friend by his Army buddies for whom he was their Commanding Officer, and they had the watch engraved for him in 1945. Even more sentimental value than its street price.

It took two days of diving but Dickie finally found the watch. There was no visibility at the bottom and all he could do was feel around with his hands for the small object. Junk, live crabs, eels and all sorts of things were in arms reach. Back and forth he scoured, like a tractor working rows in a planted field. No visibility at all and he only had a general idea of where it may lie.

Dickie was happy he finally found it and proudly presented it to the resident, who later gave it to the owner. For two days of diving effort, Dickie received $75 from the big-time executive. And the resident said 'You'll never have to buy any soda again.' Which implied the soda executive would keep Dickie supplied with soft-drinks for life. A few days later, ten cases of soda were delivered to Dickie's gas station and that was the end of it; nothing later.

Dickie was rightly pissed-off because the soda had a value of about twenty dollars but the executive likely got it for free. Cheap bastard!

***

A large boat berthed at the private marina in Sesuit Harbor incurred a problem with its shafts or propellers. It was a Sunday and with the marina closed, the boat owner could not obtain repair assistance. A local man suggested that he call Dickie Buck because he might be willing to make the repair under water if it was a simple problem like replacement of a sacrificial anode zinc.

Dickie was available and came to the marina within the hour. His proposal:

"I'd do the work for $50 but I can't do it today because it's Sunday."

"Well, I'll give you $100 if you do it today."

Dickie agreed. He dove down to assess the problem and returned to the surface in a few minutes. "I'll need a Phillips-head screwdriver."

The owner went to his car to fetch a screwdriver from the toolbox in his car. He returned with the tool and Dickie dove beneath the boat again. Soon, he surfaces and makes another request, "I need a pair of pliers." Next, it was a wrench he needed.

This was taking considerable time with repeated trips to the car for one tool at a time.

Finally, Dickie completed the repair and the owner gave him $100 and departed.

A friend of Dickie who had been watching this whole production said

'I don't get it. First you needed a screwdriver, then pliers, then other tools. Why didn't you just use an adjustable wrench rather than have that guy make all the trips for individual tools?'

"Oh Christ, I had it fixed in five minutes. If I'm going to charge him $100, I've got to stay down for a while."

***

Dickie was once summoned to the harbor because a resident reported that a body had washed in. The Dennis Police always considered Dickie the Go-To man when it came to underwater search and recovery on the north side. But on this occasion, it was a bit of a false alarm because what had washed up was only a box containing someone's cremation ashes. Not a big problem.

***

It wasn't all fun and games for Dickie when it came to his emergency diving assistance but he never declined an official request for assistance. Once he had to bring a drowned clam digger ashore who had been caught in the rising tide off Chapin Beach.

Another time he had to Scuba dive to recover the body of a college-aged girl who was in a boating accident off Dennis. Apparently, the boat had four occupants and was anchored from the stern rather than the bow. The weather quickly turned bad and the seas rose and swamped the boat. Some of the occupants were saved but two persons were drowned. A very sad accident.

The Poisoning of Scargo Lake

In the early '60s, the Massachusetts State Fish and Game Department decided that Scargo Lake had sufficient depth and water quality for hatchery-raised trout to survive the Cape's cold winters. The first step in the 'stocking' process was to rid the lake of all other fish and block the upstream end of Sesuit Creek so herring could not enter the lake for their spring spawning season.

Rotenone was and still is a federally approved piscicide for killing nuisance fish. After the poison was introduced to the lake, it was a major undertaking to remove all the dead fish that rose to the surface or lay on the bottom. Of course, the local Authorities coordinating the fish project called Dickie for assistance. Without hesitation, he agreed to do the job. Money wasn't the driver for Dickie; for him it was about doing something out of the ordinary. Neither the scale of the project nor the potential of skin burns or poisoning scared him off.

For the fish collection operation, Dickie donned his full Scuba gear and was towed on a rope behind a small motor boat. A simple procedure but many fish were collected.

National Dickie Buck Day

From his early days, Dickie amassed many friends who enjoyed his humor and pranks. A few of the most daring friends have sought opportunities to play jokes on him. One April 27th (his birthday), his closest friends from the Players Pharmacy decided to surprise him and celebrate his life and contributions for their enjoyment.

They constructed a large banner proclaiming 'National Dickie Buck Day' and posted it in the front window of the Pharmacy. Additionally, they made a large collage of everyone's favorite photos of Dickie in various states of dress, activities and mayhem. These items were hidden until the special day. The organizer also had made prior contact with local newspapers and lined up photographers and media representatives to be on-scene for his important arrival.

With this being a surprise party, the challenge was to get Dickie to arrive at the Pharmacy at the correct time. One of his closest friends, Judy Scarafile the Pharmacist, had to concoct a story about a having a secret job interview she had to attend. In the fib, her car had broken down and it was imperative that he come to the Pharmacy at a specific time to covertly shuttle her to the interview.

Upon arrival, Dickie was met with great fanfare (on a village scale). About twenty people were hiding inside the Pharmacy and gave him a rambunctious cheer when he approached the big front steps.

Given Dickie's extroverted personality, everyone would expect him to welcome the focus on he but that is not the case; he was angry with the surprise celebration. They escorted him inside and had him sit on a makeshift throne where they crowned him King for National Dickie Buck Day.

His friends celebrated Dickie because he had always been a giving person for all. But he only enjoys being on the 'giving end'; never on the receiving end. More of his caring personality will be apparent in a later Chapter that focuses on his generosity.

Harbormaster's Safety Procedure

Dickie was the Sesuit Harbormaster for many years, back in the days when the job paid $1,600 per year, there was no paid Assistant, nor vehicle or boat provided. It was a 24/7 job for at least six months per year. If there was a problem in the middle of the night in the harbor or out in Cape Cod Bay, Dickie would get the call.

It certainly was a thankless job but Dickie loved it and each year, hundreds of people appreciated his willingness to help everyone, his practical abilities and his ever-present humor.

Prior to the arrival of winter, Dickie would haul out all the floating piers and store them in the parking lot, as is done today. Only the pilings would remain when the harbor froze over.

Even without being paid during winter months, Dickie would always try to prevent problems from arising. Seeing that the harbor ice was exceptionally thick one year, he was concerned that the strong ice could grasp a piling and lift it up and out of the mud on a rising

tide. Often, boys would hang around the harbor offering to help Dickie on small projects, just for the opportunity to learn practical skills. Dickie decided to use a boy's help to cut the ice from around the pilings. He gave the boy a chainsaw to use but was concerned that he could fall into the newly cut hole around the piling. As a safety precaution, Dickie tied a four-foot-long wooden board across the boy's ass so that if he accidently fell into the hole, at least he couldn't go far under the ice.

This safety procedure probably didn't make it into the OSHA manual for winter maintenance but it was another example of Dickie finding a practical method for ensuring the safety of those who worked for him.

Halloween

Each Halloween evening, children roamed freely around the village for Trick-or-Treating and there was nothing to fear. Likewise, parents knew there was nothing to fear locally, except their own mistakes.

When the night got to be very late, the elder-teen pranksters would come out-of-the-woodwork to perform their Halloween antics. Home windows, businesses and school buses were soaped and miles of toilet paper were thrown over houses and across power lines along Route 6A. The younger men and teens would go house-to-house stealing pumpkins from doorsteps after the Trick or Treaters had gone to bed and parents had turned out the lights on front porches. Locals affectionately called the orange orbs "punkins". I can still hear Billy King's accent.

Men who had pickup trucks drove slowly down the back roads as the late-night 'pumpkin pickers' quietly ran from door to door. When a truck was full, the driver would head to the Post Office in Goodspeeds Store. The roof over the large front porch was the spot where hundreds of pumpkins would be brought each year. Pumpkins were tossed from the truck to other boys whose job was to wait on the porch roof and catch the orange monsters being thrown up to them. The police knew not to drive by the Post Office late that night.

The next morning, everyone was eager to drive to the Post Office and see how many had been piled up the night before. Everyone hoped they could see their carved beauty in full view. And parents didn't mind having theirs stolen because it meant they didn't have to add the drooling mess to their next trip to the town dump.

One year in the '40s, Charlie Hallett's entire wagon could be seen on the porch roof the morning after Halloween. In less ambitious years, only the Post Office bench accompanied the pumpkins on the roof.

That special night is fondly missed by those of us who grew up in the mid-1900s.

Mischievous Acts

Torching Derelict Boats in Sesuit Marsh

Back in the late '50s, old, abandoned boats would drift to the head of Sesuit Marsh at times of high tide when north winds were strong. On the falling tide, they'd be stranded there, adding to the collection of wooden derelicts and eyesores. At night when no one was watching, Dickie and a mischievous friend, Jimmy Drake, would fill the boats with bales of hay, pour some gas on the pile and set them afire. The boys would hide back near the tree-line of the marsh so they wouldn't be caught when the firetrucks arrived. Of course, the firemen knew which boys had pulled the prank.

Riding a Pilot Whale in Rock Harbor

Prior to enactment of the Marine Mammal Protection Act in 1972, Ad Hoc groups and local citizens would respond when marine mammals were stranded on Cape shores. For example, the Players Pharmacy was a contact point when strandings occurred in the central Cape area. Dickie was one of the key responders for such cases, regardless of season or weather. People knew he was always accessible, ready to help with any task and most importantly, fearless and willing to dive in freezing water if required.

When a citizen or the police from a local town called the Pharmacy with a sighting of a distressed mammal, the employee would immediately run next door to alert Dickie. Without hesitation, he'd throw his homemade wet- or dry suit (depending on the season) in his car and race to the location of the mammal sighting. His friends loved accompanying him on these adventures because there'd surely be a lot of commotion, police sirens and newspaper reporters involved.

Sometimes three or four cars would be close behind Dickie's as he raced to the scene.

One February day there was a call to the Pharmacy reporting that a pilot whale was trapped in Rock Harbor and unable to find its way out of the narrow channel leading to the Bay. Loving the excitement and visibility of another Mammal Rescue Mission, Dickie raced to Rock Harbor, put on his wetsuit and attempted to push the fifteen-foot mammal in the right direction but to no avail. He decided that a more extreme, Plan B, would be required. This was before the days of strict procedures for handling marine mammals. Warning: environmentalists may not wish to read further.

Dickie hopped on the broad back of the pilot whale as it was aimlessly swimming at a slow pace. His weight was insignificant to the animal but Dickie noticed that when he leaned to one side, the whale turned in that direction as it swam slowly forward. He recalls having been able to stay aboard the whale for about eight minutes and steer it closer to the harbor exit but once it reached deeper water, it dove and Dickie had to hop off.

It wasn't much longer before Dickie and many observers watched as the whale swam out the channel and northward into the vast Bay. On the following day, a pod of pilot whales beached themselves in Wellfleet but Dickie hoped his friend was far out to sea.

Spearfishing in Brewster Weirs

Back in the '50s Nathanial Wixon and a few other local fishermen had set up large weirs off Brewster, Dennis

and Barnstable. These primitive fishing apparatuses consisted of tall, thin poles (actually 2-inch diameter, branchless trees) that they hydraulically jetted into the sand flats near the low-water mark. A few dozen poles would be set in a line spaced by about twenty feet, horizontally. Additionally, a large 'bowl' was constructed with poles in a circle, adjacent to the long straight line of poles that were oriented offshore. Small-meshed netting was strung along the vertical poles, making a wall with a single, small opening to the bowl.

When the tide was high, the entire net was immersed and acted as a barrier to fish that were swimming alongshore in either direction. When they encountered the wall, they swam along and most would enter the bowl without realizing it was constructed with a second, inner circle that was very difficult for the fish to navigate their way out. Fish of all sizes entered the bowl and were trapped there, swimming in circles as the tide dropped.

Typically, the weir owner would arrive by boat near the time of low tide to collect the fish that remained in the net. Huge schools of baitfish like herring and mackerel were most common. There were no bluefish in the Bay back in those days. And striped bass were rarely found in the net as they were smart enough to escape during the six hours the tide was dropping. Sometimes, large sharks, ocean sunfish and even bluefin tuna were found in the nets.

Bluefin tuna had no value in those days as the sushi market was unknown to Cape Codders. They were often called 'horse mackerel', derogatorily. Worse yet, they were a major physical problem, often tearing the nets apart with their massive (up to 1,000-pound) size. The weir fishermen would sometimes shoot the tuna but normally they'd use a 4-inch diameter, long-handled circus mallet to whack the tuna on the head to kill them. If not, arms or legs of the fishermen could be broken by the thrashing beasts.

Imagine this maelstrom of swimming monsters in a weir bowl. Along come Dickie and Jimmy Drake in their boat after having come up empty-handed from spearfishing near Tautog Rock. Seeing the weir, they looked at each other and instantly spawned idea of diving into the bowl of the weir. Inside, they'd have their pick from all the fish that swim around and around in the circular net. Both divers climbed into the bowl with their spears loaded but within seconds they had the scare of their lives, with a ten-foot shark and a huge ocean sunfish swimming within a few feet of them. Fearing for their lives, they got out of the net instantly, realizing that was a very bad idea.

Donuts, Lawn Parties, Mailboxing and Golf Ball

Not long after Dickie obtained his Massachusetts Driving License, he and his friends would sometimes do bad things with cars. The more liquor involved, the worse the activities became.

One friend (purposely unnamed) had a great-aunt whose car he was able to borrow for evening rides with Dickie. Most everyone is familiar with the prank called 'doing donuts' which entailed driving a car onto a lawn and riding in tight, fast circles purposely to leave

circular tire marks. The result was to 'leave donuts' on the lawn. Many boys played this game and most got caught.

'Lawn parties' were a big step up on the damage-severity scale; a major problem for the victims. Picture liquored-up boys driving around at night in big cars. When they saw a lawn with outdoor furniture situated in the open area, the driver would immediately turn and run it over. It was essential that one of the perpetrators knew an escape route with their car if they dared venture into a back yard. Being caught would have led to disaster and certain loss of their driving licenses.

Also note that they were driving heavy, near-indestructible cars of the '40s and '50s. Running over an aluminum or wooden lawn chair was no problem for the tough, steel undercarriages. Today's cars would likely incur major damage.

The activity was not focused on homes of enemies; rather, just targets of opportunity. Covertly, they'd pass by the scenes of the crime the next day to see their damage, similar to gangs and graffiti artists returning to walls they had painted the night before.

A similar act of automobile-inflicted vandalism was 'mailboxing' where a car was driven closely past a mailbox located on the side of the road, typically in a private yard. Boxes perched atop thin posts were best (easiest to knock off). As the car was driven by a targeted post, the person in the passenger seat, riding 'shotgun', would open their door at the precise time to knock the mailbox off its post. Damage to the car door seemed not to have been a concern for these boys in their buzzed state. Parents probably made a big deal of it the next morning with their sons aching from their hangovers.

The moment of truth arose when the kid with his hand on the passenger-door handle had to decide 'Is the post too big?' Either the mailbox or the door would win.

An even worse activity was called 'golf ball', when the car was driven onto the finely trimmed grass of a local municipal golf course. Donuts were a dime-a-dozen on fairways but extra points could be gained from perfect circles scribed on the manicured greens. This was the Greenskeeper's biggest nightmare when arriving at sunrise to clear the morning dew from their perfect greens.

One vandal's car got stuck in a green-side sand trap. There were a few minutes when the boys figured they'd be put in jail for years but they managed to dig themselves out and escape before being caught on-scene.

Boys look back at these malicious, alcohol-fueled pranks with much shame. The reason such activities are mentioned here is to illustrate that it was not an uncommon activity back in the mid-1900s. Kids had cars and alcohol was easy to obtain before the legal drinking age. Certainly nothing to be proud of, but recognize that some of your elder male friends or relatives may have been involved in such activities.

Dangerous Activities

Targeting Street Signs

One of Dickie's guy friends buys a used car for a couple hundred dollars from a local Used Car Dealer. The Dealer was a well-known character who always had a great come-back to any question posed by a potential buyer.

From a distance, the car looked great. A big Lincoln convertible, black exterior and red leather interior. The potential buyer asked if it burned very much gas?

"With that tremendous power under the hood, you have to sacrifice a little gaaaaaaas."

"Why are the seats all rotten?" the buyer asked, although he knew he was getting the car for a good price.

"When you pick up girls on the road and they get in this fine car, they immediately commence to climax, and that rots the leather out." Quite a Dealer!

The buyer dared not ask any more questions. That night he offered to drive his new wheels to Boston for a night of fun with Dickie and one other guy aboard. They all were in their twenties.

Of course, they went directly to the Gilded Cage bar, a notorious strip-joint in the Combat Zone of South Boston. They had a raucous time; explanations are not necessary.

The drive back to the Cape was surely going to be eventful and it started by someone saying to the driver, 'Why don't you run over that sign marker on the side of the highway?' It was just a small, temporary sign indicating 'Icy Road'. With a crash, the car easily drove over the sign and kept going, with a car full of laughs and encouragement to look for a bigger sign. They even took turns driving to see who could ruin the biggest sign.

By the time they got to the Cape Cod Canal bridge, they had wiped out a half-dozen signs of progressively larger size. Initially they worried about the top of the signs coming into the car and hitting them on the heads, but it seemed not to be a problem and they had plenty of liquor on board to wash away any further fears.

As they approached Exit 2 on the Mid-Cape Highway, for Route 130, they all spotted the biggest target of the day. A massive sign indicating the entrance to Otis Air Force Base. It was at least four-by-eight-feet in dimensions and mounted on strong, four-by-four-inch wooden posts. A substantial opponent even for the Big Bad Lincoln sign smasher.

Dickie was at the helm and without needing encouragement from his friends, he aimed right for the middle of the sign. A direct hit and it all came down. The guys cheered but saw a police car far in the rear so they immediately got off the highway and took back roads to evade the police. A short distance down the road in

Sandwich, they pulled into someone's driveway and hid as the police car drove past them.

From there it was clear sailing back to East Dennis with one exception. The low-oil indicator light illuminated and the engine started making loud noises. They hadn't realized that one of the broken signposts went under the car and punctured the oil pan at the base of the engine. As they continued to drive home, all the lubricating oil drained from the engine and the sound got louder: 'nukka-nukka-nukka'.

By the time they reached Hudson Eldridge's house, there was no oil remaining in the engine crankcase. It was totally seized up and kaput. They had left a trail of oil along their entire route from Exit 2 on the Highway and now there was barely a trickle coming out when they reached their destination.

The owner was not only disturbed his engine was shot and the front-end of his nice Lincoln was all smashed, he most feared that the police could track the oil and the car's paint from the broken signs. Maybe he'd end up in jail and owe thousands for the damaged signs?

Without discussion, he hid the car behind Hudson's garage and immediately went to work cutting the car into pieces using an acetylene-oxygen torch. When he was done, they used Hudson's Ford tractor with its front-end-loader bucket to dig a deep hole then dump all traces of the car inside and cover it up.

The car was totally gone in less than twenty-four hours of when he bought it. These guys certainly were tough on their wheels!

Lost at Sea with the Coast Guard Officer's Daughter Aboard

Dickie has always been spiritual and he attended church regularly in his early years. Possibly atoning for his many (and ongoing) sins? He vividly recalls the first time he 'talked to God' when he was lost in the Bay aboard his small duck boat, expecting to die. It was a desperate plea from an eleven-year-old, promising that he'd never again be bad if God would save him. It worked or so he thought.

The second time he talked to God was more desperate, while lost in the Bay again and close to dying.

"This time God, I'm not kidding. I mean, I really will be better if you don't let me die." He explained that he didn't want to "use up many God pleas" but it was essential.

"I know I fooled you the first time, but this time I'm serious."

***

One late-summer day, Dickie took a group of guy friends out in the Bay on a spontaneous drinking cruise aboard the 31-ft Huckins cruiser that he and Hudson Eldridge co-owned. It was an enjoyable time aboard *Shirley* until they accidently hit a rock with one of the propellers. The boat started taking on water but Dickie couldn't find the source of the leak. He figured they'd just use the manual bilge pump every so often to keep the water-level below the floorboards. With a pretty good buzz, they came ashore at 4 p.m. and put the *Shirley* on its mooring in Sesuit Harbor.

Later, Dickie had to say goodbye to his pretty girlfriend from New York. To take his mind off the sadness of her departure, he invited a good friend and his girlfriend out for an evening cruise. Still dressed smartly in his sports jacket and overcoat, he also invited a nice girl who lived down the street from the Sinclair gas station where he worked. She was not another girlfriend; rather, he knew her family well as they had three boys who he had spent time with over the years. The father was a bit intimidating to Dickie because he was a Chief in the Coast Guard.

Around 8 p.m. Dickie borrowed a small open boat from the gas dock at the private marina. It was a lapstreak Penn Yan with an outboard motor on the back. He used the boat to shuttle his three friends out to the *Shirley* that was still on its harbor mooring. Once aboard, they headed out through the jetties to enjoy an evening cruise off Sesuit, then anchored about a mile north of the jetties. Eventually, they decided it was time to return to shore but the *Shirley*'s engine wouldn't start due to a dead battery. That was the beginning of a long evening for all.

Dickie was not rattled by this minor challenge because they had towed the Penn Yan behind the *Shirley* rather than leave it on the mooring for their return. Dickie chose to ride the small boat back to Sesuit Harbor to get a fresh battery from the gas station that would later become his Magic Garage.

His lady friend decided to hop in the small boat and take the ride ashore with Dickie. Before they departed, Dickie instructed his guy friend to use the manual bilge pump regularly, so the *Shirley* wouldn't fill with water. A few days later, it was determined that during his afternoon cruising, a bolt had come out of the propeller strut upon impact with the rock. The small hole could easily have been filled but Dickie hadn't found the source of the leak earlier. Nonchalantly he told his friend that he'd be back in less than an hour, so the manual pumping would not be exhausting.

The good plan took a turn for the worst when the outboard motor ran out of gas before Dickie and the girl reached the harbor. They immediately started drifting offshore under the influence of a stiff south wind. Dickie knew it was unlikely they'd drift exactly back to the *Shirley* and he was correct. They passed within a hundred years of the big boat but he had no way to close the distance. As they reached their closest point, Dickie yelled to his friend, "Keep the water below the floorboards."

The winds and waves were picking up and it kept getting darker as they drifted north to the center of the Bay in the small boat. Dickie knew it was a bad situation. The girl was getting cold in the open boat so he gave her his overcoat.

For a moment, he instinctively thought 'Maybe this will give me an opportunity to get in her pants; a first time with this girl.' Then he quickly came to his senses. 'No God, I'm not going to touch her because I know you'd get mad at me.' Whispering so she wouldn't hear his plea for help, he looked upward and said, "This time God, I'm not kidding. I mean, I really will be better if you don't let me die."

As the hours passed, they were

getting desperate, seemingly alone in the ocean. They were three to four miles offshore and the waves had risen continuously. Dickie was now concerned about stabilizing the boat. He considered disconnecting the outboard engine, tying it to a line and using it as a sea-anchor to keep the bow of the small boat headed southward toward the waves. This plan didn't work because he couldn't unfasten the outboard's mounting bolts from the transom. The biggest irony was that Dickie was unaware that an anchor and a set of oars were just inches out of sight, beneath the boat's wooden, removable deck boards.

"We're going to die, aren't we?" She was very frightened and started to repeat prayers while holding an imaginary rosary. They both were terribly cold in the dark, with a damp wind and high waves pitching the boat around. To seek shelter, they climbed into the small rope locker at the bow of the boat. 'Barely enough room for the two of them snuggled in there.

"We're going to die, aren't we?" she repeated, sobbing. He replied but not with words she wanted to hear.

"Yes, I think so. And I'll tell you how I'm going to do it. I'll take the deepest dive I've ever taken and I won't be able to make it back up to the surface. I'll just see how far down I can go." His response would have been enjoyed by his guy friends over a case of beer but not by the sobbing girl.

She started beating on his chest with her cold, little fists.

Dickie remained pessimistic but told her that a rescue would occur when the sun rose. For the moment he had to focus on keeping the boat afloat while the waves kept splashing over the low gunnel.

The small Penn Yan drifted all night, first to the northwest with the wind, then aimlessly in the central Bay as the winds dropped and the tidal currents rotated at six-hour intervals. Dickie was most concerned they'd drift farther north, between Race Point and Marshfield, effectively 'out the chute' and into broad Massachusetts Bay where the search area was huge.

Aboard the *Shirley*, Dickie's guy friend had to use the manual bilge pump every half-hour, all night long, to prevent sinking. His girlfriend had to massage his shoulders all night, which may have helped their eventual decision to marry. Romance was the last thing on their minds that night.

***

When Hudson visited the harbor after sunrise the next morning, he noticed that his big boat was gone. Quickly, he enlisted a few of his friends, who were already aboard their boats, to head out in the Bay as a search party. Within a few minutes they found the *Shirley* anchored a mile northwest of the jetties. The two passengers were glad to be saved but asked why Dickie hadn't come back out to bring the fresh battery. They were very angry he had abandoned them.

Soon it became clear that Dickie and the girl had not made it back into the harbor. Everyone knew this was terrible news, as both had been out in the small boat the entire night with strong southerly winds and substantial waves on the Bay.

Hudson was good friends with Red Lowther who was Chief of the Race Point Coast Guard Station. He dreaded making the call to Red but had no choice because that was the quickest way to engage the Coast Guard in a full Search and Rescue Mission on the Bay. Nothing less would be acceptable in this grave situation.

"We found my Huckins, the *Shirley*, but Dickie Buck is missing at sea, in a small boat. He's been out on the Bay all night."

"Well, you don't have to worry about him. He's got sea savvy. Yes, he's got savvy."

"But Red, your daughter is with him! It's true, your daughter is out there."

"Oh, Jesus Christ. Oh..." Red was panicked knowing that she and Dickie were lost at sea. Immediately, he engaged the full assets of the Coast Guard in the search: airplanes, boats, DUKWs, everything that was available. Even harbormasters of all towns on the Bay were called in for the wide-area search.

Because two villagers were lost at sea, local fishermen and other active boaters from Sesuit immediately headed out on the water to join in the search. Hours went by and the small Penn Yan had yet to be found. By late afternoon most of the private boaters had sadly returned to the harbor without good news. They figured that by then, almost twenty hours after it started its drift, the small Penn Yan would be in Massachusetts Bay and able to be found only by the Coast Guard search planes.

Dan Walker and Paul McDowell from the Dennis Garage were still out on the water in their open boat, searching. They too didn't want to give up but it was late afternoon and the sun would soon set. When they decided to search for only another half-hour, Paul spotted a small glint on the dark horizon. They motored over to the sighting and recovered the two survivors.

Dickie was half asleep in the rope locker. He thought he was dreaming when he heard the motor of a boat approaching. Not until that boat bumped into the side of his did he accept the reality that a rescue boat had found them.

Dickie and the girl were aboard Dan and Paul's boat as they entered Sesuit Harbor. Dickie still had only his suit jacket over his t-shirt; she had the overcoat to keep her somewhat warm. They obviously had been freezing all night on the water. Despite the near-tragic situation, Dickie still found energy to be playful, putting Dan's old pipe in his mouth. Actually, he craved nicotine from his smoking habit so the pipe was his only option but the onlookers thought Dickie was clowning again.

As they approached the dock, Dickie could see dozens of people waiting for their arrival, especially Red and his family who were desperate to have their daughter back on dry land.

Dickie was justifiably apprehensive about meeting Red on the dock. 'I know he's going to smash me. But I'll let him do it.'

To Dickie's great surprise, Red reached out and put his arm around Dickie. "Are you alright son?"

"Don't call me son, yet." 'Just Dickie being his flippant self.

Looking back, it was very fortunate that Dickie and his friend were found early that evening because a very intense storm arose within a few hours and their boat certainly would have capsized in Massachusetts Bay.

Stealing Champagne from a Local Nightclub

A good friend of Dickie's was a barback at a popular nightclub on Route 28 in Yarmouth. At closing hour he'd have to take all the trash cans out to the dumpster behind the club. 'Somehow' full bottles of Champagne got mixed in with all the empty wine and liquor bottles. Dickie would pick his friend up after work and they'd load all the Champagne into his car. Any chance it found its way aboard Dickie's boat?

Blame the Roma Rocket

During Dickie's years of alcohol consumption, Seagram's 7 whiskey was his favorite and Galliano Italian Liqueur was another evening choice; 'mellow yellow' for a classy guy. But in his early days when money was tight, much of his trouble and antics could be blamed on the 'Rocket', Roma Rocket Muscatel wine to be exact. The stuff was cheap and so notorious that a song[38] was written about it:

Well we don't need no Red Jockey
And Ripple is only just ok
MD 20/20 feels like kindergarten
There's only one wine that's really
got it

It's bright and red
It tastes like Draino
But it's purely lethal, Italiano

If you drink it you must be able
It'll put your ass right under the
table

Makes you throw up in your pocket,
Roma Rocket
Roma Rocket Roma Rocket
Makes you throw up in your pocket,
Roma Rocket

When you next see Dickie, ask him if he ever threw-up in his pocket like the song implies.

Jumping out a Restaurant Window

A group of local boating friends, including Dickie, were attending the 'Blessing of the Fleet' in Provincetown. The annual summer event was great fun and everyone was usually quite liquored-up by dinner time. The group decided to meet at Ciro and Sal's restaurant for dinner. As they all sat down at the table, Dickie announced he'd pick up the check when the meal was over. Everyone was pleased by his generosity.

After a few hours of dining and enjoyment, the waitress presented him with the check. With extreme showmanship he stood up, gasped while looking at the check then ran to the window and jumped out. Everyone was shocked by his acrobatic departure, especially as the group was dining on the second floor of the restaurant. When they looked out the window to see if he was injured, Dickie was nowhere in sight but they noticed a large dumpster that he must have landed in; likely a well-planned escape. He did not return to the restaurant that evening.

Note, that Dickie has always lived up to his financial obligations but sometimes his showmanship surpassed all other commitments.

Setting Scargo Hill Ablaze

Dickie has a remarkable memory for events and pranks throughout his life. Often, he links these activities with the automobiles he and his friends were driving at the time. When he described the prank below, he started with "We drove a Henry J up to Scargo Hill."

Few people nowadays know all the various models of Ford automobiles (A, T, etc.) but they recognize the name Henry Ford, the founder. But the 'Henry J' automobile has nothing to do with the Ford automobile line. Henry J. Kaiser developed an affordable car for the average American, with production from 1950 to 1954 under the company name Kaiser-Frazer Corporation. His cars were a pioneer of the American inexpensive Compact Car line.

Back to the story: Dickie and two of his guy friends enjoyed crazy stunts with no concern about their own safety as proven here. One night they drove up on the Hill with three one-gallon glass bottles, each half-full of gas. Just that image sounds dangerous enough, especially since the boys were probably buzzed to start with.

They stood on the top level of the tower, each boy holding a jug in his hand. They lit the rag that was sticking out of each jug and when the signal was given, each boy threw his jug as far as he could to the north so the bottles landed down the hill from the tower's parking level.

When the jugs burst from impact with the ground, the flame ignited the broad patch of gas and three massive blazes were started. This was exactly their plan: to start the side of the hill on fire. Quickly they drove to Newcombe's Hill and parked on the grassy knoll at the south side of Peter Road. There they watched their accomplishments as the fire spread down the hillside. Eventually they saw the firetrucks arrive on Scargo Hill and the blaze was out in less than an hour.

This prank went as 'good' as possible. Now, Dickie can see how things could have gone wrong, very wrong.

First, one of the boys could have dropped one of the jugs of gas after the rag had been lit on the top level of the tower. This would have created an inferno, incinerating the boys and igniting the wooden stairs below. If they happened to survive the explosion, they would not have been able to run down the burning stairs which was their only escape route.

The same would have occurred if one of the boys happened to hit the concrete upper edge of the tower's top rail as he tossed the jug outward: explosion and fire at the top of the tower.

Second, the fire could have spread over the entire hill and eventually to houses around the Lake. This was before the housing developments appeared on Erb Drive and Scargo Heights Road but depending upon the wind direction, the fire could have impacted the Holl's Scargo Pottery complex and a substantial part of the village.

The fire effectively burned all the underbrush over a substantial sector on the north side of the hill. The following spring, the impacted area was evident from the bright green where the fire had cleared the dead brush.

Before cell phones, texting and video games, some boys resorted to dangerous activities during their spare time!

Exploding Balloons from Scargo Tower

Some years later at his gas station, Dickie often used a cutting torch fueled by oxygen and acetylene. As a prank, he and his friends devised a plan to use the gas mixture as an explosive. Daringly, they filled large rubber balloons half-full with the mixture and tied a string to a piece of cloth beneath.

Carefully they drove these balloon bombs up to Scargo Hill, as it was their equivalent of Cape Canaveral; a perfect proving ground for missiles and bombs. From the top of the tower, they lit the cloth beneath one balloon on fire and let it drift away to the north. Fortunately, the balloon moved away from the tower's upper platform as they ran down the wooden, spiral steps.

The explosion was huge and with sufficient strength to blow out windows of a car if one had been parked nearby. Proudly, they lit off a few more balloons, knowing the entire village would have heard their good work. Then they drove as fast as they could back to Dickie's gas station to pretend innocence.

Within the hour, Detective William Kelly arrived at the gas station. "You boys been up on Scargo Tower?"

"Nope, not us." Dickie had developed a moderately convincing act of denial from years of practice.

"We know it's you. What are you blowing up?

The boys shake their heads.

"Come on, you're the ones blowing up the tower. Don't shit a shitter!"

"We'll keep our eyes open." the boys said cooperatively.

Personally, I think Bill Kelly's line should be memorialized: "Don't shit a shitter!"

Explosive Trash Cannon

At Dickie's gas station, the creative boys also built new types of contraptions to cause mayhem, make noise or simply get a few laughs. It was always harmless fun with no intention to hurt anyone nor their property. Remarkably, they didn't blow themselves up.

Having learned the explosive power of the oxygen-acetylene balloon bombs, they took it a step further. They welded a number of scrap metal pieces to the top, outer edge of a circular metal tire rim, making a sort of chimney with the vertical metal scraps. Next, they carefully placed one of the explosive balloons at the bottom of the chimney and piled lots of loose trash on top. When they lit the balloon, the explosion was tremendous as expected but this time, the power was all directed upward and the trash was blown over the top of Red Lowther's house next door. He must have loved living next to Dickie's Magic Garage!

Driving a Car into Scargo Lake

MythBusters was an American television program that aired on the

Discovery Channel from 2003 to 2016. Two special-effects experts used their scientific curiosity and engineering skills to test the validity of numerous rumors, legends and age-old myths. Dickie would have been perfect on this program because he surely would have been willing to try any test or physical stunt. Dennis' Evel Knievel!

For no reason other than curiosity, two of Dickie's friends, Chris Myland, Sr. and Phil Amero decided to test whether a person could escape from an automobile that went underwater. Scargo Lake was a perfect test site as its northeast end had a sharp drop in depth within ten feet of the shoreline.

The men were experienced Scuba divers, so they devised a plan that one person would be in the car while another would be standing-by with a Scuba tank in the event that the 'driver' was trapped inside and underwater. Adding to the excitement, they had the test car positioned on a flat-bed trailer that was backed up to the water's edge and headed toward deep water.

There was no prior advertisement nor publicity for this event but a group of locals gathered at the site when they saw a stunt was in process. Word probably spread around town quickly, 'Dickie's up to something at Scargo Lake!' Everyone would drop what they were doing to watch him, again.

Phil got into the car without Scuba gear, revved the engine to the point the tires were burning on the trailer bed, then the car shot forward, off the trailer and into the water with a big splash. Chris was in the water nearby, with Scuba gear if a rescue was needed.

They expected the car to sink immediately, but it didn't. The *MythBusters* experts probably would have anticipated this but not the East Dennis boys. The car bobbed in the water, nose down, for at least five minutes before it began to sink.

Phil easily escaped and the whole test was, for the most part, a bust. Oh well, no loss of life.

The amusing fact is that Dickie actually had very little to do with this stunt, but he got full credit for it as rumors spread around the village. His role was to assist with preparing the dive gear, nothing more.

Rappelling Scargo Tower

Dickie and some of the village boys actually developed activities at Scargo Tower that didn't involve fire or explosions; quite surprising. Sometimes they would take their girlfriends to the tower and teach them how to climb up the rocks on the outer face.

First, they would take cables or large diameter ropes to the top, tie them securely and hang the length over the outer wall of the tower. Next, they would attach a climbing belt to a girl and have her climb up with the safety harness attached. Most of the girls loved the adventure but a few did not.

Naturally the boys would show off in front of the girls, rappelling without the assistance of ropes and safety belts. Wisely, they did this only when buzzed and barefooted.

Three Auto Accidents in Two Days

One afternoon Dickie drove from East Dennis to the south side of the Cape to pick up his mother who was working as a car-hop in a restaurant at the intersection of Routes 134 and 28. In those days, you could buy a half-pint of fried clams for 75 cents. He was driving his father's 1941 Chevy ¾-ton panel truck. Sixteen years old and buzzed.

When he pulled into the restaurant's parking lot, his older brother immediately recognized Dickie's buzzed state. "Get your ass home, you're buzzed. Get the hell out of here and get your ass home."

Dickie turned the truck to head home but as he did, he leaned out of the window to spit. When he looked up, there was a telephone pole dead ahead. Fortunately, he was driving slow but took the pole dead-center in the front bumper. The middle of the bumper was bent in and the ends were sprung forward so it looked like deer horns in front of the car. The pole didn't smash the radiator or hurt the engine so he was able to drive the car home. Accident #1.

The following night he went for a ride with a guy friend, in the same neighborhood of South Dennis. His friend was driving drunk and he slurred to Dickie, 'I'll show you how to take corners. I'll show you how to take corners!' They were jointly working on a bottle of Wild Turkey bourbon, in the front seat. Both were eighteen years old.

The car they were riding in was a 1941 Ford and the boy was proud that it had airplane shock-absorbers for suspension.

Heading south on Swan River Road,

well over the speed limit, he rolled the car onto its side. Dickie remembers the car sliding down the road, on its side with sparks flying everywhere. When the car stopped, Dickie was able to climb out, unhurt. Somehow the driver had been thrown out of the car but was not hurt, possibly due to his drunken state. He came walking out of the bushes, still holding the neck of the bourbon bottle but that was all that was left. Still drunk, his first concern was not about the car, it was about his Wild Turkey. 'Somebody stole my bottle.'

Fortunately, a few people were walking down the road and they helped to tip the car upright. One side of the car was all scratched and the gas tank was leaking but the two teens were able to drive the car back to the Tydol gas station located across the street from the Dennis Public Market. They parked the car behind the station and left. Accident #2.

That same afternoon, Dickie needed to pick up his girlfriend so without asking, he borrowed the gas station owner's 1939 Cadillac LaSalle hard-top. A beautiful car with leather seats. He headed down New Boston Road then right on Beach Street but near the intersection of Whig Street he went off the road and hit the guy wire for a telephone pole, bounced off that and put a big cowl in the left-front bumper. Rather than pick up the girlfriend, he took the car back to the Tydol station and hid it in the garage. Accident #3.

The next morning the owner of the station found Dickie, shook him violently and held him up against the wall.

"Did you steel my car last night? Did you take that car?"

"Yes, I did."

"Ok. That's all I wanted to know." He knew Dickie would be honest.

Someone fixed the damaged front bumper and Dickie later bought that car and another of the exact same year, model and color that was a convertible. The seller was a very generous friend to Dickie over many years.

These three wrecks in two days were independent of the car they used to smash all the street signs and was buried within twenty-four hours of being purchased.

Stealing a Live Christmas Tree

When Dickie was renting the large brick house across Route 6A from Players Pharmacy, his children were young and he wanted to give them a joyous Christmas Holiday. His funds were limited but he devised an elaborate scheme to decorate the yard to the surprise of everyone. On the small front lawn, he wanted to place a very large tree and decorate it lavishly.

Two weeks before Christmas he had driven around town searching for a tree that would be fitting for the holiday display. It was another matter whether the tree was truly 'available'. Since there were no town-designated forests from which to harvest live trees, his search expanded to properties that were vacant or containing abandoned houses. With luck he spotted a fine tree on Scargo Hill Road near the intersection of Paddocks Path. There was a house on the property but it was vacated, with no signs of life there for many seasons, maybe years. A twenty-four-foot evergreen tree stood tall on the property and Dickie felt it would be much happier if it were all decorated

and shining brightly on busy Route 6A.

Driving his snub-nosed Willys Jeep, he covertly returned to the property after midnight with a large saw to harvest his prize. The tall tree certainly was too long to put inside or on top of the short Jeep so he used a strong line to tow it back to his property at the intersection of Route 134. Of course, there was no one on the roads that time of night.

Dickie's theft produced a highly visible trail of pine needles along the half-mile towing route but he didn't have time to sweep up his mess. It was more important that he get the tree mounted in his lawn before the sun rose. He hoped that passersby would be busy admiring the festive tree rather than pondering whether there had been a tree in that location the day before.

He scurried for hours in the darkness, digging a hole, attaching guy wires for the tree's stability and placing lights and decorations before his family awoke. As the sun started to appear down Route 6A from the east, he completed his monumental task. Standing proudly next to his creation, he felt like tired Santa climbing into his sleigh after a long night of delivering presents.

In daylight, everyone was both surprised and pleased with the tree. Dickie was happy too, although he did have concern that consequences may arise, especially in the small village where nothing goes unnoticed.

The following day he saw police cruisers parked across the street from his house and an old lady pointing toward the tree. 'Officer, that's my tree, that's my tree.' she said loudly.

They took many photographs of

Dickie's work of art then departed. It was only a few hours later when the police returned to interrogate Dickie. With no hesitation nor resistance, he admitted his wrongdoing.

The woman happened to be the mother of the Dennis Fire Chief so word of the theft spread quickly around town. He expected she'd insist on monetary compensation but she only wanted a comparable or better tree to replace her original. 'It's not the money, it's the idea that the tree is missing.'

"No problem. I'll replace the tree." Dickie replied. He was actually relieved, knowing he'd be able to find a similar, live evergreen and install it in her yard for less cost than she might have requested otherwise.

Within a few days, Dickie identified a thirty-two-foot evergreen located in the back yard of a woman he knew. (He likely had been in the back yard of many women in town, but I can only suppose.) He recalls not having to pay her, in cash.

Extraction of the large tree from the ground was a major undertaking but he and a friend from Harwich used a dump truck to lift it from its hole. Cleverly, they stood the dump body vertical, tied the side of the tree to the empty body, then lowered the body into its horizontal position on the truck so that in the process, the root ball of the tree rose from its hole via the lever action.

Next, at the scene of the crime, they removed the root ball of the original tree, dug the hole considerably larger then lowered the large tree into its new, subterranean home. Dickie returned each day for two weeks, with fifty gallons of water he poured into the tree's root pattern. With fingers crossed he prayed the tree would root. It did, with no signs of distress, and the woman was content that Dickie lived up to his promise.

Ironically a year later, the Fire Chief donated the old house to the town for firefighter training. One day it was ignited and eventually burned to the ground. The tree was lost also, which gave welcomed closure to Dickie.

Stick-Ups, Fistfights and Arrests

When we recall early Western movies, we picture gunslingers, heavy drinkers in local saloons, fistfights often for insignificant reasons, hold-ups, girls who liked masculine men and outlaws, shoot-outs, robberies and arrests.

This Chapter demonstrates that Dickie lived life as if he was in the Wild West, except at a different time and place. The notorious Wild West days were from 1865 to 1895 and it was commonplace for cowboys and outlaws to live the dangerous life, with minimal resistance except from the local Sheriff. Of course, life in the village one-hundred years later was much more civilized and laws were more protective but Dickie pretty much did as he wished, with frequent run-ins with 'the law'.

What's most remarkable and evident from the contents of this Chapter, is that he was wild and highly visible, being the only one consistently behaving like this in the small village, for decades! In the Wild West days, many men would have been just like Dickie and Dennis would have been much different and dangerous, for sure. Singlehandedly, Dickie kept the Wild West alive whether people liked it or not.

Yes, he spent many a night in jail, but he admits that with today's laws, he'd have been 'put away' more often and for much longer. The mid-1900s were just a different and more forgivable time.

The names of Dickie's partners-in-crime have purposely been eliminated to 'protect the guilty'.

Boyhood Troublemaking

Borrowing the Minister's Car during Wednesday Church Services

When Dickie was in his mid-teens, he was definitely more adventurous (wild) than most boys. He could even find trouble when participating in Church activities. For example, he and other children from East Dennis would attend the weekly Church Services on Wednesday evenings in Harwich.

Dickie and Clement Sanborn, a friend from the south side of Dennis, would meet for Services at the Cape Cod Bible Church, located at the intersection of Depot and Main Streets. Accompanying the large group of parishioners, the boys would enter the left side of the Church to attend the first half-hour of Services, then the congregation would take a break before the Sermon would be presented in the right side of the Church. During that break, everyone would exit the Church, mingle in the parking lot then enter the door on the right side. As everyone entered, the boys would remain outside, in hiding.

As the boys heard the Sermon being given, they proceeded to 'borrow' two cars: Dickie took the Minister's and Clement took the Deacon's car. In those days, everyone left their keys in the cars' ignition as there was no concern about stealing on Cape Cod.

The daring boys knew the exact schedule of the Sermon and would carefully return from their joyride in time to park the cars and greet all the parishioners as they exited the Church.

Fortunately, they did their joyriding without a single accident but their inexperience with cars proved to be a slight problem. At the beginning of each ride when they started the cars, neither boy knew how to release the hand-operated emergency brake which had been set by the owners. Consequently, when the boys drove, the asbestos brake pads were still firmly pressed against the brake drums which caused them to burn after a few minutes' driving. No flames arose but the smell of the burnt composite-asbestos pads was terrible and distinct. The boys could not understand why the Minister and Deacon hadn't associated the horrible brake smell with the Wednesday night Services.

The boys did this joyriding on eight nights without getting caught. Soon after, their luck ran out as they broke from their normal heist schedule. That fateful night, the boys got lost on the Harwich roads and were unable to return before the Services were complete. Everyone was standing outside the Church when the boys nonchalantly drove into the parking lot in the 'borrowed' cars. Calmly, the Minister and Deacon asked for the keys and called the police.

The boys were charged for 'Unauthorized use of a Motor Vehicle'. Dickie still remembers receiving the official notice in the mail, stating: 'The Registrar of Motor Vehicles has determined that you are an unfit person to operate a motor vehicle on the highways of Massachusetts, therefore you shall Cease and Desist…, signed Rudolph F. King, Registrar.'

Both boys lost their Massachusetts Drivers Licenses but Dickie was able to obtain a Florida Driver's License when he was seventeen and a re-instated Massachusetts License at eighteen.

Stolen Army Equipment from Barn that Preceded Eldred's Auction House

As mentioned in the Chapter on Notorious Characters, Bob Eldred Sr., purchased the house and barn at 1483 Route 6A which had been owned by Colonel Argo. At the end World War II, Colonel Argo had been contracted to store surplus Army equipment in his large barn, which had originally been attached to the main house on Route 6A before it was moved back from the road and expanded.

When Dickie was ten years old, he and other local boys knew that the barn contained thousands of Army surplus items including: pup tents, bolo knives, kitchen utensils, mess kits and numerous other items. Of course, the boys snuck into the barn at an opportune time and 'borrowed' dozens of pup tents and miscellaneous items. They had a great time setting up the tents in the woods some distance away. Fun for boys, pretending they were Army soldiers. Fortunately, they were not caught with the goods, likely because there was only one full-time policeman assigned to the north side of Dennis during non-summer months. Patrolman Carl Fisher had better things to do than search in the woods for 'borrowed' pup tents. Furthermore, the value of the misplaced goods would not have substantially reduced Colonel Argo's estate.

Peeing in the Radiator of a Borrowed Car

When Dickie was fourteen, one of his young guy friends drove him to a dance in Harwich. There he met a pretty girl (of course) named Judy Williams. They danced and enjoyed each other; as time went on, she felt comfortable with Dickie. Boldly, she asked if he had a car.

"Of course I do." was his answer, trying to prove that he was mature. He had neither a car nor his driving license.

"Do you want to drive me home after the dance?"

"Surely!" He figured this was his big chance - his first girl in a car, alone. Having no car was just a minor snag. His hormones surely would help him find a solution.

He quickly asked his guy friend to drive him back to Dennis where he could 'borrow' a car. He knew there was an idle car parked on the property of the Sign of the Motor Car Inn on Route 6A. It was owned by Ms. Adelaide Hayden who ran a nursery school on Sesuit Neck Road.

She was often out of town so she paid young Dickie to start her 1940 Ford station wagon once per week. He enjoyed driving it around the property as it was good practice, albeit off-road. The regular use kept the battery charged and the car running properly, or so Dickie thought.

Because he knew the Ford fairly well, he figured he could quickly drive it to Harwich and pick up the pretty girl he met at the dance. The first challenge arose when the car wouldn't start – a dead battery. That wasn't going to stop Dickie and his hormones. He and the two other boys pushed the car eastward, down Route 6A to the Town Landing at Scargo Lake. Dickie was pretty savvy, even at fourteen, knowing that if they pushed the standard-transmission vehicle downhill, he could pop the clutch in forward gear and jump-start the car despite the dead battery. He had a two-second window of opportunity for this procedure to work, or imminent disaster. Amazingly, the teen succeeded and he backed onto Route 6A to begin his journey to Harwich.

In hindsight, he knew that if he failed at jump-starting the engine, the car would have ended up in the lake and a rear tow would have been necessary to get it back out to the road. Luckily, this was not necessary.

Like most early teens, he didn't know how to navigate the town roads very well. But this didn't stop Dickie, as he made his way across the Cape and onto Route 28 in West Dennis. Then he noticed that the car was overheating, with lots of steam billowing out from under the front hood. As it was getting continually worse, he pulled over to the side of the road and lifted the big hood. The radiator was boiling over but Dickie quickly came up with a solution for cooling it off. Maybe not the right solution but it was his best plan for the moment.

He and the other boy who was riding with him stood on the big front bumper, unzipped their pants and did their best at peeing into the radiator, after Dickie had bravely removed the hot cap. He was confident that would solve the problem and he'd be driving to Harwich soon.

While they were still peeing, a State Police car approached from the east and slowed to determine the problem with the disabled car. As the officer got closer, he saw the two boys peeing on the engine.

In short order, the boys were in the back seat of the cruiser, heading to the State Police station in South Yarmouth. For a split second, Dickie realized that he probably wouldn't be able to pick up the pretty girl at the Harwich dance but his mind quickly shifted to fear of his parents when they find out what he had done.

Upon arrival at the station, the two boys were escorted into a small holding room while his parents were summoned. This was Dickie's first arrest but he missed the opportunity to be locked-up in a real jail cell, probably because he was a minor. He did, however, have many opportunities for nights in the slammer during following years.

His parents arrived and explained to the Officer that their son had not been in trouble before (or at least caught, as Dickie's eyes rolled). The senior Officer explained that Dickie could have been charged for driving without a license, operating a stolen car, indecent exposure and other charges but as a teen, he would get off easy.

Dickie still remembers November 2, 1949 (aged fourteen), the day he went to the Second District Court of Barnstable, located in Harwich. The charges were: Driving without a Driver's License and Operating a Motor Vehicle without Authorization. Additionally, he was sternly warned never to do this again and given one year's probation. Each week of probation, Dickie had to write a letter to his Probation Officer in Provincetown, James J. Cordero, stating what he had done (with selective omissions, of course).

***

Nearly seventy years after his first arrest, Dickie commented "A lot of girls got me in a lot of trouble." He surely meant it indirectly, with he being the perpetrator, often taking outlandish steps to hook-up with the next pretty girl that crossed his path. Surprisingly, he only went after 'nice girls', or at least that's what we thought.

Stick-Ups at Gunpoint

As Harbormaster, Dickie was also designated as a Special Police Officer. With that responsibility he was expected to carry a gun while on duty but soon he chose not to. Some years later, the town changed their regulations and the Harbormaster was not allowed to carry a gun. Defiant Dickie put a cap gun in his suitcase so it looked like he did possess a gun if a problem arose that needed a serious deterrent.

In his personal life, he owned a High Standard 22-caliber Supermatic Citation target pistol and in 1960 was an active competitor on the Iyannough Pistol Team, associated with the Yarmouth Police.

Stick-Up at Bill and Thelma's Restaurant

Bill and Thelma's was a very popular restaurant on Route 28 in West Yarmouth from the '50s through the '70s. Dickie remembers, "For 99-cents you could buy lunch with veal cutlets or a hamburger platter including mashed potatoes, vegetables, coffee and dessert. All that including a 15-cent tip for the waitress." Times certainly have changed.

Most of B & T's evening patrons were students and young people who gathered there after dances and local sporting events. The late crowds formed for socializing; dining was secondary. On weekend nights, fistfights were common as the boys had been drinking liquor for many hours.

What better a venue for Dickie and his friends to cause a disturbance with a big crowd of on-lookers?

Dickie and two of his friends went into B & T's wearing long trenchcoats and looking like they were gangsters, there to make a robbery. To their surprise, they noticed Dan Walker from the Dennis Garage, who was eating dinner.

He instantly became the perfect target for their charade because Dan knew that Dickie regularly pulled pranks and he'd never conduct a real robbery.

All three raised their guns and pointed them toward Dan. 'It's a stick-up! Get your hands up.'

The boys scared the hell out of everyone in the restaurant (except Dan) but Dickie and his cohorts immediately let everyone know they only had cap guns and it was meant as a big joke.

Just then, the police barged in. 'We're looking for Dickie Buck. Where's Dickie Buck?'

Dickie made his identity known and told them it was all a big joke. He and his two friends hadn't intended on bothering anyone.

The police didn't appreciate the joke. They charged Dickie and his friends for 'Inciting fear into the populace.' No jail time, but stern warnings not to pull this stunt again.

Stick-Up at the Center Theater in Hyannis

The Center Theater in Hyannis was the place to see first-run movies in the 1900s. Located on the southeast corner at the intersection of Main Street and Barnstable Road, it initially opened as the Idle Hour Theater in 1911 and changed its name to the Center Theater in the '30s. It incurred an internal fire in 1971 and another in 1972 after which the building was torn down.

Dickie and two of his daring friends decided they'd pull a prank on Main Street, hoping to create a lot of commotion. Their success was quite predictable because each of the boys was carrying a cap pistol that was very authentic looking.

One of the boys walked up to the exterior ticket window of the Center Theater, pretending he was going to make a purchase. Dickie and the other partner-in-crime suddenly came around the corner and shouted, 'Hold it right there!', looking at the boy at the ticket window.

Immediately, all three boys started firing their pistols at each other, 'Bang. Bang. Bang.'

All passing cars screeched on their brakes and came to a stop. The boys ran like hell but a Hyannis street cop happened to be nearby and stopped the boys for questioning. He was a huge man, well known in Hyannis and rightfully angry with the boys. They quickly proved their sidearms were only harmless cap guns but that didn't appease the cop.

In the end, no official arrests were made but there certainly would have been serious charges filed if the boys had pulled their prank in today's world.

As a side note, when Dickie told me this story, he stressed that 'The Hyannis cop was huge, and I wanted to fight him. Because I knew I could beat him.'

This was typical Dickie in those days, wanting to fight a big opponent just to prove he could beat him. He wouldn't back down from anyone; the bigger the better and fighting was a common sport for some.

Guns on the Bar at Dom's

One night, Dickie and a friend walked into Dom's bar acting like gun slingers from the Wild West. They slammed their guns on the bar.

"Check our weapons, we're going to do some drinking."

The manager called the police department figuring some type of problem might arise. This was unnecessary because Dickie and his friend hadn't asked for their guns back or caused any commotion.

The Police Chief, Gilbert Kelly, got pissed off just by their presentation of guns on the bar. 'I want your pistol permit. If you don't turn it over to me… ah… I'll get it.'

Dickie didn't give a damn whether he had a gun permit or not, at the time. The matter washed over.

Fistfights and Arrests

Dickie is not the largest of men but he certainly has been fearless throughout his life. This section presents only a subset of his fistfights. Everyone who has known Dickie has said he's a "scrapper" who never backed down from anyone, not even if his foe was twice his size or if two or more guys wanted to do him in. If fact, he sought fighting opportunities with the toughest opponents around. He is, by definition, a Pugilist.

Dickie actually liked fighting, as a sport. One of his closest friends would seek fight opportunities and actively propose wagers. When the opponents and betters saw Dickie's modest size, they would make substantial bets and Dickie always won the purse.

Fighting the Limey

Reputations flew around the favorite bars and in neighboring towns, especially when a guy was dangerous, a troublemaker and/or a fighter. By the time Dickie was in his mid-twenties, his reputation for being a very rough fighter was well known from the Canal to Provincetown.

In Hyannis, there was a big guy who was British and they naturally nicknamed him 'Limey". He was well known as being one of the tougher fighters in the region. He had heard about Dickie Buck as his reputation for fighting preceded him. People were looking forward to the day the two scrappers would have a fight and see who prevailed. The Limey was a large man whereas Dickie was much smaller. Those who knew Dickie well understood his attitude about his opponents: 'The bigger the better!'

People would taunt Dickie, 'The Limey is looking for you. Limey is going to get you.' And they likely told the Limey that Dickie wants to beat the hell out of him.

One night, Dickie pulled into the parking lot at Bill and Thelma's restaurant. A nearby car had its door open and it was in Dickie's way so he told the guy "Hey, shut your door."

The guy replied, "Shut it yourself."

Dickie's reply, "I'll shut you!"

So the guy said, "Come on, come on." with his fists raised, ready to fight.

Dickie didn't know it was the Limey nor did he care. And it made no difference that his opponent was a big guy. Dickie jumped up on the hood of his own car then dove at the guy.

They went at it for a long time, punching continually. At some point they learned who each other was. While under a car and still fighting, Limey said to Dickie, "I've had enough. Have you?"

Dickie replied, "Ya, I've had enough. And you?"

That's the way the fight ended and they became very good friends ever since.

Fight at Gina's Restaurant – Flying Pizza Story

Dickie and other locals would often dance at Gina's on weekend nights in the summer. One night when Dickie was there, a group of Italian men from the Little Taunton neighborhood came inside as they waited for pizzas they had ordered for take-out.

Dickie was having fun 'Dirty Dancing' with a girl and as a joke, he pretended to be gay. He enjoyed this because some patrons didn't know he was actually a tough guy and playing gay was completely out of character for him. Typical Dickie playacting.

To taunt the macho men waiting for their pizzas, Dickie really played up the gay act and spoke with a very effeminate voice. The biggest guy became very bothered by this and tried to interrupt Dickie while dancing.

Purposely adding to the tension, Dickie spoke up with a slow, high-pitched, sissy-boy tone, "I gusta have me a ride hoo-um."

"I've been wanting to give you a ride home on the end of my toe all night long." The big guy said.

Dickie replied submissively, "I don't

think you can do that." Meanwhile, Dickie had two other male friends who were there enjoying the scene.

The big guy who made the wisecrack to Dickie was carrying a tall stack of pizza boxes. Upon hearing one more comment from the guy, Dickie punched him in the mouth so hard that all the boxes went flying in the air. The guy crashed on the brick sidewalk with a thud, as the pizzas flew out of the boxes and all over him.

The outdoor walkway on which he had been standing had an edging made of standard masonry bricks that had been buried half-way in the ground and at a forty-five-degree angle so their pointed corners were facing upward. From Dickie's punch, the Italian guy fell face-first on the bricks and cut his face badly. Dickie cared not and quickly pounced on the guy to inflict a terrible beating.

Five or six of the victim's friends jumped on Dickie and started punching him from all directions. Dickie didn't care how many were swinging at him, he just kept swinging. One of Dickie's friends pulled him out of the churning pile by his feet but the remaining guys were unaware their target was gone. Dickie got on top of the pile and started hollering, "Kill him. Kill that son of a bitch!" and the damn fools continued swinging until they realized they were fighting each other.

Within minutes, two local policemen arrived, the victim hobbled over to them and pointed to Dickie. 'Arrest him, arrest him! Look what that runt did to my face. Look what that runt did to me.'

Dickie was amused that the guy called him a 'runt' because the guy had been beaten up badly by none other than he.

Quickly, Dickie drove off with the lady he had been dancing with and spent the rest of the evening at the County Fair Restaurant, of which she was its owner.

Fight at Dom's Bar – 'Pink Queer' Story

One night, Dickie was drinking at the bar in Dom's and a guy he knew from East Dennis was sitting nearby and talking to the owner. He was set on picking a fight with Dickie because of some prior arguments. Pointing toward Dickie, he spoke loudly, "Don't fuck with him, he's just a Pink Queer, a Pink Queer."

Dickie waited outside and eventually the argumentative guy came out. "Did you mean what you said in there?" Dickie poked.

The guy gave him a snide reply so Dickie immediately gave him a wicked punch and the guy fell to the ground. The guy's girlfriend jumped on Dickie's back so he reached behind, grabbed her by the hair and threw her over his head onto the ground and on top of the guy who was still stunned from Dickie's initial punch.

Another guy that Dickie knew from Yarmouth Port came over and swung at Dickie but missed. Dickie said, "You've just made a big mistake."

Knowing Dickie would beat him up, he jumped in his car and drove away rapidly. Dickie and a friend got in his car and chased the runaway down Nobscussett Road with their headlights out. Dickie wanted to catch the guy and beat the hell out of him, just for trying to punch him. The guy was very big but as usual, Dickie didn't care about the size of his opponent.

A short distance down the road they spotted the guy's car rolled over in the woods. The driver was standing on the side of the road when Dickie came up to him.

"Don't hit me, don't hit me. Please don't him me." He was more concerned about Dickie's wrath than his own car accident.

Dickie had cooled off by then. "Don't worry, I'm not going to hit you."

He helped the guy roll his car upright so it could be driven to the Tydol station down the street. They hid it there temporarily, behind the station. The next thing Dickie knew, the Dennis Police Sargent arrived and took verbal information about the fight at Dom's and the subsequent car accident.

Apparently, the guy who rolled his car over had blamed it on Dickie. In court, he pressed charges against Dickie for 'Inciting Fear into the Public' which caused his Driver's License to be revoked for a period of time. All this for a fight at Dom's. Just sporting for Dickie.

Fighting the Paul Bunyan of East Dennis

In the '60s and later, if you asked anyone from East Dennis if there was a local man who was threatening in size and his attitude, they all would have named the same person. For the present discussion, the man's name will be substituted by 'Paul Bunyan' (PB) of American folklore. Famed Paul was a giant lumberjack of North Dakota who demonstrated great strength with his 300-pound mass. In the early 1900s when the story became publicized, men

of that stature were mythical but not the case now, as many gravitate toward professional sports. Note that Paul was a 'gentle giant'; the exact opposite of the true-to-life East Dennis character.

PB was threatening to visitors of Sesuit Harbor. Any wise person would give PB a wide berth rather than chance a confrontation. The only exception was Dickie Buck who was not intimidated by PB. Harbor folks knew it was inevitable the two would someday go head-to-head.

Another point of clarification: Dickie may have weighed 150 pounds soaking wet while PB tipped the scales at 290 pounds - all muscle. Dickie was nearly forty at the time while PB was in his mid-twenties. These factors would have scared any sensible person from considering a fight with the brute. Worse yet, PB was a professional boxer who fought competitively in New Bedford. No doubt, he could land a wicked punch and 'take' many as well. Considering the size difference between he and Dickie, it would be like Dickie simultaneously fighting two professional boxers who were much younger than he.

Once, PB boasted to Dickie that he was New England's #1 Contender for the boxing title. Never missing an opportunity to verbally taunt PB, Dickie replied, "In your wildest, wettest dreams. I watched a guy in New Bedford kick the shit out of you and he was much smaller." No fight arose that day but the inevitable confrontation inched closer.

One summer day, Dickie had just completed varnishing his boat at the town dock in Sesuit Harbor. PB came by and noticed that Dickie's varnish was still wet. Realizing he could ruin the varnish work by splashing water on it, PB called to a young girl who happened to be standing on the high dock near the boat. "Come on, let me see you do a belly-flop; show me a cannon ball."

The girl jumped in the water with PB's encouragement, splashing Dickie's carful varnish work. That's when Dickie started arguing with PB as he had enough of his bullshit antics. "PB, people don't want to come down to this harbor because of your attitude."

The word 'attitude' must have triggered something in PB's brain because he instantly 'sucker punched' Dickie right in the mouth. PB's fist started low and came out-of-nowhere as far as Dickie was concerned, with no time to avoid the massive blow. Getting 'cold-cocked' in the mouth by the 290-pound brute resulted in a big split in Dickie's lip and a huge wake-up call.

Dickie started to defend himself, swinging rapidly and bobbing and weaving to miss PBs round-house attempts. He was getting over-confident because PB couldn't land a substantial punch. 'I'm way faster than him; he can't hit me.' he thought to himself. Then 'Woops!'

'I made a mistake and he got me across the top of the eye. A big punch that opened me up and later took 12-14 stitches to close.'

He had to go on the offense. 'After I realized I was getting hurt and I really was, I came into him, and I came into him hard.' (My interpretation of 'coming into him': A barrage of rapid punches, each as hard and fast as Dickie could inflict.) 'It was the only time I came up against somebody when it was like hitting a stone wall.'

Dickie started thinking of a Plan B: 'I thought if I could push or wrestle him into the water, I could beat him. I could out-swim him and I could hold my breath for two minutes no problem. Maybe drown him.'

'As I went into him again, as hard as I could one last time, PB just turned around and started walking away.

"Bid deal, big fucking deal." PB commented as he walked down the dock. 'His way of saying that Dickie's attack was insignificant.

Dennis Police did not arrive on the scene nor did Dickie press charges against PB for the fight. But a short time later, the Dennis Police filed charges against PB for his frequent fighting and disturbances. He was arrested for having more than twenty cases of Assault and Battery against him and subsequently spent time in jail. Additionally, he was banned from Barnstable County for ten years.

To this day, many locals still remember that Dickie dared to fight PB and was always fearless of the toughest opponents. Dickie's attitude remains that 'It was a good event and I have the scars to prove it.'

***

Dickie shared a secret about selecting his fighting opponents.

"I always fought a bigger guy because if I ever did get the shit kicked out of me, at least people would say I was brave enough to fight the tough guys. But I was never beaten. The bigger they are, the faster or harder they fall.

I was never afraid of PB but I was

concerned after I confronted him. I would love to reenact the whole thing, not today but back then. I was physically fit and mentally too.

If it wasn't for that first punch I received, I would have been in pretty good shape. That fight would have been the Crown Jewel if I had beaten him."

Arrested at John F. Kennedy's Nomination Ceremony

In July of 1960, John F. Kennedy made his acceptance speech in Hyannis for his Nomination as the Democratic Presidential Candidate. Of course, Dickie then twenty-five years old, could not miss this historic celebration and pre-event drinking was certainly in order.

He and a friend went to the National Guard Armory in Hyannis, pretending to be Reporters. Dickie had an expired Press Pass from *Collier's*[39] magazine which he intended to use as his ticket into the event. The magazine had recently gone out of business but he figured the police officers would not have known.

Adding an element of disguise, Dickie hid one arm in his shirt, pretending he had only one limb, but this was necessary to hide his half-empty bottle of wine. He lacked a camera but no concern.

Outside the Armory door was a cordon of officers, configured in two lines through which guests had to pass before entering a security check-point in a small room which Dickie considered the 'inner sanctum'.

When Reporters started walking through the cordon of officers, Dickie joined the line. Just as he reached door, the last two officers grabbed him by the shoulders, spun him around and paraded him out in a 'hop-skip-and-a-jump', as Dickie recalls.

When back in the street crowd with his friend, he found a ladder and tried climbing up so he could see what was unfolding on the other side of the fence. His first attempt failed as the ladder tipped backward into the crowd. On his second try, he told his friend 'Push me up harder'.

A voice replied quickly, 'I'm pushing.' but it was the voice of a State Police Officer who was actually pulling him down the ladder. Without delay, Dickie was marched to the Police cruiser because they wanted him far away from the Nomination Ceremony.

Before Dickie stepped into the back seat of the cruiser, he lit a cigarette but it was immediately knocked out of his mouth by the officer.

"No smoking in the car!"

Defiant Dickie put another cigarette in his mouth; this time, backwards and unlit.

"I told you, no smoking in the cruiser." The officer stated, louder than the first time.

As the officer went to knock it out, Dickie pulled back and said "If you knock this cigarette out of my mouth, I'll knock you out!" He was serious and would have done it, regardless of who he was addressing. That was the end of the conversation. The officer understood fully what type of character he had in custody.

Dickie and his friend were driven to the Hyannis Police Station and held in jail for the night. The opportunity to hear JFK's acceptance speech was gone.

The whole time he was in jail, he thought that 'Any moment now, I'll be released by the soon-to-be President., like the new King of England releases prisoners.' No such luck.

"Looking back, I was buzzed anyways." Dickie admits.

The charges for his arrest were 'Drunk and Inciting a Riot.'

"I didn't think the police were capable of handling such an important event so they had to have some type of charge put against me."

Later in life, Dickie became good friends with the arresting officer, Captain Clifford Taylor of the Massachusetts State Police, who was originally from Provincetown.

Fight in Provincetown

Dickie often went to Provincetown for dancing and hellraising. One evening he was dancing with a girl at the popular nightspot Crown and Anchor. There was a younger guy from Harwich at the bar who didn't like Dickie and tried interrupting him. He attempted to cut-in on Dickie's dancing and also started telling the girl private matters about Dickie, which he certainly didn't like.

Taunting Dickie in front of the girl, he said, 'Come in the men's room and I'll knock you through the shit-house wall.'

'If you've got any balls, you'll follow me down to the dock.' A typical reply from Dickie, welcoming the confrontation.

Dickie proceeded to walk to the dock and when he looked behind, he was surprised to see the guy coming towards him. 'You hot shit, you did follow me.'

Dickie said to him, eager for a fight with the cocky, younger man.

In Dickie's words: 'I started getting into it with him. I punched him in the mouth so hard it slammed him against a wall. The people inside opened the windows to see what had caused the loud crash.'

'I don't want to fight, I don't want to fight. You're the 'Killer from the North Side'! I don't want to fight you.' The guy already had his tail between his legs although Dickie had hardly begun. Because the guy was from Harwich, he knew of Dickie's reputation as a good fighter.

A police cruiser arrived and as soon as the cops walked up, the gutless opponent came after Dickie because he figured he'd be safe with the cops right there. He didn't land a punch on Dickie.

***

Rather than settle the grudge at a later date with his own hands, the guy attempted to hire a man from Harwich to fight Dickie: Davey Gonsalves, Sr. He was a U.S. Marine Corps Veteran from the Korean War days and the All-Marine Boxing Champ; he later became a professional boxer with a great reputation on Cape Cod. Davey happened to be a good friend of Dickie and declined the 'hit man' opportunity. He later told Dickie about the conversation he had with the man making the offer.

'Dickie Buck, he's a good man. You must have pissed him off. You must have fucked with him.' Consequently, the sponsored fight never occurred.

***

Apparently when Dickie landed his first punch on the guy during that evening in Provincetown, he knocked some of his teeth out and broke his dental bridge. A few weeks later, Dickie received a letter from the man's lawyer demanding $1,000 for his client's dental repairs. Dickie decided to settle the claim rather than let details of the evening in Provincetown become public.

Momentarily Lost

Dickie had many male sidekicks who partied, drank, drove fast, boated and got in lots of trouble with him. One night, he and Jimmy Drake were quite inebriated and later were 'escorted' to the town jail to sleep it off in adjacent cells.

In the middle of the night, Jimmy awoke in the dark cell, still quite buzzed and urgent. Thinking he was in a motel room, he noticed something missing. 'Hey Buckie, there's no place to pee!'

'There's no toilet because you're in jail, asshole!'

Fight and Arrest at Windswept Inn – Dickie's Last Drink Forever

Labor Day Weekend. Summer was over but there was still nightlife in the bar called Captain Luther's Liquor Locker, located in the basement of the Windswept Inn on Scarsdale Road. None of Dickie's summer friends were there but he was enjoying a 'few' drinks with a group of girls.

When he had entered the bar, he created a ruckus by pretending he was a cop who was busting the place. 'This is a raid. This is the police. Stay where you are.' Fortunately, the manager knew Dickie so he enjoyed the joke and made nothing of it. Soon after, he suggested that Dickie pull the same prank on the two brothers who owned the business and were in their apartment with a girl, two floors above.

Never missing an opportunity to pull a joke on someone, Dickie barged up the stairs, banged on the door of the brothers' room and hollered, 'Come out, come out. This is a raid. This is the police, come out now.'

They didn't come out so Dickie went back downstairs and continued drinking with the girls. Within a few minutes, someone hollered to Dickie, 'He's coming downstairs and he's going to take care of you!'

Soon after, one of the brothers came partway down the stairs and spotted Dickie. Taunting Dickie, he said 'Hey, do you always hide behind girls?'

'I don't hide behind anyone.' was Dickie's defiant answer then he ran up the stairs and charged at the guy. The other brother arrived in seconds and Dickie found himself in a brawl with the two. It's just what he wanted; another fight for sport.

After a few minutes he was on the floor still fighting with one guy, and actually laughing while he was punching because it was pure entertainment for Dickie; surely not for his opponent. The other cowardly brother decided it best to just run out the door.

Dickie still recalls the fight clearly, 'I did them both up, pretty well; both brothers!'

My translation of Dickie's fight description: he beat the hell out of both brothers, singlehandedly. Photos were taken shortly after, which showed that both had their faces cut up from multiple punches, and blood all over. Both went to the hospital for facial repairs. Dickie walked away without any significant damage.

Additionally, one of the brothers had been hitting Dickie with a nightstick (standard police-issue 'billy club') that was acquired from a third brother who was a police officer in Boston.

Outside, the escapee had climbed into his car so Dickie jumped up on the hood then onto the roof. Having great fun, he started dancing and said 'Come on out. I'm going to teach you the dance. Do you want to do the dance?'

Realizing that the coward was going to stay locked in his car, Dickie jumped down and returned to the bar to continue drinking as if nothing had happened.

Within ten minutes, the local police barged in. 'Where's the fight, where's the fight?'

Calmly and with a Cheshire smile, Dickie replied, 'There's no fight here.' He looked around as if totally surprised by the question.

The cops spoke to the manager and quickly got the gist of what had gone on. Next, one of the cops went upstairs to speak with the brothers and hear their side of the story. Dickie decided it best if he disappeared so he made a quick exit.

One significant issue was that the 'bouncer' and ID checker at the bar was a Deputy Police Officer and close friend of the two 'Bashed Brothers'. He worked for them for many years and would certainly support their case. When the on-duty cops arrived, the Deputy immediately gave his biased account of the fight, which was all Dickie's doing of course. He later took numerous photos of the brothers' condition and possibly doctored them with catsup or other red liquid to make their condition exaggerated.

Dickie intended to drive away in his Jaguar before the cops could assess his highly buzzed state but this was not possible because the police cruiser was blocking his escape. Stupidly, the cops had left their squad car running with the keys in the ignition. Elevating stupid to the next level, Dickie decided to take the cruiser for a joyride and drove north on Scarsdale Road, out of sight. Despite his buzzed state he realized that move may not have been a great idea so he drove back to Windswept. Once a wise guy, always a wise guy, Dickie thought it would be too parochial to just park the cruiser in plain sight so he drove behind the large building and parked it in the cranberry bog. Definitely a ballsy move!

Reconsidering a final drink, Dickie boldly went back into the bar. Within seconds the cop hollered, 'Who's got my cruiser?' He was really pissed off!

Like an obedient student (albeit a very buzzed student), Dickie raised his hand up. 'Yes, I had to move it a little bit.' 'Quite the understatement.

Predictably, the next words out of the cop's mouth were, 'Arrest him!'

But wise-guy couldn't keep his mouth shut, even in this predicament. 'Good idea!' Dickie replied, with glaring looks from the cops. Despite his blurred mental state, he recalled having heard that other officers were making an arrest of a prominent doctor from the village and Dickie thought it might be an enlightening experience if he spent the night in the jail cell with the doctor. Both guilty individuals did go to jail but Dickie went to the town jail while the doctor went to the State Police barracks.

After the police cruiser was recovered from the cranberry bog, Dickie was transported to the Police Station in West Dennis for processing and interrogation. Upon arrival, he was given the opportunity to make one phone call so he tried calling his girlfriend who had a Brewster 896 phone exchange. Multiple tries were unsuccessful as the call just wouldn't go through. Dickie was frustrated but the police attributed his calling failure to his inebriated state. Actually, in West Dennis he needed to dial a '1' prefix before the 896 exchange but he was not aware of this. Later in court, the police used this phone difficulty to confirm that he was buzzed.

Dickie was placed in a small jail cell for the night until arraignment the following day. Full of energy as always, Dickie proceeded to do pullups and various acrobatic moves from the overhead bars of the cell. When the officers saw him hanging upside down, they were further convinced the lunatic was drunk.

When he was ready to sleep he noticed that the support beneath the wall-mounted cot was broken so the mattress and horizontal platform frame were pitched downward at a forty-five-degree angle and thus unusable. He decided to climb under the cot and make an effective tent, covering himself with the blanket in a fetal position. Because of his small size, it looked like the cell was vacant when the night officer passed by. Immediately, an All-Cape Bulletin was transmitted to all neighboring towns to search for the escapee. His presence 'back in the cell' at daybreak had the officers confused, temporarily.

Despite Dickie's claims that the wall support of the attached cot was broken upon his arrival, he got blamed for that damage also.

Upon arraignment, he was charged for:

- Assault and Battery: two counts
- Drunkenness
- Disturbing the Peace, and
- Malicious Destruction of Public (jail) Property

It seemed that Dickie wasn't charged for Confiscating a Police Vehicle because the officer didn't report that he had left the keys in his cruiser with the engine running.

For his defense, Dickie hired a lawyer from Brewster who had a less-than-stellar reputation and he certainly lived up to his earned reputation. The case was handled in the Second District Court of Barnstable, located in Orleans.

The first problem Dickie had with his defense was that none of his friends were in the bar the night he had the 'skirmish'. They all had left the Cape before Labor Day. And the deck was stacked against him because the two brothers had the off-duty Deputy Police Officer working diligently to make a strong case for the prosecution.

The officers in the Police Station also testified on Dickie's buzzed state upon arrival. 'He was hanging upside down from the overhead bars like a wild man. And he wasn't even able to dial his own home phone number.'

Dickie raised the issue that one of his opponents was hitting him with a nightstick but this carried no weight in the argument.

The final verdict: 'Defendant Guilty on all accounts.' Into jail he went.

The next day he was discharged and had to walk all the way home from Route 28 in West Dennis to East Dennis, the full length of Route 134. It was a hot, sunny day in September and Dickie still remembers looking on the side of the road for anyone's discarded cigarette butt. Being a heavy smoker, he was craving a cigarette desperately, having gone without a smoke for two days.

When he arrived at the Players Pharmacy, he bought a bottle of Seagram's 7, a six-pack of Budweiser beer and a pack of Marlboro cigarettes. All that he needed to get back to his comfortable, normal state.

But in a remarkable epiphany, he held the bottle of booze up to the window light and reconsidered his life going forward. 'Ah, broken teeth, loss of license… is it really worth it?'

He put the cap back on the Seagram's bottle and put it in a drawer. Next, he did the same with the cigarettes. Since that day forward, he has never lit a cigarette that was going into his mouth. Often, he'd have one in his mouth, but always backwards and unlit.

Dickie has confessed that his "diabolical, sinister body craved nicotine" but all he would feed it was a little nicotine from wet tobacco under his tongue from the unlit cigarette.

Dickie appealed the case in Superior Court. He had the same ineffective lawyer but he developed a stronger defense on his own. His goal was to convince the court that he wasn't guilty of anything except being buzzed that night.

He made his non-guilty plea directly to the Judge based on the following:

- He didn't have a nightstick; the brothers had obtained it from their third brother who was a police officer.
- They were equally as responsible as he for this melee and fight, and
- Two of them ganged up on him, but he happened to be more pugilistic than they.

The brothers further claimed they had to visit the hospital as a result of their injuries, but this seemed ridiculous as they were fighting only one person and Dickie's physical stature was not daunting.

At the end of the hearing, Dickie made a final plea to Judge Knight: "Your Honor, you will never see me in this court room again for being drunk."

The Judge replied, "For your sake Mr. Buck, I hope not."

When all was said and done, Dickie again lost the case but he was given only one-year probation. Although he lost his case, he was relieved the sentence was lenient.

But soon after the guilty conviction for Assault and Battery, the brothers next decided to sue Dickie for $8,500 each. This was frightening to Dickie and he had to fight it because he could not pay this large sum if the decision went against him again.

For round three in court, Dickie hired a lawyer from the village for whom he had great respect and trust: Atty. William Ernest Crowell, who Dickie affectionately called, 'Almost Always Honest Ernest'. In court, calm tempered Atty. Crowell did a fine job representing Dickie's interests.

Near the end of the hearing, Dickie made a plea directly to the Judge about not having the nightstick, as he was accused: "Your Honor, I hope that if I'm lying to you, that I die of cancer of the throat. I pray that I'll die from that cancer."

It must have been convincing because three weeks later, Dickie received a letter in the mail with the final verdict:

'The court finds in favor of the Defendant.' That was the end of it and fortunate for Dickie, as a guilty verdict would have forced him into Bankruptcy. $17,000 was a lot of money in those days.

As Dickie looks back on that saga in 1965, he feels it was a positive experience because he has never had another drink of alcohol nor smoked a single cigarette since that day.

Fight at the Beach Party

Dickie was invited to a beach party in East Dennis by the girl who lived in the large house at the north end of Bridge Street. She and Dickie had been friends for many years. He was three years older than she and she knew that he would always protect her if any trouble arose. The majority of the partygoers were seniors in High School and thus about eighteen years old; under the legal drinking age.

An hour into the party, she rushed to Dickie very upset, 'You've got to stop that jerk over there. He's beating up his girlfriend; she's my best friend.'

Without delay, Dickie rushed over to the kid and told him to 'Cut it out!' Not harsh words but a serious beating was imminent if he didn't obey Dickie's orders. The guy had slapped his girlfriend repeatedly and he was very wrong to do it.

Because the whole group was young, they didn't know how to control themselves under the influence of alcohol.

Many of the partygoers were pleased Dickie was confronting the bad character. They saw that something was brewing and crowded in. Dickie told them all to move back but a boy named Forrest Robinson resisted Dickie's order. 'I ain't moving back for you or anybody else!'

'Ok then, I'll move you.' And Dickie did; with a barrage of punches, and the kid went to the ground. Dickie recalls his fast work, 'I lit him up', meaning that he finished the guy off quickly with no difficulty.

Then Dickie went after the young guy who had hit his own girlfriend. 'I knocked one of his teeth out; maybe it was on a bridge but it broke right off.

It ended quickly. You could get away with fighting back then.'

***

Back in the '40s and '50s (post War) it was common for boys and men to have a fistfight to settle any type of dispute. 'Let's go outside and duke it out. Put up your dukes!' Dukes or dooks are fists when they're raised for a fight.

In those days, fistfights were practically a form of exercise, like males now go to a gym to work out. Surprisingly to most women, the fighters usually became better friends after their fights.

Fight at the White Swan

Three years after the fight on the East Dennis beach, Dickie had another run-in with Forrest Robinson. Dickie and a couple of his friends had gone to the White Swan bar in West Yarmouth, located on Route 28 at the intersection of Higgins Crowell Road. The Yarmouth Police Station sat ominously across street in those days, which translated to a very short response time when fights arose at the Swan; not good for any rowdy patrons. Years later, the Station was moved farther north on Higgins Crowell Road.

The Swan was a popular spot in its day but a tad on the 'seedy' side, earning its reputation as the 'Dirty Bird'. Dickie's plan was to have a few drinks and chalk-up a stick to play some pool but the table was being used. Alcohol didn't increase his patience.

Dickie remembers the confrontation as if it were yesterday. "I really instigated the fight, I really pissed that guy off. He was playing pool and I wanted him to lose and get off the table so I taunted him.

'Oh, you're gonna miss that shot, you're gonna miss.'

When the guy finally missed the easy shot, he was pissed off and came at me with a stick.

'Let's go outside' I said. There was an old lady they called 'Ma' who ran the bar. I didn't want to cause any trouble for her.

Out the door we went. I had a couple friends who followed me outside to the parking lot, but the other guy had at least a half-dozen buddies with him. It was kind of like the North lining up to fight the South but my team had many fewer men."

The guy worked at New Seabury in Mashpee and apparently was a construction foreman of sorts. He spoke to Dickie, 'There's twenty-seven guys who work for me and every one of them could kick your ass.'

'Well maybe so, but you can't do it.' Dickie replied defiantly.

Forrest Robinson happened to be at the bar and saw Dickie's predicament. And he certainly remembered what a good fighter Dickie was, from the time at the beach party when Dickie laid him out quickly.

Forrest spoke up, 'I fucked with you once but I'm not fucking with you again. I'm on your side this time.'

It made Dickie feel good because he didn't know if he had any help at all. Forrest had become a good friend after the previous fight in East Dennis.

The riled-up opponent ran at Dickie but he was met by a wicked punch in the stomach that caused him to bend over forward. At the same time Dickie lifted him off the ground by his crotch and chest so the guy's forward momentum carried him up then he slammed down onto the hood of a nearby parked car. "Bam, you could hear the air blown out of him. And he rolled onto the ground, all done. It was a short-lived fight."

***

As a bit of local trivia, there is a link between the White Swan and a particular property in East Dennis, at 128 South Street. In the early 1900s, a windmill and tall, wooden water tower were located on the property of the Swan for provision of domestic water for the on-site resort. In the '70s, the five-story tower was purchased by Parker Turner and moved to East Dennis, restored beautifully and later converted into a habitable building. Those who had seen the tower shortly after it had been moved still remark about the large beams that were strongly bolted together inside the structure.

Parker, who passed away in 2016, was enjoyed for his storytelling but also remembered for having been guilty many years ago of stealing all the planks from the boardwalk extending into the Bass Hole from the Yarmouth Port parking lot. He had used them as wall boards for the interior of his house on Paddocks Path, opposite Cape Cod Paper Company. This same house was the first house Dickie ever lived in, starting at four years old, when his family moved from Yarmouth Port to Dennis; his brother Bertie was born in that house as well.

Fighting a Stalker at the Magic Garage

A man from Brewster went to Bucky Beaver's Magic Garage on a mission to 'settle the score' with Buckie, who he thought had been messing with his wife. Dickie was actually not-guilty in this instance.

The stalker entered the gas station carrying a .30-06 rifle. There were a few people standing around and the floor was all wet because Buckie had drained his fish tank.

The stalker spoke in a serious tone although he was definitely liquored-up.

"I'm going to have to shoot you now." He paused then continued. "Not everybody sees the bullet that's going to kill them. But you do, and this is it."

He held it up for Dickie's viewing then put it in the gun's chamber, closed the bolt and said, "Now I'm going to shoot you."

Dickie was a bit buzzed and confident as always that he'll never die. With minimal concern, he dared poke verbally at his opponent.

"All these years you've been talking about you kicking the shit out of me and now it turns out it takes a gun for you to do it?"

"No bejesus, it don't take no gun."

With gun in hand, he walked over to the front step of the next-door pharmacy and smashed it to pieces. While doing so he cut his hand from the sighting bead on the front tip of the gun then came back to Buckie with blood pouring all over.

"Now I'm going to kill you, with my bare hands."

Buckie's fearless reply, "Take another step and I'll drop ya!"

He took one more step toward Buckie with hands extended as if to grab his throat. Dickie spun him around, hit him in the face hard and the guy dropped to the floor and lay stunned in the puddle of water.

Recalling the event, Dickie admits, "I never thought I could beat him so bad as he was a Marine. But I beat him, and fast!"

Being the ultimate showman in front of his friends, Buckie put his foot on the guy's head, like in the Western movies.

"Get this pussy out of here before I really get pissed."

One of Buckie's friends who was standing nearby was a professional fighter. He was concerned.

"You killing the man. You killing the man!"

Buckie told his friends to put the guy in a chair. As the victim started to gather his wits, he mumbled.

"Argh, give me a cigarette, I need a cigarette."

Buckie gave him one of his Marlboros and spoke.

"Sorry I had to do that to you but you were going to kill me. Now let's go across the street to Hudson's and clean you up."

"I don't need you to clean me up or anything else." He paused then added, "Now I'm going to Plan B. I found out I can't beat you with my hands, I'm going to Plan B. You might see the flicker of the sun on the barrel and feel the burning pain as the bullet sears its way through your body."

"Hey, you're threatening me. I'll go to the police and tell 'em."

"No, you won't. I know your 'M O'. If you can't handle it yourself, you're not going to handle it."

He went away, with the shambles of a gun in his hand.

***

Several months later, Buckie's same opponent came back to the Magic Garage, this time with a shotgun in hand. "Buckster. I don't drink anymore. Do you want to go hunting?"

"Ya, I'll go hunting with you. We'll go duck hunting." It was blowing pretty hard but that didn't matter to Buckie.

Often, he'd walk out of his gas station during normal working hours, leaving whoever was there in charge. He was confident that he was the first person ever to have a self-service gas station, in the country. Even a little East Dennis lady in her nineties would stop and pump her own gas, knowing to leave the money in the box inside the station.

Buckie and his hunting partner drove to Brewster, got out of the car and Buckie walked ahead, up the dunes. There was only one gun on this hunting adventure and it wasn't in Buckie's hand. Was it really a duck hunting trip, or a 'Buck hunting' trip?

Buckie's mind started to race as he walked and the gun may have been pointed at him from behind. 'If he doesn't shoot me now, he never will.'

He wasn't scared because he always knew he'd never die, no matter what situation. But, there was a chance he'd be shot, right there and then. The fact that both of them had quit drinking surely increased Buckie's chance of not taking a bullet. He mentally acknowledged this was a good thing; maybe a life saver.

The two sat on top of the bluff waiting for ducks to fly over but it never happened. More importantly, Dickie said they've been best friends ever since!

Marriage and Family

I, the Author, lived in the village from birth in 1950 until my early twenties when I left to attend various graduate schools, then marriage, career, etc. During my first two decades, I'd heard of Dickie Buck and saw him occasionally around the village. We weren't friends, because of our fifteen-year age difference. Regardless, my parents frequently mentioned his antics and sometimes partied with him and other local couples. Friends openly shared their experiences with and sightings of the daredevil as it made for entertaining conversation. That was the only side of Dickie's personality that I had ever heard – the wild man of East Dennis.

From my twenties to mid-sixties, I spent holidays and annual vacations with my extended family in the village. Stories of Dickie's latest antics never ceased.

Not until 2017 did I again spend considerable time in the village, while writing my non-fiction book *Albatross and Her Crew*. And it was not until then that I first heard that Dickie was married, to one woman for fifty-four years! I was stunned. 'Dickie Buck married? To whom? How could she cope with all his risky behavior?'

This Chapter illustrates that he has been a husband and father of two daughters, interspersed with his achievements, physical stunts, daring behavior, fights and arrests. All this activity by one person and most within a few miles of Scargo Tower. Everything

he has done has been seen and/or heard by someone. It's too small a fishbowl to get away with anything unnoticed. Clearly, achieving visibility was a key element of his shtick and it often outweighed the consequences of being caught.

From my perspective, his bravery in a fistfight was matched by the bravery he demonstrated by remaining in the small village, despite the many outlandish acts associated with his name. Anyone else would have 'gotten out of Dodge' on the fastest horse, to evade 'the Law' or a gun-toting husband, sometimes both. Dickie admits that he'll always live in the village, to the very end, like Howie Newsome in Grover's Corners (from the Thornton Wilder play *Our Town*).

Dickie's Courting Days

In 1962, Dickie was twenty-seven years old and managing Bucky Beaver's Magic Garage in East Dennis. As demonstrated in previous Chapters, he had already performed hundreds of antics, ranging from amusing to dangerous and unlawful. A seasoned clown and troublemaker who was definitely high-profile. The police in all neighboring towns knew his name, as did the District and Superior Courts. And he had certainly 'befriended' girls of all ages, backgrounds and availability status during these early years.

Surely, if there was a pretty girl in next-door Brewster, he'd catch her scent and readily track her down, (as a hound, of sorts). It was likely, however, that her friends and/or parents had already warned her about "that Dickie Buck character" because his reputation often preceded his engaging smile and outlandish opening line. Most local girls (and women) knew his advances were inevitable; it was just a matter of when.

Judy Sencabaugh was exactly that girl from Brewster: very cute, blonde, seventeen, a High School senior with a driver's license and car. Dickie's dream girl!

**

Viola and Mac Sencabaugh owned and operated a small restaurant on Route 6A in Brewster called 'Vi and Mac's'. It was sold in the early '80s and renamed the Brewster Coffee Shop. The Sencabaughs originally lived in Arlington, MA but moved to Brewster when Judy was four years old. She was given a parakeet after the move and to this day, she keeps large, tropical birds in the living room of their home.

Judy attended the Brewster elementary school which had low attendance; only eleven students graduated in her eighth-grade class. All but two went to Dennis-Yarmouth Regional High School. Judy's mother did not like the Dennis-Yarmouth school system so she insisted that Judy enroll at Nauset Regional for her High School studies. She graduated but missed most of her friends during those important years.

During her mid-teens, Judy worked part-time at her parent's restaurant. Dickie, then in his mid-twenties, worked locally as a Forklift Operator and a Mason's Tender. Often, he'd work in Brewster or Orleans and would purposely stop at Vi and Mac's for lunch, hoping to see the cute, blonde girl named Judy. She can remember her mother saying, 'Here comes that crazy guy again!' when Dickie's dump truck would pull into the restaurant's parking lot.

One day when he stopped for lunch, he brought in a frog, just for amusement. Young Judy enjoyed this but it's been rumored that he flushed the frog down the toilet. Whether it was verified or not, Mac got very angry at Dickie over the suspected prank. 'Probably not the only time Judy's father was displeased with Dickie!

When Judy turned sixteen and was able to drive, she'd always go to Bucky Beaver's Magic Garage to obtain gas and predictably, receive a healthy dose of flirting from Dickie. In the fall after her High School graduation, she enrolled at Cape Cod Community College which gave her frequent need to stop for gas at Dickie's station on her way to Barnstable. To help her good friend Dickie, she'd stop at an Auto Parts store in Hyannis on her way home if he needed someone to pick up parts that he had ordered.

Another day when she stopped at the Magic Garage in her red Mercury convertible, Dickie quickly jumped in the passenger seat and hollered, 'Follow that car!' Apparently, he wanted to follow one of his ex-girlfriends but Judy couldn't keep up with the other car so the pursuit ended uneventfully. He also wanted to be alone with Judy. What she didn't know was that Dickie had been scheming for a few months about how he could get her to date him.

As they were returning to his garage in East Dennis, Dickie noticed the Cape Playhouse sign which advertised that *PT-109*. the story of John F. Kennedy during World War II, was playing at the Cape Cinema. Mustering up his bravery, Dickie asked, "Would you rather go to the movie with Peter or me?"

"You!" she quickly answered, with excitement.

Being a good daughter, she felt obligated to ask for her parents' permission to go to the movie with Dickie. Anticipating less wrath from her mother, she approached her first. With justifiable trepidation, Vi approved Judy's request for a date with Dickie.

"But you better tell your father."

Judy couldn't lie to her father so she requested his permission. To her relief, his acceptance proved much less confrontational than she had expected.

***

One thing led to another and the wild-bachelor Dickie decided he wanted to marry Judy. He was twenty-eight while she was only eighteen. Dressed nicely, he went to the Sencabaugh home one evening and announced to Vi and Mac that he and Judy wanted to get married. The sentence was quickly followed by his clarification that Judy 'needed to get married'. Dickie expected the father to 'blow a gasket'.

Mac paused for consideration then answered 'You have my blessing.' Dickie was stunned but very relieved with the positive response.

Vi and Mac had known Dickie

only from his visits to their restaurant. Fortunately, his full reputation hadn't crossed their paths by the time he proposed.

A wedding was soon planned, on Thanksgiving Day that same year, 1963. And it seemed to many locals that Dickie's wild life might finally settle down.

It is noteworthy that Judy's parents and grandparents also were married on Thanksgiving Day. A wonderful family tradition.

Pre-Wedding 'Activities'

A few weeks before the wedding, a local man thought Dickie was having an affair with his wife. Dickie was driving eastward on Route 6A to visit Judy in Brewster. Ahead of him happened to be the man's wife heading in the same direction. By coincidence, the husband's car was immediately behind Dickie's. She pulled into the gas station in Brewster and Dickie pulled off the road a couple hundred yards farther west, near his fiancé's home. The wife quickly turned around at the gas station and started driving the other way. Thinking this was odd behavior, with Dickie close by, the husband figured she was having an affair with then-infamous Dickie Buck. The husband had been drinking so his imagination was certainly well fueled. Nevertheless, the husband's rage began to grow.

***

The night before his wedding, Dickie was spending 'quality time' with two of his closest friends, drinking of course. Under the influence, his fears started to blaze.

'Why would I want to get married? I have nothing. How am I going to take care of a family?' At that moment he wanted to run away. Maybe just typical fear; maybe reality.

His close friends knew they shouldn't give Dickie an opportunity to escape his marriage commitment this late in the game. He passed out and didn't awaken until 10 a.m. the next morning – Wedding Day.

Dickie was not one to ever 'pass out' from drinking; actually, he always became the life of the party with more consumption. To this day, he's been convinced that his friends gave him something to knock him out for the night so he could not leave town. 'Probably a good move!' he adds.

Wedding Day - November 28, 1963

On the day of the wedding, Dickie and Judy's families and a large group of friends had assembled at the beautiful First Parish Church on Route 6A in Brewster. Judy was in hiding with her Bridesmaids while Dickie was standing in the church vestibule watching his Groomsmen usher guests to their seats. Meanwhile, outside the church a truck drove up and slammed into the front of the honeymoon vehicle, Dickie's Lincoln Premier; a nice luxury model of its time.

A man climbed out of the truck

wearing hip boots and proceeded to grab a five-gallon can of paint (roughly 55 pounds) from the rear of the truck and threw it through the front windshield of the beautiful Lincoln. Fortunately, the can of paint did not open but the car was certainly unusable for a honeymoon drive.

Next, the culprit grabbed a shotgun from the front seat of the truck and began walking up the front steps of the church in full sight of many who were still entering.

The Brewster policeman who was directing wedding traffic on Route 6A saw the scene unfolding and bravely ran to the gun-toting man entering the church. The policeman immediately arrested the man and escorted him to the police cruiser. As the car was driving away, the angry man in the back seat kicked out the side windows of the cruiser but the culprit could no longer interfere with the wedding. Recognizing that Brewster is a small town, it's not surprising that the cop was the brother of the assailant.

Dickie's Best Man was no less of a clown than he. When the gunman had been neutralized and removed from the church property, the Best Man went to the back of the church and hollered.

"Ladies and Gentlemen, Dick Buck has been shot, Dick Buck the Groom has been shot!"

It had been only six days since President John F. Kennedy had been shot so the Best Man thought it would be theatrically amusing to mimic the announcement of the tragic assassination. It didn't matter that Dickie was not shot; it was all about getting a laugh from the wedding participants. Definitely a bad joke but Dickie took it well as he stood bullet-free and waiting for the Bride to enter. He was buzzed of course, so that minimized any tension. When it was time for him to enter, he skipped down the aisle with a big smile on his face. Wonderful Dickie, the showman everyone came to see.

The Bride's father had witnessed the whole ordeal on the church steps and was both shocked and angry. Vi was even more furious with the man who tried to disrupt the wedding. To both parents, it raised significant concern about the type of friends and enemies 'Mr. Buck' had accumulated.

With no time to delay, the father met with the Bride and proudly escorted her down the aisle. Judy still remembers her father trembling and obviously struck with anger but it was definitely not the time for interrogation. Her mind was screaming 'What the heck happened?' but she didn't learn until hours later.

Dickie and the wedding crasher later became 'Best of Friends' and still see each other weekly. Our Groom is definitely not one to hold a grudge nor run from an aggressive opponent.

Wedding Reception

Despite Dickie's numerous, high-profile antics and local arrests, he always had a knack of befriending influential persons who moved into the village. He was the first to lend a helping hand and give advice on local amenities or obstacles. Never was he driven by the potential of financial reward; in fact, just the opposite, with many cases of he providing physical services with no attempt to obtain payment, even years later.

A relevant example was the venue of Dickie's Wedding Reception. It was arranged and choreographed by a very influential woman who was best friends with Princess Grace Kelly of Monaco, originally of Wellesley, MA. Ms. Jean Barry Ward Pochna owned a home overlooking Cape Cod Bay near Crocker's Point, between Stone's Point and Corporation Beach. Ms. Pochna graciously planned Dickie's lavish reception in a lovely grove at her home by the Bay.

Dickie first met Ms. Pochna when she would visit Dennis and sometimes entertain Grace before she married the Prince of Monaco in April 1956. For those visits, Ms. Pochna was the full-time Companion of Grace because it was improper protocol for the Royal Fiancé to ever be alone with the Prince before they were married. Ms. Pochna also was friends with Bob Hope, Bing Crosby and other Stars, from her association with Grace during her illustrious Hollywood career.

Leave it to Dickie to have friends from both Royalty (albeit indirectly) and movie fame.

***

Following the reception, Dickie's plan was to drive he and Judy to New York for their honeymoon, but the lack of a windshield certainly prevented use of his fine Lincoln. Peter Tufts, a friend of Dickie's, saved the day by offering his Ford Galaxy 500 Convertible for their honeymoon trip. All that was necessary was for the lovebirds to drop Judy's brother, Sonny, at his home in Ithaca, NY on their way to New York City.

No way was Dickie going to leave HIS party before it ended. Late in the evening after much liquor consumption, the three partygoers climbed into the Galaxy at the end of the terrific wedding reception. For the ride to New York, Dickie had a full bottle of Seagram's 7 which he figured was plenty for their evening drive but this proved not to be the case.

Although the Massachusetts Turnpike had been completed in 1957, the ride to Ithaca was very long. To Dickie it seemed like they drove through the entire night, having to stop for more Seagram's at least once. Every couple of hours Dickie asked if they were getting close.

"It's just a down the road a little" Sonny replied, repeatedly.

The distance was actually 400 miles

so it likely took eight hours. Not the best of wedding nights for the pretty Bride Judy. By the time the three arrived in Ithaca they were exhausted.

The next day, Dickie and Judy drove another 300 miles southward to New York City to begin their honeymoon. Along the way they stopped in the town of Roscoe where Dickie spent a few months in High School before transferring to North Carolina.

Daughter Linda

Dickie and Judy's first-born daughter, Linda, arrived in May 1964. From the start, he never treated her like a prissy daughter, but he was a good father.

"In many respects he was a typical

dad, teaching me how to ride a bicycle, fillet a bluefish, drive a boat and things like that." Practical things, like changing the oil in her Mustang and how to drive a jeep on Chapin Beach. "He'd be clamming and tell me to drive around on the flats on my own."

Dickie knew his grandfather Elmer's

technique for teaching someone how to swim. And he heard that Elmer threw his son-in-law Buckie (Dickie's father) into deep water to learn, so Dickie figured it would be fine for Linda too. Off the dock tiny Linda went, into Sesuit Harbor at four years old. She survived and still swims today, but only when she wants. Linda reminisces, "Early on, he tried to instill in me that there is nothing to fear but fear itself."

For nearly thirty years, Linda (and often sister Alesia too) would accompany her dad for the annual New Year's Day polar bear swim at Corporation Beach or Millway in Barnstable. His last year of participation was 2017, at age eighty-two. Wife Judy was relieved Dickie wasn't going to stress his heart again in the cold Bay water.

***

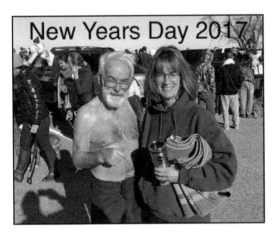

New Years Day 2017

Linda has always been emotionally close with her dad and a pal during her adult years. "When I was a little girl, we all thought our parents were perfect. Like all daughters, we start off with a certain level of hero-worship. My dad was the greatest thing on the planet to me.

As we become adults we realize that they aren't perfect and learn that people make choices about how they want to live. And that nobody is perfect. If we want to have good relations with people, and our parents, we have to make the choice and accept that they are who they are. They too are free to make their own choices.

He's my dad and no matter what crazy things have happened, I've always been proud to say he's my dad."

***

Often throughout Linda's life on the Cape, people will learn in mid-conversation that she is Dickie's daughter. Linda explains how she proudly answers, "Yes, I am!"

The normal response is, "How was that growing up?" sometimes with a tongue-in-cheek look.

"Never a dull moment." Linda replies with a smile.

Linda further comments on her father: "He's lived an extraordinary life and I just want people to know that I have a wonderful dad. He's one in a million and there's not another like him.

I had been told by a former boss that the younger guys in the village enjoyed my dad because he was like the eternal Peter Pan. He wasn't afraid to take risks. "

***

Dickie has always appreciated his firstborn's consistent love and respect. "Linda has been with me through 'thick and thin'. She can roll with the punches. She's pretty good at it, as proven many times!"

Linda certainly knows who he is and better than most anyone on the planet. He certainly has never-ending energy and has lived an ageless existence. She continues to embrace the few quirky elements of his personality and has always been his biggest fan. It has been she who's found the best doctors for his care late in life, making sure he lives forever.

Daughter Alesia

Four years after Linda's birth, her younger sister Alesia arrived, in July 1968. Alesia was the more daring of the two daughters starting at an early age and a few times it wasn't totally her doing. When just two years old and the family was living aboard their boat in Sesuit Harbor, she happened to fall overboard. This was well before she could swim but her uncle plucked her out of the water by her long hair. No problem; just part of growing up in the Buck family.

Another water event was communicated to me by a village mom who still vividly remembers seeing Alesia jump into deep water at four years old. Dickie had anchored their boat off Corporation Beach one summer day and as always, moms in their beach chairs kept their eyes wide open for any child in peril no matter whose. This particular mom knew Dickie and his family well and watched as he jumped into the deep water and began swimming to shore. She saw little Alesia stand on the bow and holler, "Daddy wait for me".

He didn't turn around at his daughter's request but with no fear, Alesia jumped off the boat and into water that was well over her head. For a couple seconds there was no sign of the little girl but she finally popped up and proceeded to dog-paddle to shore.

The shoreside mom nearly had a heart attack fearing the young child would drown but Alesia made it to shore and caught up with her Dad. None of the observers were pleased with his apparent laissez-faire attitude about his daughter's survival. Furthermore, they were unaware that it was Dickie's procedure for teaching his daughters to swim. (Learned from his father but not necessarily the best technique.)

***

During Alesia's childhood, she visited her paternal grandmother on three occasions at her home in Sarasota, FL. She was ten years old when Dickie, Judy and Judy's Mom drove south with Linda and Alesia all in a camper van (R/V) that had been borrowed from a friend of her Dad's. It was an eventful ride because the trailer they were towing lost a wheel, so all the furniture that had been in the trailer had to be moved into the crowded camper. 'Vacation from hell' was one reference to the trip, including torrential rains, cars spinning out, etc. Alesia decided at that early age that she would never again drive to Florida. But young Alesia's visit in Sarasota was actually wonderful as it was the first time she saw members of the Ringling Brothers Circus practicing across the street from her Grandma's house, as discussed earlier.

She made another trip to Sarasota at age fourteen accompanied by her sister Linda, and Alesia's third trip was at age eighteen, accompanied by her Mom and Dad. No catastrophes on either of those.

At age ten, after returning from Sarasota, Alesia became very interested in gymnastics. After school she spent many hours doing flips and other acrobatic moves in their yard. She fondly remembers her Dad purchasing equipment that she could use to further her acrobatic skills. One item was a trapeze that he carefully installed in a tree for her use. He also gave Alesia an authentic acrobatic belt/harness that she could use to perform jumps and complete flips.

He enjoyed that Alesia was interested in gymnastics and acrobatics, as did he. Some afternoons he returned from work early and joined her, creating new acrobatic moves and tricks. She most enjoyed perfecting a hand-stand on his hands as they were high above his head. This was 'quality time' with his youngest daughter. It was one of the happiest times in Alesia's life, feeling she had a bond with her Dad that she felt most other children did not have.

***

As Alesia entered adulthood, she became very independent; possibly attributed to her father's free-spirited genes? She has enjoyed pursuing her artistic talents, via painting and especially wood carvings. What's most important to her today is her husband and two wonderful children. Her daughter is severely Autistic but Alesia has embraced this major parental challenge and enjoys sharing her experiences and knowledge with other parents who have young children with the same condition.

As clarification, Alesia is often called 'Lisa' by her family and close friends.

Family Living in the Village

As a family unit, Dickie, Judy and their young daughters certainly 'lived locally' with each location within a few miles of Scargo Tower:

- Brick House at the intersection of Routes 6A and 134
- Black Ball Hill Road
- Aboard Dickie's boat in Sesuit Harbor (one summer)
- Harbor Road
- Bayberry Lane
- Fairland Circle

Interesting Mothers-In-Law

Dickie and Judy were both very fortunate to have wonderful mothers-in-law. As described in previous Chapters,

Dickie's mother Ellie was a real character throughout her life. She was very flexible, hopping around the country with her husband who was a 'drifter' of sorts. She worked a wide variety of jobs in Dennis and later in Sarasota, Florida. It's not surprising, with her independent streak, that she chose to live her latter years in the South rather than in the village with Dickie and his family.

Viola, Judy's mother, also was a wonderful lady. She has been described as always looking very prim and elegant, with her hair done nicely and fine make-up. Everyone said she was a nice woman with lots of energy.

From the beginning, Vi was justifiably concerned about the character her daughter had married but Dickie was very caring to Vi and convincingly 'won her over'. His kindness shone brightly when Vi sold her house and was considering housing options. Dickie was aware that his mother-in-law lacked the funds to purchase the house she wanted in the village so he spoke to Judy and suggested they purchase the fine, new house together with Vi so she could be happy and they could care for her if and when it became necessary. This was an extremely kind and generous gesture, agreeing to live with his mother-in-law thereafter. And it worked well, to Dickie's credit.

***

Ever since the male troublemaker from Brewster damaged the honeymoon car of Dickie and Judy, and attempted to bust up the wedding ceremony with his shotgun, Vi remained bitter toward the perpetrator. She was consistently a sweetheart in everyone's eyes but she couldn't drop her resentment for 'that man'.

As is typical for guys, Dickie and he eventually became very good friends over the next few years.

Vi and the perpetrator came face-to-face at the 1998 wedding reception of her granddaughter, Alesia. He had generously provided hundreds of fresh oysters for the wedding reception and began the laborious task of shucking them for the guests.

Vi, as the lovely Grandmother-of-the-Bride, was very active socializing with guests but she also had the opportunity to interact with the earlier perpetrator and they began to get along. He was very polite and attentive to Vi and her frigid attitude toward him gradually melted, thirty-five years after Dickie's wedding in 1963. A comfortable situation from that point on.

***

Vi worked various jobs in the village, including cooking in many local restaurants, behind the Luncheonette counter at Terpos' market and a long period at the liquor store of Players Plaza where the U.S. Post Office is located today.

55 Years of Marriage

Dickie recalls that when he was planning marriage, people in town said 'He won't last six months.' But a friend of his disagreed, 'Oh yes, he'll last better than a year.' implying not much longer.

Dickie is not hesitant to boast where credit is due. 'Judy is responsible for this longevity. Anyone else would have left me many times, many times!

Everyone tells me 'She must be a Saint. A Saint to put up with you!" A unanimous opinion.

"When I take Judy places with me, I introduce her as my daughter. She looks like she could be my daughter. But also, she's my wife." Certainly a kind compliment from a husband but with Judy, patience is the virtue that shines most brightly.

November 2018 marked Dickie and Judy's 55th wedding anniversary. Certainly, an amazing accomplishment for any couple but knowing Dickie's extraordinary lifestyle, it's even more incredible.

***

One day in the privacy of their home, I asked Judy to give me her view of their marriage. Without hesitation, she replied instantly and honestly.

"I would marry him all over again."

"A wonderful tribute to you, Judy." I replied.

"Yes, that's really all I have to say. I would do a few things different but I would marry him all over again. We have our ups and downs but everyone does. It all worked out."

Judy expressed that she has the family she wanted with two caring daughters and three grandchildren. She's happy now and has been throughout her life.

***

How Dickie and Judy have maintained their relationship is their business but those outside of their family have the opinion that Judy has been a Saint. They view her as a testament to patience and compromise.

She has amassed local friends from living in Brewster and Dennis her entire life and working in many local restaurants and markets. She still works today, part-time, in Peterson's Market in Yarmouth Port, as well as maintaining a lovely home and garden.

When I asked her friends how they'd characterize Judy, the comments were spontaneous, warm and gracious. Below is a subset of those, well-deserved:

'She's an absolute sweetheart with incredible patience.'

'Judy is kind, caring and has always been very nice looking.'

'Judy is a great gal.'

'She was wonderfully kind to both her mother and mother-in-law.'

'How was Dickie so lucky to find an angel like Judy?'

'She stuck by him and had a lot of guts.'

'Dickie was such a daredevil, poor Judy.'

'How could anyone else put up with him?'

'God bless Dickie's wife, Judy!'

Suffice to say, everyone knows that Judy is like no one else and possesses a heart of gold.

Dickie's Generosity

As I embarked on this challenge of compiling Dickie Buck's Biography, I knew my interviews with past and present residents of the village would uncover numerous stories of his antics, which proved true; actually hundreds. I anticipated that a single, consistent theme would develop from the visible part of his exceptional life story. To my pleasant surprise, I had barely begun when I encountered a barrage of positive statements about Dickie's generosity from dozens of townsfolk. Many were eager to describe acts of kindness Dickie had performed for them and others, over many decades. The stories were heartwarming and inspiring. One individual who recounted her personal experiences of Dickie's kindness and actions actually wept as her feelings were so strong. Extraordinary, especially since the prior Chapters have shown that he's probably been one of the wildest personalities ever to have lived in Dennis. Stating it lightly, some people wouldn't dare have an argument with him while others could not have made it without him.

In this Chapter, I present only a subset of real-life examples of Dickie's kindness that I heard from my interviews with over forty people, excluding his family members; twenty-five hours of discussion. The personal stories demonstrate how his kindness has affected people across a broad range of life situations.

Never were Dickie's actions about financial gain. For him, it was all about giving, with no reciprocation wanted nor accepted. And consistent with his perpetual sense of humor, Dickie would add an amusing comment or twist whenever and wherever possible.

One compassionate reason for omitting names from some stories in this Chapter is that many of the locals who Dickie helped were experiencing difficult times in their lives and it's no one's business other than their own. Suffice to say, he helped those most in need and he remains in touch with them daily.

Helping the Little Girl Whose Mother Passed Away

One of the village's favorite little girls was Annie Walker; now a middle-aged woman of 'Annie's Crannies' fame. When she was only nine years old, her mother Alice passed away. A very sad situation for the father and five children; Patricia Walker being one. Dickie was working for her father at the time, delivering home heating oil. He and many other local families helped as best they could over the next few years.

When I met with Annie recently, hoping to obtain a few stories about her interactions with Dickie, I was shocked with the outpouring of emotions and kind words Annie expressed when describing what he had meant to her, over more than four decades. A few examples are given below, in her own words:

"When I was a kid and to this very

day, Dickie is the guy that when you need something, whether you're having a hard time or need help, you go to Dickie. He's either going to do it for you or he's going to turn you to someone who can help you do it. He is the Go-To person in town and probably the most reliable person in town.

He's come forward for this town in so many ways, the town doesn't even know it. He helps things get done in the village!"

***

"Here's another example of how Dickie stepped up to the plate for me and my family. Six months after my mother died, one of my older sisters got married. Consequently, my father was left with me and my two young brothers still at home. The villagers stepped in and helped raise us kids, keeping us busy. As an example, my two brothers had sleep-overs at Bob Eldred, Sr.'s house where he taught them to play chess.

Well, Dickie and Judy took me in that year. They were living at the Dennis Inn at the time (Windswept or La Coquille back then). When I was eight or nine, I loved ice skating. Whenever I could, I'd skate before and after school at the small manmade pond at the corner of Elm Street and Route 6A.

While living with he and Judy that winter, Dickie knew how much I missed skating, so late one cold night he went out behind the Inn, turned the garden hose on and flooded the rear parking lot to make a skating rink for me. In the middle of the night, he put the floodlight on and woke me up. 'Come downstairs,

I've got a surprise.'

I'll never forget walking downstairs, then going outside and seeing my skates at the rear parking lot, ready for me to put on. He made my very own private skating rink. Dickie was so kind to me, always."

***

"When my mother was still alive, she and my father would take an annual vacation. Dickie and Judy would move into our house and take care of all us kids."

***

"I can't imagine this town without Dickie."

Finding the Young Girl's Lost Doll

Seth Crowell, a life-long friend of Dickie, told me a wonderful family story. "One day, my granddaughter was in the third grade and riding home on the school bus on Sesuit Neck. She had a doll that was a monkey and when they were tossing it back and forth, it went out the window. She was devastated; came home and in tears told her mother, 'Lost Monkey'.

Well, Dickie heard about it and went to look for it. He went to the place where she said she lost it. Of course, it wasn't lying in the road so he went knocking on doors. He found it; somebody had picked it up. He got it and brought it back to her. Made her really happy. He was full grown at the time; not a kid."

'Another case where Dickie just

happened to hear that a little girl had lost her doll. He dropped what he was doing at the moment to assure the story would have a happy ending. People were always amazed that he'd hear, in real-time, about everything happening in the village and instantly appear to solve the problem. "Like a Guardian Angel looking over us all." some have said.

Protector of Sisters at Beach Parties

Sandy and Sally Poole wanted to share their personal story about Dickie, as their protector:

"Our family had spent summers in the Corporation Road neighborhood since we were very young, then we moved there full-time during our High School years. Back then it was safe; we could walk around the town without worrying; you can't do that now. Dennis truly was a great town to grow up in.

We had a charmed childhood near Corporation Beach. We worked 'til 5 o'clock then went water skiing at Corporation Beach 'til 8 o'clock. You wouldn't catch me doing that now with the sharks.

We've known Dickie since we were little girls. He would do lawns for people; take care of cottages; lots of local jobs. He's always been around.

In our teens, we wanted to go to the summer beach parties. Our father ('Lefty' as he was known) said to us 'As long as Dickie Buck is there, I'll be fine, I won't worry about you at all'.

Well of course, Dickie was the biggest hell-raiser around. He was the 'Fox in the henhouse'. But he always protected my sister and I. He was like a Guardian Angel to me. He protected me.

Sometimes we had bonfires at Crowe's Pasture beach 'back in the day'. Dickie would organize the parties, get the wood and arrange the whole thing. He was like the Pied Piper and everyone would go. And our dad would say 'It's good that Dickie was going to be there. Yup you can go, ok.'

There were never any fights when Dickie was there. The guys knew not to mess with him.

He was always a gentleman with us. Even when he was with a different girl, he'd always keep an eye on us. The Fox in Sheep's Clothing. If a guy came up and talked to me too long, Dickie was at my side. Like an older brother but more like an Angel.

Even though he raised more hell than us, he was the Angel with Horns!

There wasn't anybody who knew him that didn't like him. A very crafty guy but very capable. If you were out in a boat and in trouble, he'd arrive to help.

And if he liked you, he was more than willing to give of his time and just be there. You didn't expect him necessarily, but he would show up when things were 'interesting', shall we say.

He was always around and he knew every nook and cranny in town. He had a real ear for being at the right place at the wrong time (to help people).

He is a legend in his own time. A Living Legend as it were, thank goodness. For many, many reasons."

Sold Car to a Friend for $19.95

Patricia Walker has been another life-long friend of Dickie, with warm feelings, respect and appreciation of his kindness and generosity; an example is given below.

"What does Dickie mean to me? He is and always has been for me, a really dependable, good friend.

At one time I was short on money and went to Dickie, 'I need a car'.

He replied, 'How much money have you got?'

'Twenty bucks.'

'Ok.'

He sold me a car for $19.95. I gave him a $20 bill and he gave me a nickel back

He sold me a Rocket 88 Oldsmobile. The driver's side door wouldn't open so you had to get in through the passenger side. But it had a brand-new battery in it!

I drove the car for a year-and-a-half. Every week I was down at Marceline's (junk yard) buying a tire for $5.

The day it died, I was over near Hamlin's garage in Harwich when the whole driveshaft fell out of the car. We pushed it in and called Louie Hamlin the next day. He said 'It's got a good battery. I'll keep it.'"

Breaking Up a High School Party that was Out of Control

Chris Myland, son of Ejner (Big Chris) Myland mentioned previously, remembers growing up around Players Plaza when his father ran the gas station.

"When I was in High School, Dickie worked for my father at the Sinclair station. He lived above the station's office for a while.

Our family had moved into a duplex on Mayfair Road. One weekend when my parents were gone, my younger sister was having a party in the basement. After a while I went out to get more beer. I borrowed a kid's car, a little Volkswagen, but I rolled it over on North Dennis Road. Thank God, the guy I was with was the President of the High School class. He happened to know the cop who came and we just said somebody ran us off the road. He drove us home with no problem.

When I got back to our house, there must have been a hundred kids and the party was getting out of control. They even stole my speargun. My sister knew to call Dickie for help. He came quickly and cleared the whole place out just like a cop would do. Everyone scattered.

Dickie was truly a legend – solving everyone's problem."

Helping a Best Friend During Boyhood

Dickie reminisces about his friends growing up in the village: "Michael Dubin was probably my best friend. He and Bobby Sears, but both have since passed away."

Michael arrived when Dickie was in sixth grade (12 years old). It was Michael's father who built the Players Pharmacy complex at the intersection of Routes 6A and 134. Because Dickie was always hanging around in that neighborhood, he and Michael became close friends. Dickie was a year older than Michael.

Michael was smart but had a slight

frame and not athletic. Dickie recalls, "Kids would pick on him. I took to liking him because he'd bring candy to school. We got along well. I announced that if anyone wanted to do anything hurtful to Michael, they'd have to come through me. And nobody wanted to. I took on the two biggest, toughest kids in school, at separate times."

Dickie was not large for his age but he quickly earned a reputation for helping his friends, while just an early teen. Dickie defended Michael for many years through school.

"Michael became my very best friend and we shared everything.

Years later, I went to Mike and Judy's wedding in Brookline. And I worked in the gas station for many years next to Mike's pharmacy. We spent lots of time together, over decades of friendship."

Dickie also helped Mike and his wife Judy during his illness which eventually led to his passing away at an early age. It was very sad for Dickie when Mike died.

Top Choice of Whom to be Stranded with on a Desert Island

Significant comments from Judy Dubin, Mike's wife:

"One of the things I have always said, since I have known Dickie, is that if I were deserted on a desert island and if I had to pick one person to be with, for my best chance of survival, it would be Dickie. He's a survivor. He's a very, very smart person. He has a tremendous amount of native intelligence, a lot of curiosity and he always seems to be there when you need him. He has an instinct for that.

He also likes women but I think it's because he gets a kick out of them. I have known about his old girlfriends and him sneaking into their houses on ladders, etc.

Everybody liked him because they wished they were him!"

Services without Requesting Payment

Additional comments from Judy Dubin, explaining that Dickie is a much greater person than is represented by his antics:

"He's honest, trustworthy and really a caring person. He's done so many things for so many people; he just shows up and does it.

Sometimes he drives people crazy because he never sends a bill for his services, no matter what he does; landscaping, yardwork, etc. He figures people will pay him when and if they can.

In some cases, he's done things like plowing snow from someone's driveway without being asked. Dickie knew they needed assistance and he knew they didn't have the wherewithal to pay for it. So, he just did it without them knowing who had been in their yard."

This has been echoed by numerous men who have worked for Dickie over the years. Apparently, an elderly woman approached Dickie's employee one day after he had mowed her lawn. She was very upset that Dickie had been taking care of her lawn for over two years and he had yet to request payment. Mostly likely because he felt she may not have the financial resources.

Daily Visits with Villagers

A long-term friend of Dickie's, Judy Scarafile who had worked at the Players Pharmacy during the days of Bucky Beaver's Magic Garage, recalls Dickie having spent nearly every day of his life in the village.

"Dickie does not like to leave Dennis or East Dennis. He'd go to Hyannis but only if he really had to. He's a bit of a fish out of water when he crosses the town line."

This was consistent with my observations. During recent conversations with many people, I asked "So, how often do you see and interact with Dickie?"

To my surprise, nearly every one of them replied, "I see him daily."

He gets around constantly, like a perpetual motion machine, from sunrise 'til dinner. And he normally goes back out cruising around town for a final check of local matters.

Some might say he's like a neighborhood dog that has his daily rounds, visiting each house for a treat. When Dickie was young, his definition of a "treat" might have had a lascivious meaning but that's off-point from this discussion.

Dickie has always possessed abundant, positive energy that he readily shares with everyone. Consequently, they all enjoy seeing him drive into their yard.

They know he'll never be asking for anything; he's just stopping by to share an item to aid their living situation or just chat about nothing in particular. Dickie is always up-beat and optimistic, to this day. That's why everyone enjoys his visits. Especially the elderly who don't have many visitors.

But don't be fooled; Dickie is always listening closely. And his mind doesn't forget an iota of local news or gossip. He processes it to fuel his anticipation of where to go next, as Johnny-on-the-Spot, when something is brewing. The 'Angel of the Village'?

Today you can still find Dickie at the 7-Eleven, the Northside Marina, the Indian Burial Ground, Scargo Tower or a dozen of his other special (some spiritual) places where he makes his daily rounds. If you don't see him, it's likely because he's visiting an elderly person who can no longer get out-and-about.

Taking Elderly Ladies for Rides on His Motorcycle

It probably would surprise most men, especially those who lived in the '40s and '50s, that many women of that period had always dreamt of taking a ride on a motorcycle. It was on their 'bucket list' before the term became popular in recent years.

Dickie was probably the only local motorcyclist who enjoyed chatting (flirting?) with elderly ladies of the village. "Want to go for a ride on my bike?" he'd ask them, even the oldest of ladies. Most said 'Yes', to his delight.

In my recent discussions with many of Dickie's friends, I heard stories of Dickie having taken three elderly ladies for rides on his big motorcycles. One was Mrs. Ruth Colby who had been the Dennis Post Master for many years, after Fred Maher retired.

Her son David fondly recalls, "Dickie was always very friendly with my Mother. The last time I saw Dickie was when we had come back to Dennis to visit. There was a band concert on the Village Green and we brought my Mother there. Dickie came over and was always very personable, of course. He really made my Mother's day, talking to her, paying attention to her.

On one of her birthdays, some years earlier when she was in her late-70s, we made arrangements with somebody from Dennis to have Dickie visit my Mother on his motorcycle. He took her for a ride when she was quite aged. That was so exciting to her."

The entire Colby family really appreciated Dickie having given his time for her enjoyment, late in life when each day can lack excitement.

***

Here's a great story about Dickie taking another elderly lady for a motorcycle ride, shared by her daughter, Alayne Hogan.

"Both of my parents were in their nineties when I met Dickie. My parents would come down to visit from Boston. My father was an ex-Police Detective; he and Dickie would have long conversations. Dickie was so wonderful to both of them.

My mother's birthday was in August. The year she turned eighty-seven, Dickie said, 'Margaret, do you want to jump on this motorcycle and go for a ride with me on your birthday?'

And she did. It became a yearly thing until she was ninety-nine years old!"

The first time Dickie took Margaret for a ride, Alayne's father looked at his daughter and said, "You think this is funny, don't you? I don't!" The riders had been gone for quite a while and he became very concerned that something had happened to her but there was never an accident.

After that initial jaunt, the father was fine and would ask to see Dickie as soon as he arrived at his daughter's home. "Call Dickie, I've got to talk with him."

Alayne recalls, "I'd call him and Dickie would reply, 'Ok, I'll be right over to see Frank.' After that, it became an annual event for Margaret, going for a ride on the motorcycle with Dickie."

The Cape Cod Times newspaper wrote a wonderful human-interest article about the happening and showed a photo of Margaret on the motorcycle, on her ninety-ninth birthday! The reporter followed Dickie and Margaret from behind, as he drove her to Sesuit Harbor, the Cape Playhouse and around the village.

"When Dickie had arrived at the house on the morning of the ride, Margaret had a group of elderly friends visiting. He entered with a black leather jacket and motorcycle helmet for her to wear but she immediately said, 'I can't put that on, I just had my hair done.' She was a real sport.

At the end of their ride, Margaret was holding onto Dickie as he was driving up the steep grade of Erb Drive, 'Dick, I think you've gained a few pounds from last year, I can't hold onto you.'

It was the funniest day."

After that ride, Dickie remembers saying to her, "You're going to be one-hundred next year."

She replied, "Yes, and next year I plan to drive this thing by myself. I can heft my leg up and over, I'll drive it myself." She was joking but it was great fun.

Dickie's kindness added significantly to this woman's later years.

Renegotiating a Better Car Purchase for a Village Woman

Joe Lowther recalls many stories about Dickie interacting with his whole family.

"I remember that my mother had gone on her own and purchased a Studebaker Lark; a stubby little car. My father was in the Coast Guard and stationed in Southwest Harbor, Maine so he was out of the picture. After the purchase, she told Dickie what she had paid for it and she felt it was too much.

'You have paid too much!' said Dickie and he took the car back to the salesman. With her, he negotiated in her best interest and she ended up purchasing a different car at a much better price."

Mentoring Village Boys

For many decades during his adult years, Dickie spent considerable time mentoring boys from the village. He has two daughters of his own but he also enjoyed mentoring boys whose fathers had left on account of divorce or having passed away. He gave each boy practical advice on diverse, everyday issues and challenges. Later, he made suggestions on possible careers to pursue and each has proven successful in their lives. They all are now adults yet Dickie maintains frequent contact with each, as friends,

one living as far away as Australia. Dickie's positive, life-long effect on these men has been profound and their individual stories are so significant that together, they could be the topic of a book of its own.

***

Dickie also mentored other boys he had met either in his neighborhood, around Sesuit Harbor or in school. Here's a first-hand account of how Dickie mentored a teen friend who later became a very successful real-estate developer. Dickie always made time to give advice although he was more than twenty-years older.

Appreciative words from Jon Gordon who manages the Lewis Gordon Senior Citizen Housing complex in South Dennis, which was founded by his father:

"Dickie was my mentor as a teen. My father had a boat in the harbor so I hung around there in the summer. Dickie often worked for my father, as captain on two of our boats.

Because my father commuted to Boston frequently for work, I had a lot of spare time at the harbor. Some days, I'd jump on the back of Dickie's motorcycle and he'd take me for a ride.

He was very good to me and took me under his wing. He was a great mentor. I learned the practical, realistic side of the world from Dickie. How people are; to treat others how you want to be treated.

He taught me about boats, tying lines and mechanical things. He'd also take me diving. He was the first person around with an Evinrude Aquanaut (the same as 'diving hookahs' of today, with a surface compressor in a tire tube that would pump air down through long hoses to a diver).

In addition to being a mentor, he's been somewhat of a father figure to me. I admire him and would do anything for him. I have a true respect for Dickie. All his different toys, all his different stories – an interesting guy. And he'd loan money to anyone.

My family was very fond of Dickie. If you're his friend, there isn't anything he wouldn't do for you."

Jon and Dickie are still close friends today, often speaking a couple times each week. Nearly fifty years of true friendship and respect.

***

Dickie also was a mentor to other boys of his age who were in school with him. One in particular was Donny Adams, a hell-raiser like Dickie at an early age, who confessed that many of the stories he most vividly remembers cannot be put in print. But he does have positive things to say about what Dickie meant to him while growing up.

"Just so you know how I think about Dickie, he was one of my mentors growing up. And I attribute much of my career success in the electronics industry to Dickie. I learned many practical things from Dickie."

In those days, Dickie wasn't an electronics whiz but his friend gained from Dickie's "practical knowledge and approach to problems, and that hard work pays off"; Donny's words.

Gift of a Free Boat Trailer to a Life-Long Friend

Seth Crowell still appreciates Dickie's frequent, unanticipated assistance, even with both in their eighties:

"Recently I was pulling my boat out of the water and the back end of my boat trailer let go; just sagged down. I got the boat home alright, got it off the trailer onto jack stands and I started looking for a trailer.

Dickie heard about that and one day, here's this trailer backing into my yard. I put my boat on it. 'How much do you want for that Dickie?'

He says 'Nothin. If you die first I'll take it. If I die first, you can have it.'"

This simple, free transaction was typical of Dickie's assistance for others. In this case, his friend hadn't even asked Dickie to locate a trailer. But with his eyes and ears always open, Dickie knows when someone is in need and immediately searches his local 'property data base' to find the right item for the person in need.

Dickie had grown up with Seth and been in the same grade through Dennis schools. In their younger years, they spent much time together.

Seth recalls, "He got in trouble now and then." and Seth beamed with a boyhood smile.

"When we were young, one of the things we did was trade items and he was pretty sharp at that. I always ended up taking a loss!"

Helping Behind the Scenes to Save Historic Houses in the Village

As explained by an unnamed person of the village:

"Here's a nice story that a lot of people don't know. It completely surprised me about Dickie.

A while back, a person bought a historic house in the village. The house was rumored to have a secret room for the Underground Railroad. (The UR was a network of safe houses established by abolitionists prior to the Civil War for those who were escaping slavery.) Of course, every old house on Cape Cod was supposed to be part of the UR.

So, they had people come look at the house. The Old King's Highway Historical District Commission and the Dennis Building Inspector concluded that the building must come down; it's unsafe.

A bunch of us wanted to appeal because we knew who the buyer was and we knew what the emphasis was. The lot was worth more than the house but it was a historic house in the center of the Historic District. A bunch of us thought it should be preserved.

So, we were talking about getting an attorney, fighting it and going all the way up to court.

There was a knock on my door. It was Dickie, he had a $100 in his hand and he said 'Here, add this to the kitty because it's not right to tear that house down.'

You could have knocked me over with a feather. Nowhere did I think he even cared. That's what kind of mystery man he is."

Loaning His Motorcycle to a Total Stranger

Dickie's daughter Alesia worked in the liquor store at the Players Plaza, where the East Dennis Post Office is located today. She worked the night shift. There was a period of two weeks when a stranger would appear regularly and sit by the phone booth under the big sign in the parking lot.

"We didn't know who he was, where he came from. We were just curious about him.

One day my Dad drove in on his motorcycle and he popped in to get a Coke. I asked my Dad, 'Hey, do you know who that guy is?'

'No, I've never seen him before.'

'He's been hanging around but we really don't know what he's doing.'

So, my Dad went over there and was talking with him for a while. The next thing I know, he handed him his helmet and the guy took off on his motorcycle.

He came back in and I asked, 'Hey, what's the deal with the guy?'

'Oh, he's down on his luck and he's living down the street in the motel. He doesn't have a phone and he's waiting for his wife and child to call him. They call him on the pay phone then he answers it and talks to them. He said he had a bunch of things to do but doesn't have a car. He's got a motorcycle license and he showed it to me, so I told him to take my bike and go do what he needed to do then fill it with gas and bring it back to me.'

Nobody does that. But my Father does that." Alesia concluded, proudly.

Dickie certainly is an amazing, trusting soul. A remarkable human being, not just a legend.

Donating an Antique Anchor to the Josiah Dennis Manse

Over his many decades of Scuba diving in Cape Cod Bay, Dickie discovered numerous anchors from vessels that sailed in the 1800s. In October 2005, Dickie donated one of his largest treasures to the Josiah Dennis Manse Museum at 61 Whig Street. The anchor still stands there today with an accompanying plaque identifying Dickie as the donor.

Emergency Assistance for Animals

Dickie's daughters remember that when their dad was delivering heating oil to homes, he'd often get calls to remove raccoons and other small animals from garages, attics or cellars. Most occasions were fun for Dickie because he appreciated animals, whether they be wild or domesticated.

His children liked their Dad's animal rescues because he'd bring the animals home as temporary pets, which was permissible back in the '60s and '70s. They still recall 'Rocky the Flying

Squirrel' who stayed with the family a few months during his convalescence. And 'Happy' the crow was nursed back to health after a broken wing.

Racoons were the most common borders. 'Sasha', 'Pebbles', 'JuJu' and the huge 'Bonkers' all spent time in the Buck home, after their initial rabies vaccination of course. All were released to the wild with a happy ending.

***

Elsewhere in this book, it was mentioned that Dickie often responded to calls about Marine Mammal strandings in Cape Cod Bay. No matter what time of year, nor harsh weather, Dickie would always head to the scene with his wet suit and jump in the water to assist a mammal in distress.

Loaning Money to Friends in Need

As described in the Notorious Characters Chapter, Dickie often gave $100 cash to Lester Hallett when asked for financial help. Dickie knew it would probably be used for F'Lester's next bottle of Muscatel but he couldn't say no to kindhearted Lester whose life was often 'on the rocks'.

Dickie was equally generous with locals who periodically fell on 'hard times'. To those he liked most, he'd know when they were low on funds and always give them some cash without their asking. To others, he'd extend a cash loan over a handshake. But he made it clear that it was a loan, stating "Pay me back when you can. But pay me back." To these persons, he wasn't being tough; he was just teaching them to be responsible.

Dickie never wanted to support a freeloader. He was quite frugal with his own money so he felt that no one else should be a spendthrift, especially with money he had loaned.

Gift of Operable Appliances for Persons Without Funds

Similar to the story above, Dickie somehow 'gets wind' that an older or destitute person had a major kitchen appliance die. He instantly calls his friend Jon Gordon, who manages the Lewis Gordon Senior Citizens Housing complex, to inquire whether he has any operable appliances in his inventory of used or discarded items. Within minutes, Dickie appears at Jon's facility, loads the appliance in his truck and delivers it to the person in need. The fortunate recipient is shocked that Dickie is there, like Santa Clause or Robin Hood, with a solution for their biggest problem. All free, again.

Responding to a Call about a Flooding Basement

Dave Howes also has been a life-long friend of Dickie's, both having grown up in the village and spent every summer around Sesuit Harbor. One time when Dave was at-sea for his maritime employment, his wife had gone into the cellar and noticed that it was flooded. She called Dave who knew the quickest solution: 'Call Dickie Buck. He'll find a way to solve the problem.'

Within the hour, Dickie was in the cellar rigging up a bilge pump and hoses to solve the problem until Dave was able to return and implement a long-term solution.

Dickie's comment: 'I revel in helping people out when they have a bad situation and need someone to solve the problem.'

Dumpster Diving for a Friend

Linda Peterson recalled a funny story about Dickie helping her and Pete at the harbor:

"Dickie was willing to help anybody, without question. The first time I learned this was when I wanted to build a fishpond in my back yard. Maybe for a starter, a good-sized piece of shrinkwrap would work.

It was late spring when the marina employees were taking all the shrinkwrap off the boats. We went down to the marina and were looking around. Dickie came up, knowing me and my husband, and asked:

'What's going on, what are you looking for?'

'I'm looking for a decent-sized piece of shrinkwrap to line a fishpond with.'

'Ah, no problem' Dickie replied and into the dumpster he went. Who would do that? Out he came with this big, beautiful piece of shrinkwrap for my fishpond."

$5 Tip to the Toll Booth Attendant at the Ted Williams Tunnel

"When Dickie was driving a group of villagers in his Limo to catch their departing flight from Logan Airport in Boston, he stopped at the Ted Williams Tunnel toll booth to pay the fee. Before pulling away, Dickie gave the operator a $5 tip and the man was shocked.

Dickie asked, 'What's the matter, hasn't a white man ever given you a tip before?'"

Loaning a Tuxedo for a Wedding

Carole and Billy Bell recall when Dickie helped them out in a wardrobe crisis:

"We were invited to a black-tie wedding in Oyster Harbors and Billy needed a tuxedo. It was in the days when Dickie was driving his limousines so we put out an All-Points-Bulletin for Dickie. He arrived the next day with two tuxes to choose from. Fortunately, Billy was the same size as Dickie.

'You don't need to buy one; just borrow it.' Dickie said.

We did, had it dry-cleaned and returned it."

Another case of Dickie making other persons' lives a bit easier.

Carole continued, "Sometime later, Dickie drove his limo for our daughter's wedding and wouldn't take a cent. That's the kind of guy he is."

Assisting at an Accidental Death at Northside Marina

Quite often when there was a serious problem or injury in the village, Dickie would appear on the scene almost instantly to help as best he could. Another example of he being the Guardian Angel? He didn't appear at only the best of times.

In an earlier Chapter, it was explained that Dickie was at Russell Bearse's side when he died from a gunshot wound inflicted by other boys. Below is another case of Dickie being on-site at another terrible accident.

One day at the Northside Marina, a large loader was being used to move heavy equipment. When the equipment operator was backing the machine, the young manager of the marina attempted to climb onto the machine to give directions. As he jumped up on the ladder beside the operator's cab, his foot slipped and his leg went down and under the large wheel.

The accident was not the operator's fault. Regardless, it was a terrible bodily injury to the victim and he spoke with Dickie within seconds of the accident happening. The wife of one of the marina owners tried to assist but there was nothing she nor Dickie could do to save the man's life.

Dickie has been Everyone's 911 to Call for Help

His daughter's view: "He was the guy everyone called at dinner time to go rescue them when their car got stuck on Chapin Beach. Dad was 911."

Another person in the village said,

"He has a real good heart. He's helped a lot of people who were born with a little less than the rest of us. If he likes you, he'll do anything for you, whenever."

Still Diving to Replace Bottom Zincs on Boats

Last year, an elderly long-term friend, Pete Schimmel, was at the harbor talking with Dickie and another boater about his sailboat. Apparently, on the 'high-course' (spring) tides, his sailboat's keel penetrated into the mud a couple feet because of the shallow depth in his boat slip. He was concerned that he needed to change the zincs (sacrificial anodes) but didn't want to haul the boat out for that small job.

"I'll go down and do it." Dickie offered.

He performed that diving job as well as similar work for other individuals and the Northside Marina, at age eighty-two!

Shoveling Out a Horse Stall for A Girl in Need

One day recently, I was taking to Dickie but he had to leave for a commitment he had made. "I need to dig out the horse stable for a girl. She's sick in the hospital and she can't take care of her horses. I'm going over there to dig out the stalls and carry away the shit; there's a lot of it!

She'll try to pay me but I won't take it."

Typical Dickie, helping another villager who needed assistance. He never refuses, even if it requires back-breaking work at age eighty-three.

The Robin Hood Syndrome

Robin Hood was an English Lord who became a champion of the people in the 12th century. He robbed the rich to help the poor and stood with the rightful King of England; King Richard, (Richard the Lionheart) against King John and the Sheriff of Nottingham. The legend of Robin Hood portrays him as a good-natured, generous and kind person who was loved by the local folk.

His additional preoccupation was pursuit of the lovely Maid Marian. (Always necessary to have a pretty girl woven into the story.)

When gathering input from Dickie's friends about his personality traits, a number of persons likened him to Robin Hood. This analogy is very appropriate with regard to Dickie's generosity and lifelong trait of helping the needy or handicapped, as shown above. But it is incorrect if anyone carelessly or meaningfully tries to associate Dickie's actions as having stolen from the rich or tax-hungry government. He certainly is patriotic, conservative and has strong political views, but he lives within local laws and the U.S. Constitution.

But you can bet your ass that if a Maid Marian ever had passed through the village (his Nottingham) he surely would have been first in line to lay down his cape with chivalry and a devilish Dickie Buck smile!

Personality Traits

When I asked over forty of Dickie's friends to describe his personality, in one or two words, the replies were highly diverse. Below are eighty-four descriptions that could easily be grouped into four personality categories: Active, Daring, Kind and *Flirtatious*. It's astounding that all these traits are represented in a single person. Imagine the adjectives his 'enemies' might add.

Acrobat   Adagio Performer   *Adulterer*   *Angel with Horns*

Automated Cash Machine   Attention Getter   Ballroom Dancer   Biker

Brew Master   *Butterfly - Flitting from Girl to Girl*   *Cad*

Can-Do Guy   Capable   Cash-Only   Charmer   Collector

Crafty   Daredevil   Dependable   Dirty-Dancer   Enterprising

Entrepreneur   Evel Knievel   Extrovert   Fearless   Fighter

Flirt   *Fox in the Henhouse*   Frugal

Fruitfly – Appearing When Women Arrive

Generous   Go-To Guy   Guardian Angel   Health Conscious   Hellraiser

Helper   *Honey Bee Pollinating*   Jester   Impersonator   Instigator

Johnny-on-the-Spot   Kind – Innately So   *Ladies' Man*   Legend in His Own

Time   Mayor   Mentor   Non-Drinker   Non-Smoker   Opportunist

Organizer

Peter Pan

Patriot   Performer   Philanthropist   *Philanderer*   Pianist

Pied Piper   Practical   Prankster   Problem Solver   Protector   Rascal

Reliable   Respectful of Elders, Natives & Indians   Risk Taker

Robin Hood

Rooster in the Neighborhood   Saint   Scallywag   *Scoundrel*   Show Off

Street Wise   *Stud*   Survivor   *Swinger*   Town Clown

Town Promoter   Trampoliner   Trumpeter   Wild Man   Wise Guy

Wizard – Predictor of Happenings   *Wolf in Sheep's Clothes*   911

Dickie's Hobbies and Personality at Home

In those rare moments when Dickie is home with spare time, he might be involved in activities you may not have guessed. Here's a bit more about how he lives.

- ✓ Plays many musical instruments (piano, trumpet, clarinet, sax, drums) by ear
- ✓ Enjoys cooking
- ✓ No longer drinks alcohol or smokes cigarettes; gave up in 1965
- ✓ No longer drinks coffee; gave up in 1973
- ✓ Not religious but is spiritual; like Native Americans
- ✓ Doesn't believe in afterlife
- ✓ Never buys a new car
- ✓ Recites works from his favorite poets
- ✓ Always pays cash from a wad in his pocket
- ✓ Likes to fix things and situations
- ✓ Disillusioned by most politicians
- ✓ Displays Oriental furnishings in their home
- ✓ Shirks off affection; characteristic of his generation
- ✓ Took annual Birthday swims in Sesuit Creek up to middle-age
- ✓ Speaks Japanese
- ✓ Enjoys dogs as his companion
- ✓ Likes tropical fish
- ✓ Ends phone conversations abruptly: "Bye" followed by an immediate 'click'
- ✓ Has a trusting mindset
- ✓ Took New Year's Day swims at Corporation and Millway Beaches with his daughters, for 30 years ending in 2017
- ✓ Likes everyone to be happy

Peter Pan Analysis

The Peter Pan story originated within a British novel titled "*The Little White Bird*", published in 1902[40]. The book achieved prominence and market longevity because of several chapters that introduced the mythical character of Peter Pan. Subsequently, those chapters were published as a children's book titled, "*Peter Pan in Kensington Gardens*".

Disney released the animated adventure-fantasy film "*Peter Pan*" in 1953 with tremendous popularity[41]. In the story, the magical boy Peter flew into the life of three children in pursuit of his rebellious shadow. He and his fairy friend, Tinkerbell, came from a far-off place called Neverland where children stay perpetually young.

The Peter character was a childhood dream of the author J. M. Barrie. It is believed the name Pan was associated with a deity of Greek Mythology – Pan, god of 'The Wild', shepherds and flocks, mountains, rustic music and the companion of Nymphs. He had horns and the legs and hindquarters of a goat as did satyrs. He often played a musical pipe as he traveled. (Note that Dickie played instruments and enjoyed associating with Nymphs, as well. And everyone knew he had 'horns'.)

Literary scholars and psychologists have studied the story of Peter Pan for over one-hundred years, as it portrays the boy who refused to grow up. With free spirit and perpetual youth, Peter is brave yet avoids moral responsibility. Certain psychologists attribute Peter's childlike actions and belief that only the self exists, was fueled by his running away from his parents when he was very young. (Dickie did exactly that, at age sixteen).

Because a number of people have likened Dickie to Peter Pan, I have listed below (in no particular order), many of Peter's traits as extracted from various on-line literary reviews of the original novel. Those common to Dickie's personality traits (from prior page) have been indicated with a check mark. Recognize that some traits were prominent only during his first few decades then waned, in his best interests and those of others.

Draw your own conclusion whether there is similarity between our friend Dickie and the fictional Peter Pan. It's all in fun.

- ✓ *Free-spirited*
- ✓ *Brave – wanted to fight everyone*
- ✓ *Loves playing jokes and having fun with others*
- ✓ *Fearlessly cocky when putting himself in danger*

Absolutely refuses to grow up
Teaches others to fly

- ✓ *Never-ending youth and innocence*

- ✓ *Humorous*
- ✓ *Associates with fairies, pirates, mermaids, and Native Americans*
- ✓ *Incredibly adventurous and daring*

Boastful
Careless

- ✓ *Able to feel danger when it is near*
- ✓ *Kind*
- ✓ *Mischievous*
- ✓ *If rescuing friends, he is far more mature than any adult*

Claims greatness, when claims are questionable

Forgetful and self-centered

- ✓ *Happy and nonchalant attitude*
- ✓ *Able to imagine things into existence*
- ✓ *Stubborn*
- ✓ *When thought he was going to die, he felt only one shudder*

Impractical at times
Escapist

- ✓ **Respected and loved by <u>nearly</u> everyone**

Dickie's Introspection and Comments on Life

Being Peter Pan and Staying Young

People certainly view Dickie as similar to Peter Pan but as the Author, I was compelled to ask his opinion. "After you've seen the list of Peter Pan's personality traits, do you feel any similarities?"

"Yes it's true, I'm like him. I never wanted to grow up. I'd go out of my way to do things that were childish as a way of keeping my youth. I never wanted to be old."

This is exactly how we've all viewed Dickie and it's reassuring that he knows himself so well and is willing to speak openly about it.

He continues (remember, he's speaking as an eighty-three-year-old man), "It's kind of discouraging now, to not have that vitality. I'd go out every morning and jump on the trampoline 150 times. I still do it some days; actually, yesterday I was out jumping with my dog. My neighbor is in his seventies and he said he couldn't keep up with me, so I guess I'm not doing too bad."

Labor Day Depressions

Although Dickie and I were born fifteen years apart, certain elements of our core personality are similar and fully attributable to having grown up beside Cape Cod Bay, especially our Labor Day Depressions as described below.

Dickie explains. "Every year on Labor Day, I was hit with an emotional depression. An empty feeling like everyone had gone. It was like having the life sucked out of me by a vacuum cleaner.

All my summer friends had left the Cape and all the available summer girls were gone too. The village mothers would keep their beautiful daughters indoors after Labor Day rather than let them roam the beach in their bikinis."

He expressed exactly how I felt during my teens, with the arrival of Labor Day. I disliked school, which was only a few days away. All there was for fall enjoyment was sports and fishing. At least the bass fishing improved in September but that was no substitute for the absence of summer girls.

Dickie had more to say: "I still remember the Labor Day I was released from the Dennis Police Station and had to walk the full length of Route 134 to get back home after having spent the night in jail. It was the day I quit drinking alcohol and smoking cigarettes. I felt bad from the night before but the Labor Day Depression that hit me was the same big deal every year, jail or no jail." Sober or buzzed.

He still dreads the end of summer and its predictable drop in community activity − proof that he's still got lots of energy to expend at eighty-three!

Missing Life as it was Before Political Correctness

"As good as it gets!" was Dickie's reply when I asked "What was it like living in the village in the '50s and '60s". He immediately thought of Jack Nicholson's character fully enjoying life in the 1997 hit movie of the same name. And come-to-think-of-it, Dickie has the same kind of rock-solid, ear-to-ear, devilish smile as Jack.

"In recent years, Political Correctness has ruined many things." Dickie added.

We discussed that PC in the U.S. has helped certain (but not all) conditions of humanity but for this discussion with Dickie, we agreed that many things that were commonplace, enjoyable and accepted in the village during the '50s are forbidden today.

"Hell, I'd be in jail, given all the fights I had in those days and I wouldn't be alone. And most of the active couples in the village partied regularly in those days. It was definitely like *Peyton Place!*"

In that context, Dickie meant that many couples were 'swinging'. All consensual but definitely an active village, socially. Nothing more needs to be said.

Resenting Physical Change in the Village

"I hate change. Especially the big houses on the beach. I wish Dennis could stay the same, like Grover's Corners and I'm Howie Newsome.

I hate the proliferation of all the huge edifices, mega-mansions.

If I had eminent death, I would like to get a horse with saddlebags full of railroad flares and ride down the beach and chuck one in each window, with a strong northeast wind blowing.

I was familiar with little cottages and rose-covered houses. Now it's changed to see who can build the biggest house.

$12-million houses at Crowe's Pasture and they don't even own the land under it."

Death and Afterlife

Considering that Dickie has taken risk on hundreds of occasions in his life, I had to ask the question, "Do you believe in afterlife, reincarnation?"

"No, I don't. I think when the lights go out, the lights go out. I think because we run on so much electricity." The speed at which he answered proved this was his credo, always at the front of his brain.

I continued questioning. "So, you figure you've got one shot at life. Did you ever worry about taking risks? Worry about dying?"

"No, I never thought I was going to die. That's why when I walked up the side of the sand dune with the wedding troublemaker from Brewster following me with a shotgun in his hand, I felt he wasn't going to shoot me."

Dickie's ability to correctly anticipate the actions of his enemies has certainly contributed to his longevity. (The sole exception being the sucker-punch from the Paul Bunyan of East Dennis.)

It Mustn't Be Told!

When I conducted discussions with dozens of villagers to obtain input for this Biography, the majority chuckled then responded with the same general opinion:

'Oh Boy, have I got stories!' then quickly followed up with 'But I cannot discuss nor reveal those secrets. They mustn't ever get into print.'

Dickie's premarital years were busy to say the least, with many 'oats sewn'. 'More ass than a public toilet seat.' the old timers often said, as they saw Dickie driving around with a new girl in his convertible Jaguar.

A fair number of men resented Dickie. Explained easiest by the local women: 'It's simple. They were jealous.' Or they had a score to settle with him, as he may have 'mowed their lawn'.

Someone summed it up, 'He could charm the birds out of the trees, ladies too.'

One lady shared a brief story about Dickie.

'I was at the beach with a woman who was new in town. I tried to warn her. 'Oh, here comes Dickie Buck. Whenever a new girl arrives in town, even if she's only twenty-one, word will spread that she must be having an affair with Dickie!''

Comments from others:

'Even if Dickie hadn't done anything lewd or made sexual advances, people would assume he had. And he never denies anything. When a rumor catches up with him, he'll smile and say 'I'm a real hot ticket, aren't I?''

'He's the ultimate big horny fish in a small pond.'

'It doesn't matter if they're 18 or 100 years old, every woman is in love with Dickie.'

'I didn't know you were married.' stated by many.

***

I initiated a chat with Dickie on the topic of women:

"So Dickie, it's obvious you enjoy women. Tell me what's it's like being you, what do you think about with women around?"

"I'm drawn to attractive women like a magnet; always have been. When they're around I can sense it."

I thought to myself, 'That's exactly consistent with the observations of others, as mentioned in prior Chapters.'

Dickie continued, "I can't help myself because I adore attractive women. They know it and some are comfortable with it.

But they have to be attractive. I've never been interested in a woman that is not beautiful."

I recall more than one woman saying that 'As engaging as Dickie is with women, fortunately he has an innate ability to sense if a woman is interested in him or not. He knows when to back off and leave a woman to herself. He is respectful.'

***

***

In this Biography, we should be able to publish the cute, flirtatious story about Dickie inside the 7-Eleven and greeting the lady wearing her face pack. He certainly left lasting impressions. Her story:

"A few years back, I returned home after an exhausting weekend off-Cape. I quickly got my daughter ready for bed and she fell asleep. I was so tired that I sat on my sofa to watch TV but fell asleep as well. I woke up at 10:50 p.m. and realized I did not have milk for the next morning's breakfast. I had only ten minutes to jump in my car and get to Tedeschi's market (now 7-Eleven) to buy milk before the store closed.

I ran in, grabbed a bottle of milk and went up to the register where Dickie happened to be standing while talking to the cashier. I said 'Hello'. He got within three inches of my face and said 'What the heck do you have all over your face?'

Well, it seems that I had forgotten I put on a facial mask that turns green when it dries. I was so embarrassed. I paid for the milk, ran out to my car and realized I left the keys on the counter in the store. I had to run back in and get them but they were not there.

I looked at Dickie and he was holding up my keys, pointing to his cheek and smiling. He wanted a kiss on the cheek! Even with all my green on!

I gave him a quick peck, grabbed my keys and said to him 'You must never repeat this story!' He never did but I had fun telling it to all my friends that know Dickie. They all had a good laugh and said, 'It's so Dickie!'" Harmless fun.

Should we not publish the story about Dickie and a few of his best buddies having a contest on a summer afternoon? Well, maybe - it's harmless and only a bit sexual. Boys in their early twenties, pre-marriage.

The rules were simple as Dickie recalls: "Whoever could visit a girlfriend, have sex and return to the Tydol gas station (opposite from Louie's market in those days) with undeniable proof in the shortest time would be the winner. No bikes nor cars for transportation; you had to hoof-it. Me, Bobby Sears, Alfred Rudolph and two others who shall remain nameless. And there was some 'small change' involved too.

We all headed off in the directions of our 'most reliable' girlfriends. In less than an hour, I was back at the 'check-in' location with absolute proof of my accomplishment. I was not the first to arrive. Nor did I win but I was quite satisfied, nevertheless. Lots of laughs!"

***

Here I sit with dozens of stories depicting Dickie's most outlandish sexual escapades. Some funny, others lewd and still others you could only shake your head at.

Many of you probably bought this book with hopes of reading these 'Dirty Dickie' stories and probably nothing else. They'd fill hundreds of pages for sure. A whole year of listening on my part.

As the Author, I could change the names to protect the GUILTY, or

I could redact key words in stories

containing strong sexual content (nearly
all the words).

DO NOT TURN THE PAGE

DO NOT READ ANY FURTHER

I have been told that these stories were based on Dickie's early, pre-marital years but nevertheless, the book Contract I established with the Buck family states that this Biography SHALL NOT include content that could offend and/or embarrass Judy, their daughters or Dickie (albeit unlikely). A deal's a deal!

Maybe someday, permission will be granted to reveal the truth about Dickie's most outlandish activities, but now is not the time.

The End

Notes

1. For folks who are not well versed in U.S. history, Prohibition of Alcohol extended from 1920 to 1933. Liquor had to be smuggled into towns, often from coastal vessels under darkness. No public drinking was allowed, to the dismay of many citizens on Cape Cod and elsewhere.

2. *Corporation Beach at Nobscusset Harbor*. Patricia A. Walker. Harvest Home Books. 2005. Note that the author correctly spells the Harbor with one 't', whereas Nobscussett Road was officially named with two 't's.

3. The last major smallpox epidemic in the United States occurred in Boston between 1901-1903. During this period, 1596 cases were diagnosed and nearly 300 people died. The epidemic had a fatality rate of nearly 20%.

4. *Remembering the Mill Hill Pavilion*. CapeCod.com. September 20, 2018

5. *Dennis, Cape Cod. From Firstcomers to Newcomers 1639-1993*. Nancy Thacher Reid. Dennis Historical Society. Dennis, MA. 1996

6. When elder locals chuckle about the juxtaposition of Dennis' villages, they quickly recall Philo Rockwell ('Rocky') King, a much-enjoyed singer/songwriter who performed for 54 years at the Sand Bar restaurant near West Dennis Beach. One of his classic songs poked fun at the geographic location of the villages versus their names: North Dennis being west of East Dennis; South Dennis being north of Dennis Port and West Dennis; etc. His lyrics were geographically accurate while presented with great humor. Rocky will forever be missed.

7. According to the original documents from Plymouth County in the early 1600s, the correct spelling of the Nobscusset Indian Chief is Mashantampaine. However, the word Mashantum, including the letter 'u' rather than an 'a', has been used subsequently for many purposes in the village. The reason is unknown.

8. *Mashantum Tennis Club celebrates '70 years in Dennis*. Susan Vaughn. Cape Cod Times. July 8, 2016

9. Although the Nobscusset Tribe had no written language, Mashantampaine had to sign deeds when land was transferred to the town and settlers. Interestingly, his signature looked very much like the number five followed by an equilateral triangle, both inverted and connected.[9]

10. *Dennis: Postcard History*. Scott I. Walker and Robin E. Walker. 2007

11. One of the small kennel buildings of the Bleak House property was relocated by my father, Paul McDowell. It was lifted by the large wrecker of the Dennis Garage, placed on log rollers, towed eastward

through the woods then down Peter Road. That 'shed' still sits behind the house I grew up in at 20 Paul Street. I recall shingling over the six small doors where Patrol Dogs would exit for duty on the beach.

12. John Murphy was also the mason who constructed Scargo Tower using individual, local stones in 1901.

13. Two references for the Dennis Village Improvement Society: www.dennisvis.org (primary VIS website) https://dennisculture.wordpress.com/2011/11/03/village-improvement-society/

14. Mr. Walter S. Morley began teaching Language Arts to Grades 7 and 8 at Ezra H. Baker in 1951, and later became Principal in 1966. He retired in 1983 after providing outstanding education and guidance to students for thirty-two years. In 1981 he completed a thorough and impressive book titled "The Continuing History of the Ezra H. Baker School" which can be viewed in the Dennis Historical Society's collections on the second floor of the West Dennis Public Library.

15. My great-great-grandfather Samuel McDowell immigrated from Scotland in the early 1800s and bought land on Seaside Avenue about 200 feet east of the present Willows Inn. An 1856 map of Seaside Avenue, with his property identified, is shown in Patricia Walker's Nobscusset Harbor book, pages 8 and 123.

16. SOCONY was the acronym for Standard Oil Company of New York, originating back in the 1880s, becoming SOCONY-Mobil in 1955, just Mobil in 1966 and finally ExxonMobil after the merger in 1998.

17. Words from my father as he taught me how to drive, on the beach. Riding in soft sand with a manual shift Jeep certainly teaches you how to shift quickly, or you stop instantly and have to start all over.

18. Late in life, Walter boasted to his son Peter that he was the Valedictorian in his 1912 graduating class at North Dennis High School (located near the present Dennis Union Church). Peter quickly deflated his father's ego by clarifying that Walter had grades higher than only five other students his age (his entire class).

19. Old timers called the Drive-In an 'Open Air' theater. And I can remember my grandfather calling golf 'Cow Pasture Pool'. "Damn foolish game" he said.

20. Dickie recalls that white suits were intended to demonstrate that the Drive-In's management was progressive, this being around the time of atomic bombs and thus, concern was high for the safety of its employees (albeit minimal protection at best). The suits did, however, allow Dickie and his coworker to hide bottles of rum in the loose coveralls. While sitting on the roof of the restaurant for hours, they managed to get very buzzed during the movies. Not the best condition for directing traffic at the end of the show.

21. www.friendsofdennisseniors.com/marguerite-ickis

22. *The Standard Book of Quilt Making and Collecting.* Marguerite Ickis. 1949

23. For the Commemorative Opening Round of the Dennis Pines Golf Course in 1965, the Author caddied for Mr. Thibeault. Pete Kirouac, Jr., the Course Superintendent, was the other player. Many eager members of the new course followed their awe-inspiring Pro, as he drove the ball to spots that were out of reach by mere mortals (or at least it seemed in those days, when I was 14).

24. The Author had the good fortune of being an evening bartender at Joe Mac's during summers of the early '70s – the bar's heydays. He and Joe Brennan greatly enjoyed serving the diverse clientele and their thirsty friends. Also, the fact that my mother dated Joe at Barnstable High School during the mid-40s likely helped with the job connection. Additionally, my sister worked in the small grocery store within the building and my Uncle Joe Hassett and his wife Susan (of Cape Cod radio fame) lived in the one-room apartment above the pizza ovens for one summer.

25. The Stageway Restaurant bought fresh fish from local fishermen for their entrees. In the late '60s, the Author sold personally caught striped bass to the restaurant. Nick's son Peter was a hard-bargaining buyer, often trying to pay me less than the 25-cents-per-pound that I asked. Sometimes I won, obtaining $5 for a 20-pounder.

26. *Whose Boy Be You? A Parcel of Recollections of Cape Cod Yesterdays.* Ben Thacher, East Dennis, MA. 2007

27. William Ernest Crowell was a highly respected man in town. Nevertheless, many local characters would poke fun at him with the nickname, "Almost Always Honest Ernest".

28. *History of Race Point Light, Provincetown, Massachusetts.* www.newenglandlighthouses.net/race-point-light-history.html

29. Bridge Street in East Dennis originally had no name. When street signs were being produced at the Town Barn during Dennis' early years, a sign was created for 'Bridge Street' but this was to be placed in West Dennis at Weir Creek near Lighthouse Point. By mistake, the sign was installed at the intersection of Routes 6A and 134, to indicate the northward extension of Route 134. The plan was to place a different sign, indicating "Road To Beach", but it never materialized. Consequently, there is no Bridge Street in West Dennis.

30. *The Eastwind Collision.* http://www.jacksjoint.com/eastwind.htm

31. Don Knotts, actor of the TV character Barney Fife, was a part-time comedian while enlisted in the Army. He apparently got tired of performing his ventriloquist act, "playing straight man for a hunk of wood". According to Knotts, he tossed the dummy overboard as his ship was crossing the Pacific but

"I could hear the dummy calling for help as the ship steamed away, leaving him bobbing helplessly in the waves".

32. The skilled and high-spirited Berrien sisters were greatly enjoyed. Like most residents of Dennis, they would attend the Town Meetings and voice their opinions on town matters of the day. Kay had a son with the nickname 'Dinky'. On one occasion during town discussion of reducing the size regulation of outboard motors on Scargo Lake, Kay stood up and made a comment about her son's boating, which made the crowd roar: "…My Dink rides his boats on Scargo…

33. *An Analysis of Ball Lightning – Aircraft Incidents*. Doe, Keul and Bychkov. American Geophysical Union, Fall Meeting 2009. December 2009.

34. In 1919, the 'supercharger' was invented to increase the pressure of the fuel-air mixture for internal-combustion engines. When the device was added to an engine, the result was a much faster, 'souped-up' engine. Thus, the origin of the expression for improved performance of 'hot rods'. It's odd that it wasn't spelled 'suped-up'.

35. The Indian Motorcycle Company began manufacturing high performance motorcycles in 1907, with their famous 633-cc, 42-degree, V-Twin, then stepped up to the 1,000-cc Powerplus engine in 1910. During WW I, they provided 50,000 motorcycles to the U.S. Military from 1917-1919. After WW II, they produced primarily Chief models but ended production in 1953. The company changed hands many times over the past few decades but Indian is again a competitive manufacturer on the world market.

36. *Poor Howard's Wednesday Afternoon Post*. 1966 http://www.provincetownhistoryproject.com/archives/5966

37. *Ten Million Steps on Route 6. A fresh look at America & Americans from Cape Cod to California*. Joe Hurley. Arkett Publishing. 2014

38. VKTMS, pronounced 'victims', was a popular punk group from San Francisco that started in 1979.

39. *Collier*'s was a leading American magazine published from 1888 to 1957. It popularized the short-short story format of journalism, with single-page features. More significantly, the magazine gained a reputation for advocating social reform. Numerous legal suits from private companies failed, thereafter giving print magazines more journalistic freedom, which President Teddy Roosevelt called "muckraking journalism".

40. *The Little White Bird*. Sir James M. Barrie. 1902. Chapters 13-18 were extracted and republished in 1906 under the title, *Peter Pan in Kensington Gardens*.

41. *Peter Pan*. Animated fantasy-adventure movie produced by Walt Disney. 1953.

Photographs

Acknowledgements

The concept of developing the Biography of Dickie Buck came to me indirectly. In February of 2018, I had recently completed the non-fiction book about the *Albatross and Her Crew*, the fishing boat in East Dennis, when my cousin Patrick McDowell approached me and said "You've got to write the book about Dickie Buck."

"Why would I want to do that? He's certainly been the wildest guy to ever have lived in Dennis but the book could only be a collection of wild stories and most of these couldn't be published for various and lewd reasons."

Patrick didn't give up. "Speak to these people (he gave me a short list) and you'll get a different impression of who Dickie really is. He's been a great contributor to our village and people don't want his legend to be lost."

I spoke to four people and my view of Dickie changed 180° as supported in numerous Chapters of this book. Next, I convened an initial Skype session with Dickie and his family to discuss the book concept and what it could (and could not) be. From that very positive session, I accepted the project to write Dickie's Biography.

During our initial collaboration, Dickie explained that over the past twenty or so years, a number of persons had approached him with offers to write his Biography but he ended up choosing me. His selection criteria were his own business but after our first face-to-face meeting in March 2018, we were convinced we could work well together. He'd mention the name of a prominent person or place in the village from the '50s or '60s and I could finish his sentence. He'd name the bars, where he drank and had fistfights and I could recall the bartenders' first names. Tautog Rock, Beach Buggies with bald tires at Chapin, schools of herring under Bridge Street; I knew them all. Although he's fifteen years my elder, we have tremendous overlap in space and time, as I too grew up locally, near Scargo Lake, when Dickie was at the peak of his hell-raising years.

Dickie has been a joy to work with on this project. His memory is still amazing and he's provided details about the models of cars he's owned, the names of police officers who've arrested him, the price of the lunch specials at Bill and Thelma's in the '50s, even details about his first time with a girl – TMI. We met dozens of times in spring and summer of 2018 and since then, we've followed up with phone calls when I've been off-Cape writing.

Herein, the body of text pertaining to his life exceeds 100,000 words and this represents a subset of the information he and others provided. Many stories were not included, for reasons which you can guess.

Who other than Dickie would be so brave to tell the world about all the outlandish activities he's conducted over his years in the village. And he even said that after he dies, I should publish

Part II with all the stories that were inappropriate to include in Part I. His family can make that decision; I will abstain.

Additional thanks are due to Judy, Linda and Alesia for their contributions to the Biography but more importantly, for their trust that I would produce a quality book that does justice to the husband and father they dearly love. The girls also compiled the old photos and delivered hardcopies of draft Chapters to Dickie for his review.

I also wish to thank my wife, Susan Bacoyanis, who provided excellent editorial support during iterations of the voluminous text. Also for having patience while I was mentally 'away' during many months of book creation.

Carole Walker Bell and Peter McDowell graciously provided review of the Chapters on Landmarks and Notorious Characters. They were well suited for this task, having lived their entire lives in the village. Their memories were essential for fact-checking the topics for which my memory was vague, having lived away from Dennis for many years although I return annually. Carole also provided many early, relevant photographs.

Input from Dickie and numerous individuals represented the raw material for this Biography. Early in the process, Dickie suggested specific persons I should speak with for gathering stories and memories about his antics. Sadly, he admitted that nearly all of his closest friends are no longer with us. That didn't deter him. He actively called dozens of people and 'warned' them that I'd be calling or visiting to solicit their candid input. Much of this was via knocking on doors to visit people I hadn't seen since I was a teen, fifty years ago. It was all fun and the outpouring of stories about Dickie was heartwarming.

I truly enjoyed this information-gathering phase but when I caught my breath, I realized that I had way more terrific material than I needed. From the tape recordings of my discussions, I made a spreadsheet with key points that arose so I could return to each recording segment and extract the information for each story. This Excel table of information was over 4,500 lines tall.

Most importantly, I list below those persons who graciously gave their time and candid input about Dickie. Some contributors had only a few minutes of useful comments whereas others spent more than two hours with me because they felt very strongly that they and the entire village, should make this book a tribute to Dickie for all the positive things he has done for many people.

Thank you to the following people for their contributions:

Adams, Donny

Bassett, Royce

Bell, Billy

Bell, Carole Walker

Boucher, Joy

Byron, Kate

Colby, David

Corsini, Frank

Crowell, Joshua

Crowell, Seth

Drake, Jimmy

Dubin, Judy

Elland, John

Gordon, Jon

Hogan, Alayne

Howes, Dave

Howes, Rich

Incutto, Jean

King, Billy

King, John

Lowther, Joe

Ludwig, Dale

Machon, George

McDowell, Patrick

McDowell, Peter

McDowell, Scott

Morley, Kevin

Myland, Chris

Pessa, Toni

Peterson, Linda

Peterson, Pete

Poole, Sally

Poole, Sandy

Riley, Larry

Scarafile, Judy

Schimmel, Pete

Sears, Billy

Sears, Dickie

Sears, Linda

Smithers, Maryann

Thatcher, Jonathan

Walker, Annie

Walker, Joseph P. II

Walker, Patricia A.

~

Lastly, special thanks to my daughter, Danielle, and the North Dennis Fire Department and Rescue Squad for reviving me, thirty minutes after total cardiac arrest on the ice of Scargo Lake, February 10, 2007. It's all been a bonus ever since. Consider this book as my gift to the village.

- Scott McDowell

Author Biography
Scott E. McDowell

Published Author
Ph.D. – Ocean Physics
100-Ton Licensed Vessel Captain

Dr. McDowell is retired from a successful, 30-year career in physical oceanography that entailed diverse research in coastal regions and the deep ocean around the globe. Additionally, as a licensed vessel Captain, he has operated vessels in U.S. Coastal waters offshore New England, California and Florida, in addition to The Bahamas. Now he enjoys full-time writing on oceanographic and maritime topics, as well as fiction suspense-thrillers on ocean espionage and selected Biographies. He writes from practical marine experience – five decades on the sea.

Author

Marinas – The Complete Guide for Marina Selection   *2015*
     Non-fiction – Boating   Pages: 288
     Publisher: Atlantic Publishing Group, Inc.
     Recipient of FAPA 2016 Gold Metal Award for Best Sporting Book

Deep Vorticity   *2015*
     Fiction – Suspense Thriller with oceanographic/science content
     Self-Published via Amazon CreateSpace   Pages: 315

Albatross and Her Crew   *2018*
     Non-fiction – Boating, fishing
     Self-Published via Amazon CreateSpace   Pages: 176

Dickie Buck – Robin Hood of Dennis   *2019*
     Non-fiction – Authorized Biography
     Self-Published via Amazon CreateSpace   Pages: 236

Sea Knowledge   Non-fiction – Popular Science   In process

Education and Oceanographic Research (see Scott's website)

Professional Experience in the Oceanographic Industry

Dr. McDowell was initially employed by the Woods Hole Oceanographic Institution (WHOI) to participate as scientific crew on a 7-month geophysical investigation in the South Atlantic to assess the Mid-Atlantic Ridge and the volcanic seafloor at the Triple Junction of the Antarctic Ocean. Soon after, he conducted oceanographic measurements aboard a Navy vessel during a seafloor study in the Caribbean while Dr. Robert Ballard (*Titanic* discoverer) conducted simultaneous measurements within a research submarine operated by the U.S. Navy. During his three-year period at WHOI, Dr. McDowell participated in numerous deep-ocean studies and was co-author on research papers published in peer-reviewed Oceanographic Journals. Proudly he participated in over 300 days of mid-ocean research during one fifteen-month period.

After earning his Ph.D. in Ocean Physics, he was employed by private industry for the next 27 years, conducting complex oceanographic measurement programs for state and federal agencies as well as commercial clients, worldwide. During his final years of employment, Dr. McDowell managed a Marine Sciences and Environmental Planning Division with 120 staff located in 7 offices nationwide. Forty staff had M.S. and Ph.D. degrees, exemplifying the high scientific caliber of the organization he led, with annual revenues of $23M from professional services. His responsibilities included technical and financial management, strategic planning, business development and recruiting but oceanographic work was always his key interest.

Vessel Experience

- Grew up on Cape Cod, worked aboard fishing boats during summer of teen years
- Mate and giant bluefin tuna Guide aboard private sport-fishing boat during summers of college years; all tuna caught were between 425 and 700 pounds
- Oceanographic research on numerous vessels in all oceans during 30-yr career
- For contracted research, chartered dozens of vessels between 40- and 110-ft
- Cruised coastal California and lived aboard his 46-ft vessel
- Obtained U.S.C.G. 100-Ton Master License
- Cruised southeast Florida, The Keys and The Bahamas, while living aboard his 60-ft vessel

Contact Information

scott_e_mcdowell@yahoo.com

805-320-0848

www.scottemcdowell.com

Made in the USA
Middletown, DE
09 June 2019